Walking Home

My Family and Other Rambles

CLARE BALDING

VIKING
an imprint of
PENGUIN BOOKS

VIKING

Published by the Penguin Group

Penguin Books Ltd, 80 Strand, London WC2R 0RL, England

Penguin Group (USA) Inc., 375 Hudson Street, New York, New York 10014, USA

Penguin Group (Canada), 90 Eglinton Avenue East, Suite 700, Toronto, Ontario, Canada M4P 2Y3
(a division of Pearson Penguin Canada Inc.)

Penguin Ireland, 25 St Stephen's Green, Dublin 2, Ireland (a division of Penguin Books Ltd)

Penguin Group (Australia), 707 Collins Street, Melbourne, Victoria 3008, Australia
(a division of Pearson Australia Group Pty Ltd)

Penguin Books India Pvt Ltd, 11 Community Centre, Panchsheel Park, New Delhi – 110 017, India

Penguin Group (NZ), 67 Apollo Drive, Rosedale, Auckland 0632, New Zealand
(a division of Pearson New Zealand Ltd)

Penguin Books (South Africa) (Pty) Ltd, Block D, Rosebank Office Park,
181 Jan Smuts Avenue, Parktown North, Gauteng 2193, South Africa

Penguin Books Ltd, Registered Offices: 80 Strand, London WC2R 0RL, England

www.penguin.com

First published 2014

001

Set in 12/14.75 pt Dante MT Std
Typeset by Jouve (UK), Milton Keynes
Printed in Great Britain by Clays Ltd, St Ives plc

A CIP catalogue record for this book is available from the British Library

HARDBACK ISBN: 978-0-670-92147-8
TRADE PAPERBACK ISBN: 978-0-241-18425-7

www.greenpenguin.co.uk

To Lucy, for Walking

To Mum and Dad, for Home

Now shall I walk
or shall I ride?
'Ride,' Pleasure said;
'Walk,' Joy replied.

W. H. Davies

Contents

List of Maps

Pre-Ramble

I used to think walking was something you did purely out of necessity. You had to take the dog for a walk or, trapped without a car, you had to walk home.

I spent my childhood at a faster pace. I galloped through the countryside and I galloped through life. I always wanted to rush on to the next thing before I'd finished what I was doing or saying. I was, as they say if they're being kind, 'irrepressible'. Or, if they're not, 'a pain in the arse'.

Up on the Downs above my family home, Kingsclere, there's a sign I would see nearly every day. It read 'Wayfarer's Walk'. The arrow pointing left read 'Emsworth, 58 miles'. The one pointing right read 'Inkpen Beacon, 12 miles'.

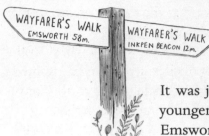

I had sometimes wondered what it would be like to walk the whole thing. I never actually planned to do it, of course. It was just an idle thought. Andrew, my younger brother, always asked me where Emsworth was.

'At the end of the Wayfarer's Walk,' I said, while giving him a Chinese burn.

'Or at the beginning,' he hissed, trying to pretend it didn't hurt.

I let go of his arm. He had a point.

'Maybe we should find out,' he said.

I waved my hand airily. 'One day.'

In fact, growing up in a racing yard, I used to know the geography of the UK only by racecourses.

I knew where Alton Towers was because you can see it from Uttoxeter racecourse, which is on the A50, midway between Stoke and Derby. I knew that there were two places called Bangor because a jockey once kept driving over and back across the Menai Bridge into Anglesey, looking urgently for the racecourse, when he should have been walking into the paddock at Bangor on Dee, just south-east of Wrexham.

I could plot my way down the east coast of Scotland and northern England via Perth, Musselburgh, Kelso, Newcastle, Sedgefield and Redcar, but I had no reason to know where Durham was. I could point to Southwell on a map, but I wasn't entirely sure about the location of Lincoln (the racecourse closed in 1965). I knew Great Yarmouth, where the racecourse sits around a caravan park, but I had never even heard of Lowestoft or Aldeburgh, or experienced any of the joys of the Suffolk coast.

I thought it was perfectly normal to have never travelled to Cornwall, because there are no racecourses west of Newton Abbot. A bit like my brother thought the seasons of the year were Flat and

National Hunt, I regarded Newmarket as the capital of the world and Lambourn as a major city of industry.

I didn't have time to just *walk*. I never had time. I was too busy rushing on to the next adventure, jumping the next fence. Then, I wanted to take risks, I wanted an adrenalin rush. I didn't want to walk anywhere, I wanted to gallop. In my family, walking just took too long.

'Why would you walk without a dog or a pitchfork?' my father would ask.

The pitchfork might seem a bit odd to you if you live on the Fulham Road, although I can imagine Dad, four-pronged fork over his shoulder, strolling past the shop that's always got a sale on mirrors and writes the prices all over the front of them. He'd consider them quite good value but then wander on to the shop that designs expensive kitchens.

'Twenty grand for a kitchen? You could buy a bloody nice horse for that. I just don't understand it.'

He'd huff at the insanity and then look for divots in the pavement to repair. That's why he carries a pitchfork, you see. To repair hoof marks in the gallops. It's called 'treading in'. You'll have seen the scene in *Pretty Woman* where they do it at the polo match in short skirts and high heels. My dad does it properly – with a four-pronged pitchfork. Get the prongs in under the divot, lift it up, then tread it level with the grass around it.

'No point doing a job unless you do it properly.' This is the mantra of his life and, consequently, the background music of mine. Dad is a doer, not a thinker.

'You won't catch me sitting like a saddo drinking at lunchtime,' he says, pouring quarter of a bottle of sherry into his Cup-a-Soup. He offers me his mug.

'You should taste this. It's really excellent, you know.'

I turn up my top lip. I hate sherry and I don't want to drink out of Dad's cup. Much as I love him, I have never wanted to share his food and I've never wanted him to share mine either. That bit is harder to prevent. My father sees himself as the official taster to the world. He will make you a gin and tonic, drop in the ice and a slice, then take a sip of it to 'check it's all right' before handing it to you.

'*Stop drinking my drink!*' I shout at him from the other room, because I know he's doing it without even seeing him. He comes in, looking bemused.

'But I have to check it's good enough for you,' he says before handing it over. 'There. That is the best gin and tonic you . . . will . . . ever . . . have.'

My sister-in-law knew she had gained full acceptance when Dad started eating from her plate without asking permission. He just wanted to check hers tasted as good as his. She nearly stabbed her fork into the back of his hand by mistake, but that's the risk you run if you steal food from under other people's noses, and my father has been a risk-taker all his life. Maybe that's why walking never appealed to him. He couldn't see the risk, or the point.

My mother likes walking, with the dogs or the grandchildren. She takes an old ice-cream container to pick blackberries or mushrooms and checks the hedgerows for hidden gems. She doesn't walk with my father because he can't stroll or forage. He'd be diving off into a field to pull up ragwort, checking on horses, or rushing home to change for a game of golf.

If something awful happens or she needs time to think, Mum will take the dogs for a walk. When our puppy was hit by a car on the road outside our house and died in my arms, my partner, Alice, and I were in that state of shocked grief that you never forget.

We drove him home to Kingsclere, where Mum had organized for a grave to be dug out. After we had buried him – I still feel a catch in my throat at the horror of it all – Mum took us for a walk. We trudged in silence, tears blurring our vision, until Ruby the boxer snuffled up, her back end waggling with joy. We had to smile at her and we had to keep moving, one foot in front of the other, away from the ghastliness of what we had witnessed.

Mum believes, as Hippocrates did, that walking is the best medicine for all ailments, mental and physical. She is a lone walker. I cannot imagine her joining a group of strangers or going very far out of her territory. The word 'ramblers' makes her come out in a cold sweat.

'They have all that *kit*. Those stupid socks and poles and a map covered in plastic and a compass. Then, when I tell them that they're not on the footpath they get aggressive.'

So I didn't exactly grow up with ambulophobia, but there *was* a degree of ramblerophobia. (I realize this may not be a word – until now.)

This all changed with a single phone call. In 1999 I was contacted by a BBC Radio 4 producer called Lucy Lunt. She had seen me on TV doing an interview with Terry Wogan for *Auntie's Sporting Bloomers* and thought I looked like fun. As I was a 'country sort', she wondered if I might be the right presenter for a new series she was making.

'Do you walk?' Lucy asked.

'Well, I walk the dogs,' I said.

I had moved to London, where my feet were mainly deployed on pavements and tunnels in Tube stations. I did go home to Kingsclere regularly, and when I was there I made sure I always took the dogs out, so I figured that counted. I had no idea there were people who walked for the sake of it, and groups who went out regularly to conquer the footpaths of Great Britain.

I sounded more confident than my experience warranted. But yes, in my understanding of the word, I was a walker.

'Excellent,' she said. 'Now, can you read a map?'

I replied, a little too hastily, 'Of course I can.'

This was in the days before satnavs and GPS, and I had an uncanny knack of memorizing a page from a road atlas so that I didn't have to look at it en route. I failed to realize she was talking about Ordnance Survey maps. A decade and a half later, I will still turn to Lucy as we're about to announce the starting-grid reference and say, 'Just remind me. Is it along the corridor and up the stairs, or up the stairs and along the corridor?'

'The day you know that is the day you'll probably have to stop,' she'll reply.

Truth be told, I never want to stop. The Radio 4 series Lucy was signing me up for was called *Ramblings*. It's a half-hour programme in which I walk with people all over the country. Lucy was hoping she might have found a format that would last for a few series, maybe even a couple of years, if we were lucky. Fifteen years and forty-five series later, it is still going strong.

Of all the things I work on, of all the programmes I have ever presented, *Ramblings* is my favourite. You might think half an hour on radio of two people (sometimes more) walking around the countryside is an odd concept for a series, but it works.

At a rough estimate, I have covered about fifteen hundred miles of footpaths, for *Ramblings*, or just for myself. I have tackled apocalyptic thunderstorms, struggled with blisters, a bad back, a twisted ankle and the wrong clothes, and traipsed through the snow of the Perthshire mountains with no voice (me, not the mountains – they always speak).

All these miles have changed my perception of the countryside, as well as revolutionizing my knowledge of it. I realize that I spent my childhood looking at a skeleton of Britain in which I knew obscure bones but not about the spine of the Pennine Way, or anything about the capillaries of tiny footpaths that take us deep into the woods and along the riverbanks of our landscape.

I have felt the delights of the North-east Coastal Path, the Highland Way from Milngavie to Fort William, the South-west Coast Path and the South Downs Way. I have bounced on spring dews and crunched on autumn leaves, I have felt the brutal wind bend me like a misshapen hawthorn bush, and I have strolled for miles with the sun warming my cheeks and refracting off chalk and water.

For *Ramblings*, my companions are always interestingly chosen. I have walked with historians, geologists, twitchers, botanists, poets, artists and adventurers. They usually have boundless knowledge and endless enthusiasm, so I always learn something new. With every step I discover more about the land in which we live.

We usually cover at least seven or eight miles, but sometimes we venture further and are encased in our boots for most of the day. I love the stories that people reveal over those miles. I have told people all sorts of things during the course of a walk, and they have told me things they probably never thought they would open up about.

That's because walking side by side is very different from sitting opposite someone. There is only occasional eye contact, so none of that awkward looking up and away if you think you've caught their eye for too long. You are sharing an experience, looking at a view together, puffing up a hill or watching the waves crash into the rocks below. You face the weather together, and as two or three hours unfold the layers peel back.

It is therapy for the soul. It's as if walking has unlocked a part of my brain the way that riding did when I was a child, and walking with other people gives me a chance to satisfy my inquisitive mind. I can ask all the questions I want to ask, and they, for the most part, seem fairly willing to answer them.

I also try to walk alone as much as possible, or just with Alice. Except we're not quite on our own – we're with Archie, our Tibetan terrier. The other day in a London park I suddenly noticed a tree I had never seen before: it looked like a twisted rope leading up to a shaggy head of hair. I stopped and stared, lost in the moment. Archie sniffed the tree and cocked his leg. He does have a way of bursting your bubble.

Walking slows me down, it gives me time to think, time to explore the land, the seasons, the person and the dog I share my life with, and the beauty in every day.

There is a frequency your brain tunes into after about two hours, as the rhythm of your footfall becomes its only beat. It is like meditation, a means of earthing your body and your mind.

This is the story of the paths I have walked, the people I have met, how my understanding of our country has changed, and how walking has shaped my life.

I love it, and I need it. Now I make sure that I start every day with an hour-long walk with Archie, and I always look forward to the evening, when I get the chance to walk him again. And whether or not we're recording for radio, I never need an excuse to get out there and discover a new path.

I am at home with my brother, Andrew, and my sister-in-law, banging on about the joys of walking. Abruptly, my brother says, 'You should do the Wayfarer's Walk. We always talked about it, do you remember?'

So I start thinking about it seriously.

I haven't seen that much of Andrew in recent years, so he's less annoying. He falls asleep at the dinner table and he wears terrible shoes but, apart from that, he's OK. He lives at Park House in Kingsclere with his wife, Anna Lisa, and their three children, and he trains about 170 horses, which consumes his life. I sometimes wonder what would have happened if he hadn't wanted to take over the business and train racehorses.

Once he had passed through his phase of calling himself Alan and licking radiators because they tasted of tea, he turned out to be quite creative. He drew things all the time and his artwork is rather good. Where my dad has always been a chart man – neat lines with his all-colour biro, endless lists and signs that he had to write himself because no one else could do it properly – Andrew is more free form. If he hadn't ended up training, I think he would have been an artist or run a gallery.

He's also a bit of a dreamer. So when he said he wanted to walk the Wayfarer's Walk, I didn't really pay any attention. Not for twenty years. Then, suddenly, I decided it was something we *had* to do.

I wanted to share with my family some of the pleasure I had got from walking all over the country and I had a crazy idea that it might be a fun way to re-create our childhood.

So I say to Andrew, 'Why don't we walk it together?'

Alice and Anna Lisa swap the kind of glance that only those who live with dreamers can understand. It is a look that says 'Here they go again.' They sensibly decide not to dissuade us – they know that will make it more likely we might follow our latest idea.

But I'm serious, and I think Andrew is too. We want to go to Emsworth and walk home from there. It is seventy miles in total from Emsworth to Inkpen Beacon. It will be a great family adventure. Won't it?

Brown Candover–Dummer

'Why don't we walk it together?'

The question hangs in the air as we sit around the kitchen table at Park House in Kingsclere. It's a different table from when I was growing up, and the window seats have gone, but the kitchen vibe is the same.

People come in and out all day long, Lindy pops in from the office next door to make her coffee, Tonto the boxer sniffs around in case anyone has dropped a morsel of food, and Henry the Labrador wags his tail and looks a bit stupid. He's a failed guide dog and, frankly, I'm not surprised he didn't pass his exams: it might give someone a thrill to be towed along by him, but on a whim he'd drag them into the road or fling them into a bush.

My nephews, Jonno (seven) and Toby (five), are adjusting their Velcro Premier League table on the wall, squawking loudly about

Wayfarer's Walk

Southampton's star players and what a good season they've had. Andrew and I are looking at a road map as we sit in the bay window. Anna Lisa has removed the curtains we'd had as children, mainly because she found a chocolate stain where Andrew had wiped his mouth when he was ten. She'd replaced them with shutters, largely because age wouldn't guarantee that he might not do it again.

Alice is reading my niece, Flora, who is just three, a Paddington Bear book.

'Deepest, darkest Peru is a long, long way away, isn't it?' says Flora.

'Yes,' Alice replies.

'Is it near Emsworth?' she asks. 'Because Auntie Clare says that's a long way away as well.'

'Peru's a bit further,' says Alice. 'Emsworth's only sixty or so miles but Peru is more like six *thousand* miles.'

'Oh, can you walk to Peru?' Flora asks.

'Your daddy can,' I say. 'And it would probably only take him a week.'

This is because Andrew has a slightly unrealistic view of how long it will take us to do the Wayfarer's Walk. He has never been much of a walker, but he likes the idea of the challenge: he now wants to do the whole thing.

So we come up with a plan. We will start on the south coast at Emsworth, in the market square, and walk home through Hampshire. Brother and sister planning it all together. It will be an adventure, a challenge, a bonding experience. The only trouble is that he thinks a road map is a walking map.

'Look, Clarey,' he says. 'It's no distance from Emsworth to Alresford. We'll do that in a day. Then there to home will only take us another day and a half. All done and dusted in two and a half days.'

I know he's dyslexic, but my brother's also developed a worry-ing blindness to scale. From an artist, I expect better.

'You numpty, that's a road map. Everything looks close together, and it doesn't show the hills or where the footpath goes. It's sixty miles away. I promise you it will take us longer than two and a half days.'

'Daddy is a numpty, Daddy is a numpty!' the boys start sing-ing. My sister-in-law gives me an old-fashioned look.

'Well done, Auntie Clare,' she says.

Alice and I go back to London, but I want to keep the Wayfarer's idea alive. To kick things off, I send Andrew a plan of the sections of the walk. I think it will take three and a half days minimum, if we are to actually enjoy it and not feel as if we're on a forced route march.

He's still keen, so we decide we will embark on our journey in March 2014, soon after I return from the Winter Olympics in Sochi. I block out the days in my diary and keep up my fitness in Russia by walking every morning before I head off to write my scripts.

Wayfarer's Walk

I phone Andrew when I get home to see how his preparations are going. He has agreed to run the London Marathon for the first time, so he's been jogging all round the local lanes. He is fitter than he has been in years.

'I reckon we can do it in two days,' he declares. He has looked again at the AA road map and concluded that all the villages named on the route look very close together. Now that he can run ten miles in under two hours, he thinks he can walk to Edinburgh and back. Emsworth – ha! That will be a walk in the park.

I still think that's a tad ambitious, but if we walk home, rather than to Inkpen Beacon at the end, it works out at twenty miles a day – for three days. As long as we don't get lost or injured, it is just about achievable.

A few weeks pass, then Andrew calls me as I'm on my way to Cheltenham.

'Clarey, we need to talk about this walk. What are we doing?'

Ah yes, the old 'What are we doing?', which translates as 'What are *you* doing?'

A week before we are due to start, it seems that Andrew only has two days spare. I had blocked out Sunday (after my Radio 2 show) to Wednesday, but I now realize I have to be back in London on Monday night for a charity dinner. No problem, I can be back in Hampshire by Tuesday morning and we'll pick up wherever we left off. Then Andrew announces he has to be home on Tuesday night because the vet is doing a presentation to the yard about how to spot signs of colic. Our window of opportunity is shrinking.

'And it looks as if I'll have a runner at Kempton on Monday, so

I'll have to go racing,' he says. 'But how about we drive the first half from Emsworth to New Alresford and then walk the rest?'

I tell him that we can't drive it because footpaths are not roads. That's the point.

This is typical of my brother. He admits himself that he's not blessed with the powers of logic. I found a letter he wrote me when I was at university to wish me luck in my Finals:

I hope that you are working very hard and that you will pass your exams so that you can earn lots and lots of money so that you can support your poor dyslexic brother, which is a poor educationaly (sic) sub-normal farmer (with very little common sense).

Good luck and remember that getting a degree is a loser's game – My Daddy told me that.

Dad had managed to get into Cambridge with no A levels but sharp enough reflexes to catch the book that was hurled at him during his interview. He had failed his degree in land economy but got a blue for rugby union and was part of the unbeaten Cambridge side of 1959. His master at Christ's seemed happy with that outcome, and so was he. After all, training racehorses doesn't require a degree in anything other than patience.

I tell Andrew I will work it all out on the Saturday after the Cheltenham Festival and let him know.

'Excellent,' he says. 'I just think it's better if you plan it all and tell me what to do.'

Tristan Gooley, author of *The Natural Navigator*, says that we

Wayfarer's Walk

are all either navigators or passengers in life. I would quite like to be a passenger every now and again, but it seems I am, not necessarily by choice, a navigator. I scale back our ambitions and decide that if we can do half or even a third of the whole route, it will be a miracle. If we can't walk the beginning section, we'll have to start later and try to walk home.

Alice has printed off a guide and it looks like we can do a relatively easy stretch on Sunday morning with all the kids and anyone else who wants to come, stop at a pub for lunch, and then Andrew and I can carry on and walk as far as we can towards home. Then we'll finish the last bit the next morning before he goes off racing at Kempton.

The major challenge of any linear walk is logistics. Where will you leave a car, and how will you pick it up when you've finished? But I have worked it out: as long as there is room for me, Alice and Archie to squeeze into the other cars, we can leave ours at the finish of the first section and just use it to take back the drivers.

We have a big team – my brother and Anna Lisa with Jonno and Toby, Tonto the boxer and Henry the stupid Labrador, Anna Lisa's mother, Suzie, and two of her other grandchildren, Jacobi and Elisia, plus family friends the Mackinnons, with three children and one yellow Lab. Children and dogs seem very excited. Adults seem very wary.

I do my Radio 2 show in the morning, pick up Alice from home and head off down the M3. We meet at the Sun Inn just off the

A30 on the edge of Dummer, apart from Andrew and Anna Lisa, who are running late and go straight to the start. As we make our wiggly way by car towards the Candovers, I keep telling everyone that the footpath back is actually more direct and will be shorter than the route we are driving. I hope to hell, for the sake of the younger ones, I am not telling fibs.

I had been away for the whole of February so had missed the endless rain that had given Britain its wettest ever winter, and I had been rather fooled by a warm and sunny Cheltenham. It meant I hadn't banked on the roads through Preston Candover, Chilton Candover and Brown Candover being closed because of flooding. The Candover valley sits along a tributary of the River Itchen. It is verdant land, a mixture of agricultural and grass fields with parkland surrounding the large estates. It is also very prone to flooding.

We ignore the red signs, drive through the floods and find the church in Brown Candover, which I know is right next to the Wayfarer's Walk. We find the church hall. A man comes out to tell us that we can't park there, but then changes his mind, saying he likes to encourage people to do the Wayfarer's Walk. We shout a cheery 'thank you' and download the dogs, children and kit.

The church hall is hosting a 'bring and buy' sale later that morning, so the man warns us the car park may get a little squished. Archie checks out the early items brought to buy and I grab him just as he is cocking his leg on a box of CDs. Luckily, the nice man who let us park doesn't see. I take Archie on to the large green field where he can cock his leg to his heart's content.

Wayfarer's Walk

The church has a slight Gothic look to it, with its tall cone of a spire, but it's classically English, with flint walls and a long, sloping, red-tiled roof. It's so easy to forget that other countries don't have villages, as we do, built around a church. I visited a hamlet recently in West Sussex that has a church large enough for a hundred people and only seven houses anywhere near it.

We have been examining the church and its glorious windows for quite a while when, eventually, my brother and sister-in-law arrive, full of apologies that they'd got the time wrong. That brings our walking team up to seven adults, seven children and four dogs. The sun is shining, spring flowers are appearing and there's the faint aroma of a freshly mown lawn. That and a whiff of dog poo, which I've picked up and deposited in a bin.

Andrew seems to have come dressed as a footballer who has just finished a training session and doesn't want to be recognized. He's wearing blue tracksuit bottoms, a red hooded sweatshirt, a baseball cap pulled low over his eyes and trainers. Admittedly, I look like I am heading off on a Scout's camping mission: khaki shorts, trainers and a blue polo shirt, with a khaki canvas rucksack that I bought last summer in a shop in Chagford, Devon, that sells everything.

'Have you got an OS map?' I ask my brother, knowing what the answer will be.

'No,' he says. 'I thought you had all that stuff.'

Of course, I would have had a map if we'd been attempting the whole walk, but the section I'd picked was reputed to be well marked. Plus, I'd taken photos on my phone of the bits I thought we needed. So, although I didn't physically have a map, I did have a sort of route planner.

The dogs are sniffing bottoms and scampering around, while the children do pretty much the same. Alice is keeping an eye on Archie in case he sparks canine warfare. He can be a bit fractious if he's threatened, but all seems fine as we set off up a gentle slope to the left side of the church.

The boys chatter about how they want to build a time machine so they can go back and see what the route would've looked like in medieval times. We come to the conclusion that it would have appeared pretty much as it does now, which is part of the attraction. We are walking in the footsteps of stockmen who would've taken their sheep or cows in the other direction to market at New Alresford or Emsworth, from where they would have been shipped abroad.

Despite the floods in the village below, the chalk path is dry and even. The first couple of miles fly by, with a hum of birds singing, people chatting and children falling over. The older boys chuck a rugby ball backwards and forwards and, as the path emerges from its tunnel of hawthorn trees, we spot a herd of about thirty fallow deer running in their strange hoppy, jumpy way across a drilled field.

We walk three abreast, groups changing and children running up to ask questions. Seven-year-old Jamie Mackinnon decides he likes long-distance walking and wants to plan a walking and camping trip along the South Downs Way. Eight-year-old Jacobi thinks he might like to cycle it instead.

Wayfarer's Walk

'If I pushed myself to my limit,' he says earnestly, 'I think I could cycle for twelve hours a day and I would cover quite a lot of ground.'

'But you wouldn't see the countryside like we're seeing it now,' responds Jamie. 'I think it's nicer to go slower and take it all in, and if you're cycling you don't get to enjoy this – listen! It's so quiet.'

Ah, the wisdom of youth. Sometimes I think we spend so much time revering the old for supposedly being wise that we miss the direct truthfulness of the young. Mind you, I interviewed Baroness Trumpington recently and she is of the opinion that you earn the right to honesty with age. She says what she means and means what she says. I told her I plan to be dangerously honest by the time I am fifty.

'You'll get into trouble,' she told me. 'But the beauty of it is that you won't care!'

The chalky path is wide enough for three or four people to walk alongside, and even wide enough for the buggy containing the youngest Mackinnon child, Ella. I hadn't factored a buggy into my planning. As I hadn't done a recce, I had no idea if this was a route with a stile every hundred yards, or none at all. I love children, without ever having wanted one of my own, but I am not in tune with the needs of people with little legs.

As luck would have it, we only have to pick up the buggy once on the whole walk.

The children are remarkably cheery, don't complain about blisters or cramp, and seem to enjoy the wide views towards the South Downs behind us and across to Winchester on our left. I explain to Jonno and Toby that it's better to do a walk from south to north so that the sun is behind you and lighting up the way ahead, rather than shining in your face and making you squint. They think Auntie Clare is very clever for knowing that, but I am fairly certain that – like most things – I've cribbed it from someone else.

Toby is the first to crack. Mothers have a way of knowing exactly how much their children can take, and Anna Lisa turns back after two or three miles to get the car and meet us on the one road we cross before Dummer.

Toby bails out with fellow five-year-old Daisy and her little sister, Ella, while the rest of us carry on up the track towards Dummer Grange Farm. As we have covered about four miles, with just over two to go, for the first time I relax and think we might all make it in one piece without the children being put off walking for life. I smile as I hear Jamie and Jonno decide that, when they embark on their long-distance walk, they will use a company to take their kit from one stop to the next.

We skirt around Tidley Hill, turn left down a track, and meet a dog walker coming the other way.

'That's the first person we've seen,' says Jonno.

Coming into Dummer, we stop to say hello to three donkeys in a field. The two brown ones look healthy, but the old grey one is clearly bowing to the effects of old age. We ponder the uses for donkeys and decide they are rather lovely companions but their practical uses might be limited, outside the obvious acting role in the local Nativity play.

Wayfarer's Walk

'I think that one might actually have been in Nazareth carrying Jesus,' says my brother, pointing at the old fellow.

Dummer is less than a mile from the M3, but the hum of constant traffic hits you only as you turn left and head towards the motorway. We cross right underneath it and then do a good impression of the shepherds who would have used the Wayfarer's Walk as we gather up the children and the dogs to cross the A30 to the Sun Inn.

The kids are thrilled that they've completed the challenge, and I have to say, if I was going to recommend a child-friendly walk with a good pub at the end of it (with a play area), Brown Candover to Dummer ticks all the boxes.

'Now listen, girl,' says my brother as we sit down to lunch. 'I think we should make it all the way home, so don't hang about. If we set off by three, we'll do it easy.'

'Don't be ridiculous,' Alice interrupts. 'You won't get all the way to Kingsclere tonight. I'll come and collect you from North Oakley or Hannington, or wherever you end up.'

My natural optimism was being tested by Andrew's imagination and lack of long-distance-walking experience. I knew it was about fifteen miles home and the light would start to fade at six o'clock. We had three hours to get there, which meant cracking on at racing pace. It also meant we had no time to get lost or be diverted by flooding.

I

New Boots

I have bought new boots off t'Internet. I tried them on briefly at home and, if I say so myself, they look great. I have decided that brown or black is dull, so I've gone for a light-maroon pair that were, to my surprise, on offer. As a committed saver of cling film and peeler-off of stamps, I cannot resist an offer.

I am so busy admiring my new boots that I nearly miss my stop. My *Ramblings* producer, Lucy, is picking me up at Tiverton Parkway, our new favourite railway station, because it's so close to the M5 that it's barely a deviation.

'Nice boots,' says Lucy. 'Are they new?'

I puff out my chest like a budgerigar. 'Oh yes. Aren't they smart? And do you know what? They only cost thirty quid!'

Lucy stifles a laugh. I have no idea why. 'You surprise me,' she says, in a voice that doesn't sound surprised at all.

'I'll drive,' I say.

It's the rule when we're on the road. Much as I'd love to study my notes, gossip, twiddle the radio dial and check Twitter, Lucy's driving is so awful that it's easier if I do it. Watching her try to select a gear is like watching the little white ball decide which section it's going to fall into on the roulette wheel. Will it be fourth, fifth, possibly third? A lurch from the abused engine suggests it's second gear. Again. Always fun at 60mph.

Lucy and I have been walking together for most of our adult lives and have seen each other through all sorts of personal triumphs and tragedies. We randomly change topics of conversation without having to explain the logic of jumping from bonsai trees to the Winter Olympics, to her son's girlfriend, who is currently singing in the Far East. (The link, if you're interested, is Nagano – the Japanese host city of the Winter Olympics in 1998.)

Lucy knows that I don't like ham, tomato or pineapple, she will put up with a bit of BBC Radio 5 Live, for my sake, before re-tuning to Radio 4, and we both get a bit hyper if we drink too much coffee. When we first met, in 1999, I was very nervous and I made the mistake of taking a work phone call just before we started walking, the subject of which then distracted me for the next hour. She then banned me from having my phone on until after we have finished recording. I think the ban still stands, but she doesn't know that I sometimes keep it on silent in my pocket . . .

Twelve years ago, when we got adventurous and did a few walks abroad, we got tipsy on sangria in Spain and revealed far too much information to each other. There was no going back after that. We have giggled hysterically at ridiculous situations and people, we have been outraged, impressed or touched by others and we have cried into each other's arms when things have got tough. We have got lost – many times – but we always find our way back again.

I do, though, sometimes question her party-planning skills. Alice and I invited her to our civil-partnership party in 2006. I had urged her to stay in London, but she didn't want to spend money on a hotel. She had such a good time that she missed the last train home and ended up in Northampton, two hours away from where she lives. She then had to pay over a hundred quid for a taxi to take her home. I didn't need to point out that any hotel near us would have been cheaper, and more comfortable.

Then there was the time she came to the launch party for my first book, *My Animals and Other Family*. Worried about creasing her new linen dress on the train, she'd decided to put it into a carry-bag, which she promptly left at home. I remember thinking that her white trench coat was very nice, but a bit of an odd choice for a drinks party.

Anyhow, my brand-new boots got their first *Ramblings* outing in Somerset, with a poet. The sky looked a little grumpy, and so was the poet, who seemed surprised that we were there at all, almost as if she'd forgotten we were coming. We trudged out of her freezing house, which had no electricity, and set off through a gap in the hedge towards a river. She wasn't exactly forthcoming, so, despite my feet feeling a little cramped, I went on a full charm offensive, determined to warm her up.

On the train to Tiverton Parkway, I'd been reading her work, much of which was about her husband. So I thought it perfectly natural to enquire after his whereabouts.

'Why are you asking about my husband?' she said, slightly spitting between gritted teeth.

'Well, because you write about him so beautifully,' I replied, with what I thought was a winning smile.

'I'd rather you didn't. The bastard left me last month and I don't want to talk about it.'

Right, well, there we are.

I may have said these words out loud, in that way you do when you have absolutely no idea how you are going to fill the next three hours, which were meant to be spent in warm, radio-friendly conversation. My toes had curled in embarrassment and I couldn't seem to straighten them again. Ow.

Just as the poet was finally defrosting, the heavens opened. Now that it had started, however, Lucy didn't want to interrupt the flow of conversation. I pointed at my legs and at her rucksack (where I'd shoved my waterproof trousers) and at the sky, but she shook her head and did that thing where her eyes tell me what I'm meant to do next. Message received – I kept asking questions and the poet kept responding. Fifteen minutes later I was soaked to the skin and, as well as cramp, I had foot rot.

We came to a road and had to stop, so I seized my chance.

'My trousers are soaked,' I said. 'I'm going to have to take them off and put the waterproofs on instead. I think my new boots are a bit tight as well. I'll go into that bus shelter.'

Lucy followed me with the rucksack, and kept recording. I let out a sigh of relief as I unlaced my boots, my feet finally released, like a horse being turned out into the paddock. Ooh, that felt good! I covered the red bits in blister plasters (about five of them on each foot). Lucy was surprisingly unsympathetic. I commentated on the stripping-off of wet trousers and the pulling-on of dry waterproofs, more as a joke for us than for broadcast. I didn't realize Lucy was going to put it in the programme.

This little interlude is what prompted the strangest fan letter I have ever received:

Dear Miss Balding,

I would like to congratulate you on the most erotic radio I have ever listened to.

I have not listened to Ramblings *before but I will certainly be tuning in from now on, particularly if you continue in this manner. They say the pictures are better on the radio and I now know exactly what they mean. It was quite thrilling.*

Many congratulations. An alternative career most definitely awaits, should you desire one.

Yours sincerely,

*Major Jonathan Harrington-Harvey**

* Not his real name, of course. At least I hope it's not.

We walk whatever the weather.

Only once in fifteen years have we had to postpone an adventure. We were in the North Pennines, planning a spectacular walk from High Force Waterfall to Low Force and back again. But when we stepped out from the protective shield of the visitor centre, the wind nearly blew us off the hilltop.

I looked at the sheep huddled into the base of the stone walls that divided their field and figured that they weren't as stupid as they looked. We *could* walk in the wind, but the microphone (even with its fluffy cover) could not handle the buffeting. The wind took our voices and deposited them on the ears of sheep a mile away. There was no point in recording, so we drew stumps and came back another day.

Apart from that occasion, we will walk in rain, snow and ice, through mud and through sand.

I arrive home and tell Alice that we must move to Yorkshire or Cornwall or the Orkneys. She nods and says, 'Of course we must,' before sending Lucy a text: 'She wants to move again. Must have been a good walk.'

I am better now at assessing distance than when we first started. I remember trudging along Hadrian's Wall with a student from Newcastle University who turned to me after a short descriptive monologue during which I'd incorrectly assessed how far we had travelled.

'Do you do this for effect,' he asked, 'or are you just stupid?'

It's quite tricky to carry on polite conversation with someone after they've said that to your face. It's even harder to do so while walking through featureless countryside on a horrid day trying to make a programme in which you are meant to sound as if you're enjoying the experience.

Lucy shot me a look of supportive horror and let me drop back to lick my wounds while she sweet-talked old clever clogs into a kinder mood. This was early in our walking relationship, and it was the moment I knew we would be friends for life.

Sometimes, Lucy switches off the tape machine for ten minutes, partly because it's not practical to record when we're all in single file and partly because it means she can talk to members of the group and warm them up, finding out information for the next 'scene'. Lucy thinks in scenes, like in a play, and fades out of one and into the next, but the work she does 'backstage', talking to the walkers before we start and during the walk, is as important as the recording or the editing.

Between us, we try to start each programme slightly differently. Some will start with someone else talking – for example, the leader telling the group where we are walking – and some will start with me already on the move, or on my way to meet the walkers.

Once we started in a café, trying to decide whether it was safe to climb up the north face of Tryfan in the pouring rain. Luckily, the answer was in the negative and, although we didn't stay where I wanted to (in the warm and dry of the café, eating cake and drinking coffee), we did go on a slightly less challenging, lateral route.

Lucy was most offended by a letter she received complaining about the loudness of the sound effects on a walk we did in Dorset. We were traipsing through a particularly deep and sticky ploughed field, discussing Thomas Hardy.

'Sound effects? What sound effects?' she spluttered. 'What an outrageous slur! I'm going to write back and tell him that we've never used any sound effects and, if he doesn't know what walking across a sopping-wet ploughed field sounds like, then he needs to get out more. Preferably in the rain.'

Lucy records 'wild track' every so often. We all have to be quiet while she looks into the middle distance and I mouth, 'Are you sure it's recording?' The ambient sound, whether it be a river flowing, sheep baaing or aeroplanes overhead, is the glue that holds the programme together. Any jumps in conversation can be covered with a little bit of wild track. So no, we don't use sound effects, but we do use the soundtrack of the day.

As she does that, I try to live those moments more fully, mainly thanks to a doctor we walked with in the hills near Hay-on-Wye who tried to teach me 'mindfulness'.

I didn't arrive in the best frame of mind. I'd been filming until 2 a.m. the day before in a studio in Salford and the journey to Hay had taken about three hours longer than I wanted it to. The wind was too strong to follow our original plan of walking up to Lord Hereford's Knob, so we walked on lower ground on the border with Wales. I was grumpy with Lucy, grumpy with the weather and grumpy with life. Not myself at all.

Right at that moment, I felt I didn't need to be out on a windy hill recording *Ramblings*. After about ten minutes, I realized it was the thing I needed more than anything else. If ever there was a 'wake-up call', this walk was it.

It doesn't come naturally to me to walk in silence. It doesn't come naturally to me to do anything much in silence. But Dr Kate Kirkwood made me understand that walking was a chance to break the cycle of 'all the talking, all the thinking and all the interacting we spend all our waking hours doing'. She made me concentrate on my footsteps, made me feel the ground beneath my feet, listen to my breathing and feel the wind on my face. This wasn't a walk so much as a couple of hours' free therapy.

Kate explained that you need to practise mindfulness, to escape thoughts, to just *be*: 'Even in the middle of a busy day surrounded by people, you can remind yourself to be conscious of the sensation of your feet within your shoes on the ground, or the feeling of the chair against your thighs. You can dip into the body at any time and, strangely, that seems to help to anchor me and keep me calm.'

I *am* conscious of my body, but only when it's hurting. I don't appreciate it for the things it does every day without complaining. The joy of simply being able to walk is something I have recently tried not to take for granted. I now refer to my morning perambulations as my 'freedom walks'. Not just because I feel that they are an escape from the phone and the computer, but because I am free to walk. I can do it without pain, my dodgy back and knees having improved for regular gentle exertion, and my head is clearer.

Talking of the head, Kate said something that I'd never considered before: 'Thinking is overrated. We think so much, but if we really look at what we're thinking, isn't it the same old things over and over again? Where has all your thinking got you? For me, I would say not very far. What has been more useful to me has been trying to cultivate some sort of calm by sinking beneath the thinking. Cultivating "being" rather than constantly "doing" – whether that's doing physically or mentally.'

I thought about the things I thought about and immediately got a headache. Usually, it's a vicious little vortex of decisions I have to make about how many work commitments I can fit into a given day, stress about letters I haven't replied to or meetings I'm being persuaded to attend . . . It's not that I don't like a meeting (I love them), but there are just so many of them, and few of them seem to achieve anything.

I tried to practise putting my mind on standby. Kate explained that I wouldn't be able to stop thinking, but the trick was not to follow the thoughts. I could notice that thoughts had sprung up but I was not to develop them. I tried it, for at least a minute. I chanted to myself, 'I am here, I am now.' It made me more aware of everything around me, the feel of my feet within my boots, the sound of the mud squelching beneath them, the change in wind direction and the sudden warmth of light from the sun.

'I am here, I am now.'

(Take two steps.)

'I am here, I am now.'

When the minute was up, my mind was bursting with even more ideas than before. I started thinking about the mental benefits of sport, the way it gives people time to concentrate purely on the game being played or the race being run. Sport creates a sort of meditation, and it feeds into my belief that concentration is the key to happiness. I am sure the same is true of playing music, or gardening, or sewing, or indeed reading – they offer our brains the chance to zero in on the thing in front of us and not be distracted by fast, random thoughts that flash into our heads.

Maybe that's why children are so captivated by video games and why even adults get addicted to their PlayStations. When I interviewed Usain Bolt I was surprised that the fastest man in the world is an obsessive 'gamer'. His passion for video games is matched only by his appreciation of Manchester United, both giving him a thrill and a sense of jeopardy that can't hurt him. I've also heard of footballers who stay up all night playing games and go straight to a match the next day.

I can see why their brains need that fix. I'd rather go for a walk.

Lucy gave me a framed photograph for my fortieth birthday. It shows five of us walking along a beach, wearing caps and many layers of clothing. There is enough light to cast shadows of our frames on the shimmering sand ahead of us. The sand is glistening not with sunlight but with rain. It is a grim day and, not surprisingly, there is no one else daft enough to be walking anywhere near us.

Luckily for one who lives on our fair isle, I like the rain. When I was young I used to run out into the garden with my mouth open and my face turned up to the sky, catching droplets on my tongue. I had a quote copied in my teenage diary that read 'Life is not about waiting for the storm to pass – it's about learning to dance in the rain,' and I took it literally. As soon as it started to rain, I was out there *dancing*.

(My mother is of the school that says there is no such thing as bad weather, only bad clothing. She is a no-nonsense kind of a mum. If you've had a fall and you're not unconscious, you should just get up and carry on. Mum listened to an early edition of *Ramblings* but didn't like it because I was, apparently, 'constantly out of breath'. I don't think she's listened since.)

Anyway, the photo Lucy gave me is of a walk we did on the east coast of Scotland, just north of Aberdeen. We were exploring a natural phenomenon known as the Sands of Forvie. It's a national nature reserve and unique because of the sand dunes, which stretch for three and a half miles in length and one mile in width.

There is no protection from the wind on the sands, and on the

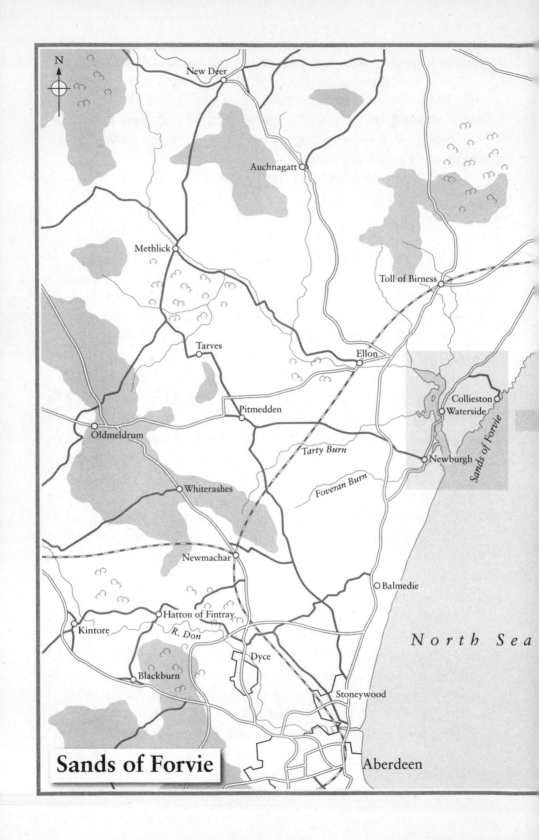

N

New Deer

Auchnagatt

Methlick

Toll of Birness

Tarves

Ellon

Pitmedden

Collieston
Waterside

Oldmeldrum

Tarty Burn

Newburgh

Sands of Forvie

Whiterashes

Foveran Burn

Newmachar

Balmedie

Hatton of Fintray

R. Don

Kintore

North Sea

Dyce

Blackburn

Stoneywood

Aberdeen

Sands of Forvie

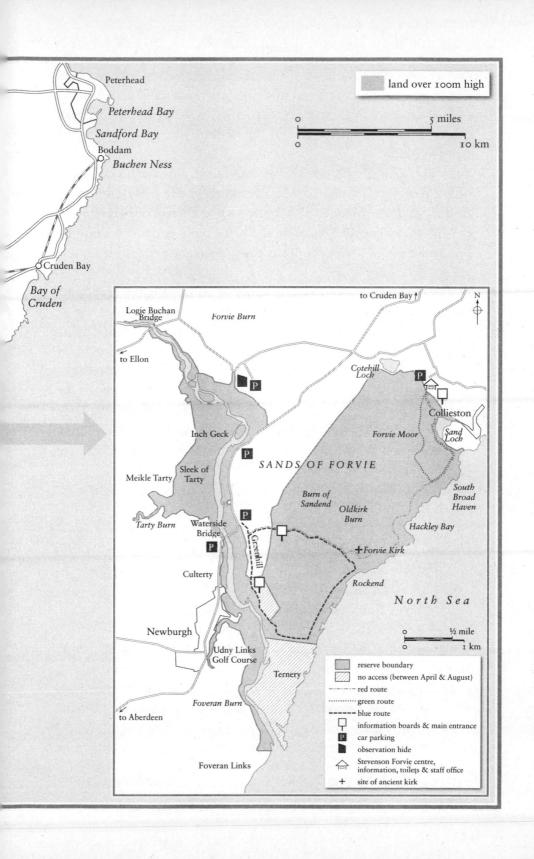

land over 100m high

Peterhead
Peterhead Bay
Sandford Bay
Boddam
Buchen Ness

Cruden Bay

Bay of
Cruden

0 ____ 5 miles
0 ____ 10 km

to Cruden Bay

N

Logie Buchan
Bridge
Forvie Burn

to Ellon

Cotehill
Loch

Collieston

Inch Geck

Forvie Moor

Sand
Loch

SANDS OF FORVIE

Meikle Tarty

Sleek of
Tarty

South
Broad
Haven

Burn of
Sandend

Oldkirk
Burn

Hackley Bay

Tarty Burn

Waterside
Bridge

Forvie Kirk

Greenhill

Culterty

Rockend

North Sea

Newburgh

0 ____ ½ mile
0 ____ 1 km

Udny Links
Golf Course

Ternery

Foveran Burn

to Aberdeen

reserve boundary

no access (between April & August)

red route

green route

blue route

information boards & main entrance

car parking

observation hide

Stevenson Forvie centre,
information, toilets & staff office

site of ancient kirk

Foveran Links

day we visited we could see the dunes moving, along with our hair. The formation is revised and reworked by the wind daily. Even the trees are stunted in growth because of it. I was beginning to think I might shrink over the course of the walk, I was bending into the wind so much.

I was walking with one of Forvie's finest, Elizabeth Hay. Elizabeth's family had come to Aberdeenshire in the early eighteenth century and she told me she has always had a sense of belonging.

'This is my part of Scotland,' she explained, 'and it's like putting on an old pair of slippers. It's a place that always changes but is always the same.'

The landscape looked as if an army of children had built a sandcastle village and a giant had come along and kicked it in. I wasn't too far off the truth, because there was, explained my guides, a hidden village under the sand. That spooked me – the thought of buildings and bones beneath us.

My sense of discomfort increased when they spoke about the 'Curse of Forvie'. The daughter of the laird had inherited a large tract of land and her uncle was not impressed. In what he thought was an entirely reasonable response, he put her 'out to sea': he sent her off on a boat, never to return.

As the winds filled the sails, the unlucky heiress put a curse on Forvie, shouting:

> If ever maydenis malysone
> Dyd licht upon dry land,
> Lat nocht bee fund in Furvye's glebys
> bot thystl, bente and sande.

Meaning that if she was never allowed to return to dry land, the village would never be the same. The curse came to fruition in 1413, when a sandstorm covered the whole thing, burying the buildings. All of them. No one was killed, which makes it a fairly humane curse, in my view.

The eeriness of Forvie seeped under my skin as we stood on the dunes. There are times when landscapes move you, touch you deep within and leave you with a lasting sense of something special. You can't appreciate it from the windows of a car, or a train. You can't take a short cut and pull over into a lay-by to take a photo. The only way really to *feel* the landscape is to walk it.

That's especially true of walking on sand, which gives you that feeling as you sink with each step. And as long as it's packed firm, walking on sand is easier, because it's flat terrain. Unless you are stupid and decide to scale the dunes themselves, which of course I did. The protest from my calves lasted for days.

If you walk where the sand is dry, your feet slip back with every stride, so it's like walking on a treadmill. The hard, wet sand is the best option, which is where my Forvie companions stayed and where, finally, I rejoined them. We strolled happily, five abreast, the Scottish wind whipping our faces.

Elizabeth told me how she used to play Arabs in the Desert when she was a child, and shared a rather alarming story of her son heading out to collect sea shells and driftwood and coming home proudly with an incendiary bomb, a remnant of the Second World War use of the Forvie Sands as an artillery range. She seemed unfussed: it was just one of those things you find.

It was a grey day, but Ellie Ingram, an artist who was also with us, told me that if she were painting the scene she would dip into a palette of orange and brown, yellow, coral, blue, green and white. I love walking with artists, because they see so much more.

'It looks grey on first glimpse,' she explained, 'but that's just our lazy eye interpretation. Look closer and you'll see the colours.'

The marram grass rose above the dunes, giving them a shifting Mohican hairstyle. The sky loomed, full of angry grey clouds. The seahorses were jumping imaginary fences, landing in a bath of North Sea foam.

We stopped for what Elizabeth called a 'chittery bite' – when she swam in the North Sea as a child, her teeth would chatter when she came out and she'd snack on her food with a staccato nibble. She told me that if I were to swim in the bay I should pick the north side. As the rain continued to fall with steady determination, I pointed out that the very idea of swimming in the bay was about as attractive as dancing naked on the North Pole.

The coastline had turned from a sweet, benign child into a bit of a stroppy teenager, with rocks and rugged bays. I love that the coast of Britain does that. In the space of an hour your feet can take you from broad, open, flat sands to rocky inlets with steep climbs and slippery descents.

I have joined a few different people taking on the challenge of walking the whole of Britain's coastline (them, not me) – just over eleven thousand miles if you follow the footpaths. They all proclaim how varied it is from one day to the next. Nerdy fact alert: did you know that nowhere in the UK is more than seventy miles from the coast?

I was soon planning to move to the east coast of Scotland and visit the Sands of Forvie every day.

Only one thing put me off. Normally at the end of a walk we head to a pub for a warming bowl of soup and a glass of ginger beer. (Drinking alcohol in the daytime makes me sleepy, but this at least sounds as if I'm drinking beer and it has a little kick of ginger to make my taste buds feel naughty.) Buffeted and blown by the Aberdeenshire air, I was mentally choosing between French onion with a Parmesan crouton, blue Stilton and broccoli with ground black pepper, and creamy cauliflower.

I may have been over-optimistic in my culinary expectations. On the south–north route we'd taken along the Sands of Forvie our end point was the village of Collieston. It sounded promising. It sounded just like a village with two or three pubs, a roaring fire in each and a buxom landlady ready to wrap exhausted walkers in a tartan rug.

I discovered that Collieston was the burial place of a renowned smuggler. It's also known for a folk dance called the 'Lang Reel of Collieston', a favourite at local weddings. All well and good, but the crucial information for walkers is that Collieston is rare in Scotland (and in the UK in general) for not having a pub. *Not a single pub.*

My home village of Kingsclere has the Crown, the George and Horn, the Swan, the Star and probably another couple I don't even know about. It should lend one of them to Collieston.

Apparently, there was once a fine and alcoholically ambitious local hotel. But in 1911 the women of Collieston got fed up with their menfolk indulging a little too enthusiastically in the spirits on offer. They formed a temperance group and had the hotel closed down. There has been no replacement since. Not in over a hundred years has anyone dared to trample on the desires of that temperance group.

Now, I am a proud feminist and fully respect the women of Collieston for wanting their men to work a little harder, but all I wanted was a bowl of soup, a ginger beer and a warm place to sit down and dry out.

Short of knocking on doors, that wasn't going to happen. We went back to Elizabeth's house and I peeled off my wet clothes, this time without Lucy recording me as I did so. I thought of Major Harrington-Harvey and wondered how on earth anyone could think taking off wet clothes constituted erotic radio.

Each to their own.

2

The Whisky Walkers

You would think that all you need to record a walking programme, apart from good walking boots, a microphone and the promise of a pub at the end . . . is a voice.

It helps. It really does. But Lucy and I have proved that you don't necessarily have to be able to speak to make a radio programme. Whether it's any good or not is open to debate (this one ended up being discussed on Radio 4's *Feedback*, and the reviews were, let's say, 'varied').

It was March 2003 and we were on our way up to Scotland. The night before, I had rung Lucy and croaked, 'I've lost my voice.'

For some reason, I was expecting her to show me some compassion, suggest we postpone our trip to Scotland and send me a bunch of flowers to make me feel better, or at least a packet of throat lozenges.

'You'll be fine. And I've already paid for the tickets' is what she actually said, before launching into travel arrangements and where she would meet me at Edinburgh Airport.

My throat in those days was often a little tender. Perhaps it was my body's early warning system and I should have noticed sooner. I would routinely lose my voice or get an ear infection (probably from always having an earpiece in my left ear with TV talkback blasting its way into my brain). In 2006, I was diagnosed with thyroid cancer and had three operations over the next couple of years to remove my thyroid and then lymph nodes in my throat. It's not much fun when a surgeon is about to slice into your neck and you have to sign a piece of paper saying that you understand you may suffer permanent damage to your voicebox. I asked him to be careful.

When I was suffering from just a sore throat, I could usually fix it 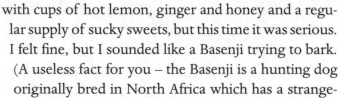 with cups of hot lemon, ginger and honey and a regular supply of sucky sweets, but this time it was serious. I felt fine, but I sounded like a Basenji trying to bark. (A useless fact for you – the Basenji is a hunting dog originally bred in North Africa which has a strange-shaped larynx. Instead of barking, it comes out with a croaky sort of yodel.)

In those days, we had a sound assistant, whose job it was to carry the microphone and monitor the sound quality so that Lucy, attached by a pair of headphones to the DAT (Digital Audio Tape) machine, could concentrate on the content. Our soundman was called Pete and he was very kind. I could guarantee a more sensitive reaction from him.

When I arrived at Edinburgh Airport, I walked sheepishly across to Lucy and Pete, who were waiting for the microphone pole to appear on the baggage carousel from their flight from Birmingham. (It has to be checked into the hold, I guess, in case it's used to assault the pilot. Is that a thing? Has that ever actually happened?)

'Hello,' I whispered.

'Jeez,' said Pete. 'What's happened to you?'

I pointed at my throat. 'Gone,' I mouthed. 'Can't talk.'

He looked at Lucy, who ignored him and offered me a coffee – as if that would magically solve the problem.

'She'll be fine,' she said, with a confidence I suspected she did not feel.

Pete furrowed his brow and shook his head at me. I sipped the sugared coffee and wondered what the hell we were all doing.

We broke one of our golden rules of *Ramblings* on that trip. Usually, we try not to spend any time with the people we're walking with before we start recording, not because Lucy and I are unfriendly, but because they tend to share all their best stories as soon as you meet them. However good a storyteller you are, it's hard to tell a person a tale for the first time twice.

On this occasion, we were intending to walk near Lochearnhead (OS Explorer Map 365, if you're interested) with a group of women who called themselves 'The Monday Walkers'.

That would be because they walk together – you guessed it – every Monday.

We had come across them while we were recording another programme in Lanark. We heard them in the woods because they were loud and lost. We'd got chatting, they offered us some whisky and asked us to come and walk with them. So we did, two months later.

The Monday Walkers liked to *really* walk. Not for them a 6- or 7-mile stroll. No, they were 14- to 16-milers. They didn't care if they were out on the hillside for seven hours.

Keenly aware that it was going to be a long day in Perthshire, we had come up the night before. We'd accepted an offer from Ulla Ross and her husband, who run a B&B, of a room and dinner. Ulla held out two keys.

'Now, one's a double and one's a twin,' she said, 'so who's sharing with who?'

She looked at Pete and then at me. Then at Lucy and then at Pete. His life flashed before his eyes at the prospect of being forced to share a room – or worse, a bed – with either of us.

Finally, Lucy grabbed a key and said, 'Clare and I will share. Pete, you're on your own.'

We took our bags up to our room, to find two twin beds side by side. I like Lucy very much but I didn't really want to sleep right next to her. She felt the same, so without saying a word we moved to the side of the twin beds and pulled them apart, leaving a respectable gap of a couple of feet.

I tried not to worry about making strange noises in the night that might destroy our working partnership. At the very least, losing my voice might mean I wouldn't snore.

We had dinner with the whole gang. My voice was working just fine at midnight when the wine was flowing and they were telling tales about their expeditions, husbands, first boyfriends and various illnesses. I think Pete learned more about women in that one evening than he had in his previous thirty-five years on earth.

By nine o'clock the following morning, I wasn't feeling so clever. My head throbbed and my voice had disappeared completely. It would have been fine if we were just walking, but walking *and* talking was going to be a challenge.

Ulla was from Sweden and told me she had never really walked there, but since she had come to Scotland and met Anne, Annette and the others she was a convert. She was quite wild, with an extended Swedish family who seemed to get naked at any opportunity. She had skinny-dipped in the sea, in various rivers and in many lakes.

Call me a prude, but I am not generally a fan of nudity.

At school I perfected the art of taking off or putting on clothes without revealing any skin to the outside world. I can take a shirt off from under a jumper, remove a bra from under three layers, and use a towel to protect my lower half in case anyone should ever know that I have a bottom. On my occasional visits to the gym, I am the only one who uses the corner changing room with the door that shuts. Everyone else stands there applying talcum powder all over, chatting about the new Zumba instructor, and I just want to scream, '*Put some clothes on!*'

I started to worry that the Monday Walkers would begin to strip off halfway up a Munro and insist that we join in. At least we had Pete with us, who although in touch with his feminine side in a kind and gentle way was, undeniably, a man. That should be enough to save us all, I hoped.

Anne Hunter and Annette Mackintosh seemed to be the leaders of the gang. Anne was tall, with dark hair, and possessed an innate elegance, even in walking gear. Her voice was soft and deep, with enough of a Scottish accent to indicate where she came from but not so strong to make it difficult for an English ear to understand. She explained the genesis of the group.

'We've been friends for a lot of years. We used to meet on a Monday for lunch, then we discovered we were all getting a bit fat, so we started walking.

'We started by always walking six or seven miles. Sometimes we would start one walk and then change plans and "chase the blue skies", which started to take us further. Now, we're quite adventurous. I can't say any of it has made us any thinner, but it's been great.'

Annette was the life and soul of the party. She was the naughty one, the one who would talk the rest of the group into drinking shots and start dancing on the table. Her day's walking would usually end up with her and Ulla back at her house, drinking whisky and singing along loudly with a 1950s singer I'd never heard of called Freddy Fender. She had the quick one-liners and the warped outlook on life.

'Don't be taking a photo from behind me,' she shouted. 'It'll be all backside.'

Annette liked metaphorically to throw the map away and take 'interesting tracks'. Her knowledge of the various landmarks would ensure that 'although we're lost, we know where we are'. It made perfect sense to her, if not to me.

She also seemed to be a walking distillery.

'As we've got older, we need a few little bottles of malt whisky in our bags,' said Annette. She wasn't joking. I could hear the rucksacks clinking as they pulled them on the next morning. A better name for the group might have been 'The Whisky Walkers'.

They were surprisingly jolly, considering the night before. Maybe they were just more used to heavy drinking than I was. The average age of the group was sixty, and they had all been through the sort of experiences you would expect from women who have lived and loved. Ulla had recently had breast cancer and a mastectomy.

'She just did it to get one up on me,' said Annette. 'I mean, I was leading, because I'd had a hysterectomy, and you can't join this group unless you've had a sexual organ surgically removed.'

'Does a cartilage count?' I asked.

'Not unless you've been having sex with your knee,' laughed Annette. 'Also, you have to be half blind, losing your memory, be having or have had your menopause, have varicose veins and have had them done. And, of course, be a whisky drinker.'

That's the kind of group they were. I loved them and wanted to be one of them. As we set off into the Perthshire hills, I realized I might be younger than all of them, but I certainly wasn't fitter. I was breathing deeply after a mile and hadn't been able to talk even before I'd started puffing.

I learned a valuable lesson that day. Although it's not ideal to broadcast when you can't speak, there's a lot to be said for leaving room for others to talk.

Anne was immediately protective and took over for me, by giving most of the descriptions. Annette jollied me along with whisky and jokes while Ulla recommended a spot of skinny-dipping in the burn.

'You just take your cloves ov and dive in,' she enthused. 'It's so invigorating.'

I smiled nervously. Lucy saved me.

'It's a lovely idea, Ulla,' she said, 'but I think we'll leave it for now. The BBC Health and Safety regulations don't really cover skinny-dipping in freezing water.'

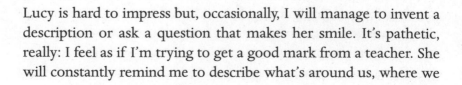

Lucy is hard to impress but, occasionally, I will manage to invent a description or ask a question that makes her smile. It's pathetic, really: I feel as if I'm trying to get a good mark from a teacher. She will constantly remind me to describe what's around us, where we are, where we are going, so that the listener can feel the progress of the walk.

My vocabulary varies depending on the book I'm reading, so I try to read something on the train that will help the descriptive side of things – poetry is particularly good. Once, I'd been reading some U. A. Fanthorpe and then described a moody, purple-grey sky as looking as if it was 'bruised'.

'That was quite good,' Lucy said. 'Sometimes I can see why you're worth it.'

'Just trying to make your life easier,' I replied. 'I know you're an above-average producer, but I'd hate you to do any actual work in the edit.'

Lucy is in charge of editing down the material we record into a 24-minute programme. Sometimes this is easy (she tells me) and sometimes it's a struggle, usually because good conversations have to be left out, or she decides there are too many voices and has to lose one. This is hard when we've spent the best part of a day walking with a person and we've really liked them. But Lucy is unsentimental when it comes to the cut.

In the old days, when I first learned to cut tape, you really did cut it – with a razor blade. There were razors all over the office at Broadcasting House and reel-to-reel tape recorders on which you listened to an interview, made a mark in chalk on the ribbon at the beginning of the word or sentence you wanted to remove, made another at the end of it, sliced through with the razor and then patched the remaining bits of ribbon together with a thin white piece of sticky tape. It was quite an art.

I loved de-umming an interview, taking out all the hesitations, false starts and irrelevant words to make a person sound perfectly fluent. It was a good idea to keep a few breaths on little bits of tape, stuck to the side of the machine, so that you could put one in if it was needed. Believe me, an interview with no breaths at all islikeasentencewithnospaces – hard to decipher.

Now, editing is all done digitally and it's a fair bit easier to repair mistakes if you accidentally chop out a crucial sentence. There's also no danger of putting the tape in upside down and back to front, which I did once with an interview with Alex Ferguson. I couldn't understand why he kept talking about a 'log'. Then I worked out I'd put the word 'goal' in backwards.

This is one of the many reasons why I do not interfere in the editing process. I trust Lucy to make it all sound the best it can. And I know it would *really* annoy her if I started questioning why she had left one section in and dropped another.

The recording kit itself has shrunk over the years. In the days when we had Pete, he carried a complicated piece of kit across his chest and held the microphone expertly in front of him for miles on end. Now, the digital recorder is barely as big as my hand. Lucy carries that, the microphone on a pole and a rucksack containing the first-aid kit, water and a few flapjacks. I sometimes offer to take the rucksack if I'm feeling really generous, but usually I just fill it with the things I don't want to carry.

I'm always worried that she has forgotten to press record and that we'll have to retrace our steps.

'Are you sure it's on?' I say, about five times during the course of the walk.

'Yes, it's on. I'm not an idiot,' Lucy replies, although I notice her checking that the red light is blinking.

In the days of Pete, neither of us had to worry. We just trusted him, then grilled him about his love life during breaks in recording. Pete is married now and runs his own company. I suspect we miss him more than he misses us.

After three hours with Pete, Lucy and the Whisky Walkers, I asked, tentatively, how far we had to go. The women were rather vague. Annette said we were at least halfway; Anne gestured to the view and said, 'Isn't it just wonderful?'; Ulla veered off dangerously towards the burn; and the others were skipping ahead. An hour later, I asked again: 'How far do you think we've got to go?'

'Well,' said Anne, 'I reckon we've done about nine miles now, so just another seven or so to go.'

'Seven?' I croaked. 'Bloody hell. You don't muck about.'

Once I'd accepted that we were going to be out in the wilds of Scotland for the best part of eight hours, I relaxed. I started to appreciate the vast open spaces around us, the lack of traffic noise, people and houses, and the strength of the friendship around me. We didn't need to speak all the time, so Pete could swing the boom microphone over his shoulder and stride on with the rest of the group. He quite enjoyed being an honorary woman for the day.

'It's kept us all young, and it's kept us sane,' Jess, who had taken over the lead, explained. 'Getting away on a Monday and talking through our losses and our problems – the ones everyone has – has been so valuable. We really talk and we share everything. You get to know people on a deeper level because you're not just seeing them in easy, comfortable situations. We come up against all kinds of weather and all kinds of circumstances, and we get through them. I think we give each other an inner strength.'

They joked with each other that 'a friend in need is a pain in the arse' but, from what I saw, these women would help each other out whatever the circumstances without even blinking. They knew when to encourage or cajole and when to back off. We stopped for lunch – and whisky – hunkering up to a rock for a bit of protection from the breeze. We could hear the water rushing by, feel the wind and see the big brown head of Ben Vorlich in the distance. It could only be a Scottish landscape. As Anne said, it was 'so Brigadoonish'.

'The best thing about Mondays,' she added, 'is that unless it's a bank holiday or we're on a Munro, you'll never see another soul.'

The Monday Walkers had climbed plenty of Munros, but they were not 'Munro Baggers'. That's the term for the folk who are determined to climb every peak over three thousand feet. There are 282 peaks above this height, and they were first listed in 1891 by Sir Hugh Munro, a founding member of the Scottish Mountaineering Club. Give a person a list and of course they will want to tick it off, peak by peak. More than five thousand people have climbed all the Munros, some starting or finishing with Ben Nevis, because it's the best known. The youngest 'Munroist' or 'completionist' was only ten when he finished the challenge. Ten years old!

The Monday Walkers were hard core, but at least they took their time to enjoy it.

That's the way it should be, because walking is something we can all do. It's not competitive – not unless you're with a particularly assertive group which wants to get to the next spot on the map as fast as it can and tick it off in the little black book. We have made that mistake before – I had paused to describe the Snowdonian scenery, and by the time I'd finished the group had disappeared over the brow of the hill. Lucy and I ran after them, cursing.

'It's not meant to be a bloody race,' she whispered. 'What's the point of walking through a landscape like this if you don't actually look at it?'

As we caught them up, I saw the gathering of brightly coloured socks and sensed a murmur of disapproval.

'We thought we'd lost you,' the leader said. 'Are we going too fast for you?' There was a hint of triumphalism in her face that made me want to prod her sharply with her two-tone walking pole.

The trouble is that, for some people, it *is* a race. There is a breed of walker out there that is all about covering the miles, ticking off the mountains scaled or the rivers forded. If they could wrestle crocodiles and eat raw meat along the way, they would. I call them 'the Alpha Ramblers'. They are very fit, have all the kit and use walking as a way of proving themselves to the world. They are – and I will be honest here – quite dull.

I'm sure there is room for all of us in the great big outdoors, but Lucy and I are not Alpha Ramblers. What we are, we're still trying to work out, but we do our best to take in our surroundings and enjoy ourselves, bearing in mind that Lucy's always carrying a pole with a furry microphone on the end:

'Ooh, look, it's a feather duster!'

'Is that a rabbit?'

'Ah, can I stroke it?'

And, 'Go on, Bonzo, *kill!*'

Yes, we've heard them all. Telling your Rottweiler to kill a BBC microphone is really not a very helpful thing to do, sir. In fact, it's irresponsible. Just plain irresponsible.

Archie occasionally comes along with me when I'm recording *Ramblings*. He's not averse to a bit of mild barking – particularly at people in hats or hoods – but he's never tried to attack the microphone. Nor has he peed on it, which can cause even more damage.

I always have to make sure the listener knows Archie is there. That helps to explain the 'noises off' as I urge him to keep up, scream at him to come back, or berate him – as I did on Hampstead Heath when I took him to meet a walking book-club – for sinking into the smelliest, muddiest puddle he could find. He lay there grinning at me, the white hair on his neck and around his nose turning black as he wallowed like a Gloucester Old Spot on a hot day. He then went loopy loo, running round and round the bemused book-club members, shaking himself and barking as he rushed by.

I think Lucy prefers it when Archie stays at home.

In my more energetic moments I can see the attraction of Munro bagging, and I have plenty of admiration for those who have done all 282 peaks, particularly those who have walked or cycled in between and slept out on the hillside. But I'm not sure it's really for me. I'm a bit too partial to a proper mattress and a hot shower, and I like a cup of hot tea in the morning, preferably brought to me in bed. A soft southerner? Yes, if you say so. Yes, I am.

Anne and Annette were forcing me to drink more whisky, while Ulla told me about them all stripping off to skinny-dip in a burn (honestly, the woman is obsessed) when a group of Scouts suddenly appeared.

'Vey must 'ave got the shock ov vare lives!'

The music of friendship echoed around the rocks as we started our descent. I was a little tiddly, but the dram worked well enough to allow me to finish the programme and the walk.

I will never forget the experience – I just wish I could remember the route. A combination of being hung-over, feeling like I was dying of laryngitis and being so tired I could barely see meant that I had no idea where we had been. Trust me, though, if you head up to Lochearnhead and stride out in pretty much any direction, you can't go wrong.

I went back recently to meet up with the Monday Walkers, ten years after our epic journey. Their adventures are a little more conservative now – they restrict themselves to six or seven miles on more kindly terrain. Three of them have been widowed, including Ulla, whose husband, Bill, had looked after us so well. Some of them have had hips or knees replaced, and one is contending with the early stages of Parkinson's disease.

But still they walk on. Every Monday.

Dummer–Kingsclere

At the pub in Dummer, the kids are discussing their plans for long-distance walks along the South Downs Way or the Appalachian Trail, which I have told them is the longest walk in the world. Andrew looks at his watch and tells me it is time to go. I may have planned the route, but he is the referee with the stopwatch in his hand.

So, at 3 p.m. on the dot, with my brother in his football disguise and me looking like a Boy Scout, we set off in search of the Wayfarer's Walk. I tell him it will be the longest time we've spent on our own together since we were teenagers.

'Bollocks,' he says. 'I sat next to you on the plane to America a couple of years ago.'

As I recall, he was either asleep or watching a film for most of that flight. I hadn't really stored it as a strong bonding experience.

Wayfarer's Walk

Over the years, we'd played a few rounds of golf together and occasionally shared a car journey, but one of us was always distracted by phone calls, or the radio, or hitting a golf ball. This will be different.

I sort of know the direction we're heading in, but my research had told me that this section of the walk isn't as well marked as our first six miles. We get a few funny looks from the customers at the garden centre as we walk up its drive and cut right to the edge of the field. I am fairly sure we can walk on the grassy edge and pick up the footpath at the top, which will eventually link across to our WW path. Andrew is on a mission, and I am soon fighting stitch from my roast-chicken lunch as I struggle to keep up.

The miles are ticking over at about four an hour. To be fair to my brother, he takes only one phone call, from a racehorse owner, and doesn't get cross with me when we take a right fork instead of going through Bull's Bushes Copse. We head along a damp tunnel under the railway line just south of Oakley, and hang left towards Deane, where we encounter our first major hurdle.

The road out of Deane is flooded. And I don't just mean the deep puddles of the Candovers. It is properly sunk in water maybe two or three feet high. Andrew thinks we can get through.

'You're all right, in those daft shorts,' he says. 'And I can roll up my tracksuit bottoms. Let's just wade through it and put our shoes and socks back on when we get to the other side.'

I am game to give it a go until I notice the fence posts have disappeared under the water. We would end up swimming rather than wading.

'There's got to be another way,' I say, 'even if we end up on the road for a bit. We've just got to get to the next railway crossing and, after that, we'll be much higher and we should be fine.'

With the benefit of hindsight, taking the road is definitely what we should have done. But hindsight is a glorious thing. Instead, Andrew decides he can see a path where other people have ducked through the trees and climbed the metal fence into a huge field that banks steeply up towards a wood. I can see from my 'route planner' that it is vaguely in the right direction but, without the benefit of an OS map, I don't have any contours or proper landmarks. We hop into the field and I start praying that the landowner won't come charging out of the large house below and start shooting at us.

As it is, around fifty sheep decide we are the most interesting thing that has happened in their lives for a long time. They come steadily towards us, baa-ing loudly, in a mood that is hard to define.

'I can't decide whether they want to eat me or make love to me,' says Andrew, who seems to be the main object of their attention.

'Go away!' he says firmly. 'I have nothing for you. Now go away.'

I imagine the headline – 'QUEEN'S RACEHORSE TRAINER FOUND TRES-PASSING TRAMPLED BY SHEEP' – but they get the message and politely retreat, leaving us to climb over another fence into a wood. We can see where the Wayfarer's Walk is meant to be, but instead

Wayfarer's Walk

of a path there is a swan gliding elegantly over our route. We are stuck.

There is a point in any walk of a decent length where you stop trying to make conversation and concentrate on the important details: where are we going and how are we going to get there? We have reached that point.

We ponder our options, which aren't plentiful, and decide to cut back to the road, which is the way we should have taken half an hour ago, before we decided to trespass and make friends with the sheep.

So we are tramping along the road in single file, dealing with the things you deal with – like a bug flying into Andrew's eye and blinding him, or my feet feeling dangerously close to blistering – when we pass a farm which I knew I'd seen marked on the map. The trouble is, on the map, it wasn't on the road I thought we were on. We are about to cross the railway for a second time, about four miles south of where we wanted to be.

'It doesn't matter,' says Andrew. 'I know where we are. I've run out this way, and if we stay on the road we'll hit North Oakley, and then we're nearly home.'

Our original plan had been to follow faithfully the Wayfarer's Walk from Emsworth to Kingsclere. But the rules had gone out the window when we ditched the first forty miles, so who was I to argue that we weren't being true to our purpose now?

As we pass Ashe Warren House, which is marked on an OS map for those clever enough to have one, a woman is shooing her dog back behind the gates.

'Hello, you two!' she says, a look of complete surprise on her face. 'What are you doing here?'

'We're walking home,' I reply. 'From Dummer,' I add, smiling, to try to show that it was a choice and that we hadn't been thrown out of the car by our parents for fighting on the back seat.

The woman says, 'Are you looking for the Wayfarer's Walk?'

We nod.

'Just take the next right, and you'll hit it up by those trees. It's not far. I take the dogs that way every morning.'

We walk on, and I show Andrew the photos of the map on my phone.

'But that takes us on a loop we don't need to do,' he says. 'If we carry straight on up this road, we'll hit North Oakley and we can join it there.'

He points at the map, and I can't fault his argument, although I'm hardly feeling the romance of our trek home if we do it all on a road. Barely twenty minutes of shin-splitting road trudging later, and we do indeed hit North Oakley, a pretty village I have never visited in my life because it's not on any route I would normally take to Kingsclere. Andrew confesses he hadn't known it existed either until he started his marathon training.

He is still setting quite a pace, striding along in his tracksuit bottoms, knapsack on his back. I can't pretend we have a series of deep and meaningful conversations – you can't when you're walking in single file along a road. Alice asked me later what we'd talked about, and I couldn't really remember.

Wayfarer's Walk

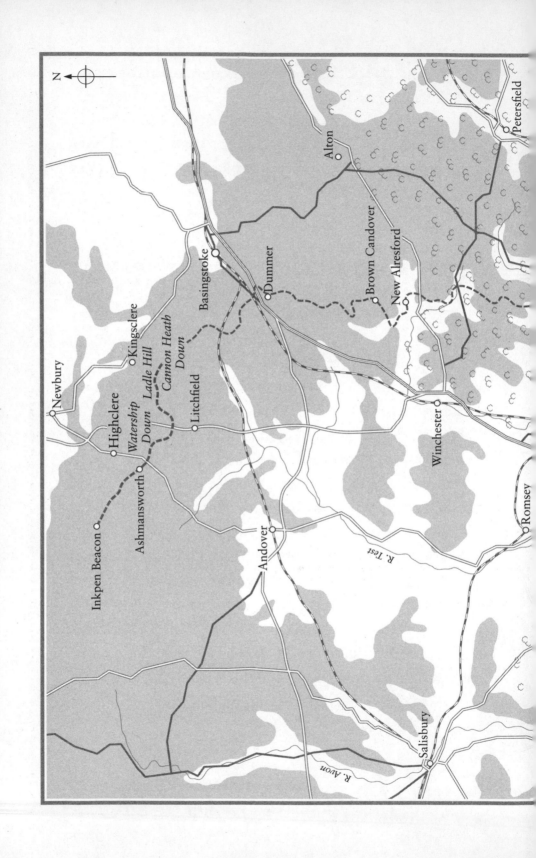

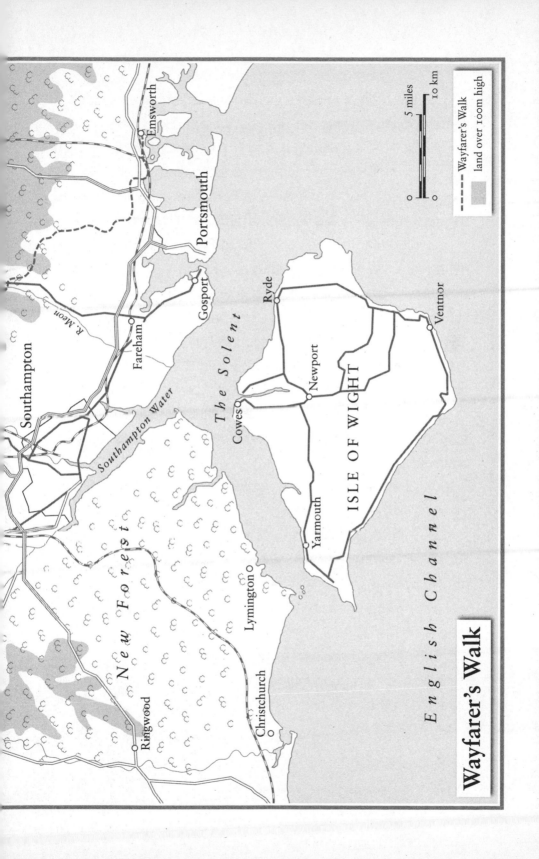

Wayfarer's Walk

Southampton

Portsmouth

Emsworth

Gosport

Fareham

R. Meon

Southampton Water

New Forest

Ringwood

Christchurch

Lymington

The Solent

Cowes

Newport

Ryde

Ventnor

Yarmouth

ISLE OF WIGHT

English Channel

- - - - Wayfarer's Walk
land over 100m high

5 miles

10 km

'Oh, everything and nothing,' I said.

I find it weird that Andrew and I have the same genes, had the same upbringing, and yet are so different. He is very patient, and I'm not. He is a diplomat, and I'm a freedom fighter. He is a non-confrontational traditionalist, and I want to change the world. He can follow the same pattern every day, and I need constant variety. He is a homing pigeon, and I'm a traveller.

I wasn't really thinking about this at the time, I was just wondering how he had such a long stride and wishing he would slow down. Then he says, 'I'm not sure I'd really be interested in this walking lark if it wasn't local. I mean, why would you want to go to Scotland when you can have this?'

I try to explain that walking in Scotland is sensational, but Andrew is like Dad: they are suspicious of praise for other places, in case you might somehow be denigrating the beauty of Kingsclere by mentioning that the area around Aberdeen is quite pretty.

'Don't be ridiculous,' Dad would baulk. 'You can't get anywhere finer than right here.'

I used to argue and show him photos of Northumberland, Yorkshire, Devon, Cornwall, Jersey, the Isle of Wight or Ireland – but he wouldn't have it. I wasn't suggesting that Kingsclere wasn't beautiful or that he ought to move, merely that there were other landscapes to be admired.

'Pah!' he would say. 'Not as good as this.'

I suppose it's a good thing for him and for Andrew that they don't hanker after other views, because this is the one they get on a daily basis and it's not bad. Not bad at all.

We finally fork off the road back on to a footpath and glimpse the edge of Cannon Heath Down in the distance. We turn right to see a long, gently sloping tunnel path, tree roots below and branches overhead. The sort of place you'd take an American if you wanted to show them what footpaths look like.

We have lost sight of the television mast that had worked as our North Pole throughout the walk. We had seen it from Dummer, Deane and North Oakley, and I knew it had to be hidden just behind the trees. Andrew's children call it 'Two Lights' and think of it, as I used to, as their own private beacon.

The sun has lost its warmth and is beginning to dip, but if we can get to Hannington it will be downhill from there. We might just make it before dark. We pass a group of caravans mounted on concrete blocks and come out at a road crossing I recognize.

'Look! The mast's just there!' I say, pointing to the right.

We are less than two miles from home, haven't got lost, haven't needed to be picked up, haven't injured ourselves. We are still talking – infrequently, but only because we've been walking for nearly four hours and we've run out of things to say. We walk up the border of a huge wheatfield on our final climb as the sun starts to set on our left behind the Downs. The gallops and

Wayfarer's Walk

the Team Chase course look different from this angle. I am over-whelmed by the desire to jump on a horse and thunder off in that direction.

Andrew decides that it will be quicker to carry straight on than take the Wayfarer's Walk, which turns left towards White Hill car park then cuts right down the Phoenix Reach gallop (named after a globetrotting Group 1-winning horse he trained). It isn't. Quicker, I mean.

As we climb over the fence on to 'our side' of the hill, I suggest that we give thanks to the land for not killing our father when he had a fall up there eight years ago and broke his neck.

Dad was jumping the tyres he'd built for the drag hunt. He can't resist 'popping' a few little jumps, even on an ex-flat horse that can't really lift its feet off the ground or a spooky hunter that shies at its own shadow. There were rabbit holes all around the tyres. Sam, the horse he was riding, put his front foot in a hole on take-off and catapulted Dad over the fence into the ground on the landing side, head first. He broke his C2, known as the Hang-man's Bone. In A&E at Basingstoke Hospital he said, 'I suppose I'm lucky not to be paralysed.'

The doctor replied, 'No, you're lucky not to be dead.'

He was in a brace for four months, during which time he swore a lot and behaved like a child, demanding attention, sym-pathy and food. Poor Mum.

Dad still has a bit of trouble turning to look both ways when he pulls out of a road junction, and he wouldn't be best placed side on to a tennis match, but he's pretty well recovered and still rides out every day, plays tennis and golf. He'd even ski – if anyone would let him near a mountain.

I pause and think about my father lying there in agony, incapable of moving, as his horse farted and trotted off home. Andrew has turned his back on me and is facing the hedge.

'Are you giving thanks?' I say.

'No,' he replies. 'I'm having a pee.'

A thanks of sorts, I suppose.

The trouble with the route my brother had chosen for our final section is that not only is it not shorter than taking the actual footpath, it is also unbearably steep – unbearable if your toes have been pressed up against the end of your shoes for longer than is comfortable and you fear you may have shin splints. I potter as best I can down the slope and think about doing it backwards because it will hurt less, but then decide against it because I will inevitably fall over and break my neck. Then my brother will come back in a few years and pee on the spot where it happened.

It is dark by the time we walk through the garden gate and I can barely put one foot in front of the other.

'Come on, Clarey,' says Andrew. 'You can have a cup of tea in a minute.'

We burst through the playroom door to find Toby and Flora watching cartoons.

'We walked all the way home from lunch!' I announce, proud as Punch that we've done it.

Wayfarer's Walk

Flora turns to assess us. After a beat she says, 'Why?'

'Why indeed?' my feet reply.

We walked because we never had done, because it was an adventure, and because we had time on our side. We walked because it's the simplest, most natural thing to do. We walked because, like breathing and rational thought, it makes us human.

We walked because my brother has never wanted to leave home and because I wanted to come home. We may have different sides, but we are the same coin.

3

Irish Miles

I've always liked Ireland. Andrew and I had an Irish nanny called Liz who took us there on holiday when we were about ten and eight. We loved its essential messiness. It didn't matter if we got muddy or grazed or ripped our clothes. We could play outside for hours and no one seemed to mind. The general message was 'Only come back if yer bleedin' or yer knocked out.'

I never stopped to worry about how we would get back if either of us was knocked out, and carried on taking swipes at my little brother's head with a broom.

Whenever I walk in Ireland I look at the hedgerows and imagine them as people with mad, wild hair that has never been brushed. The countryside has that air of chaos about it. The roads don't lead where you think they're going to lead and the footpaths could take you anywhere.

When Alice and I first got together I took her to Ireland on a short holiday. We started in Dublin, where I wanted her to meet some fabulous friends of mine. They showed us the hot spots of the city, then we headed out into the country to the K Club, a very smart golf club in County Kildare. Alice is a keen golfer and I was trying to impress her. When we got there, I thought it would be good to get a feel of the countryside around the K Club, not just the golf course. So we went for a walk.

I had looked at a map and figured out a route that should have taken us forty-five minutes. An hour later, we were completely lost. I had not brought the map with us and had no signal on my phone to work out where we were, but I refused to panic. After all, Alice may not even have noticed we were lost, even though I was sure we had been past this tree once before. (I tend to survive under the misguided belief that I can 'feel' the right way to go. It doesn't always work.)

After Alice had suggested for the third time that we ask for directions, I followed a signpost to a village in the hope that it might have a pub with people in it. I need not have worried. Every village in Ireland has a pub with people in it.

'Excuse me,' I said to a man dragging on a cigarette outside. 'So sorry to disturb you, but I wondered if you could help us. We're trying to get to the K Club.'

He looked at us and up into the sky, then back at us, then right and left down the road. He leaned towards us and fixed me with a concentrated stare.

'The K Club?' he said.

I nodded.

'The one where the Ryder Cup was held?'

I nodded again.

'I know it. Ah yes, I know it.'

We waited, assuming that he was assessing the shortest and most direct route we should take. After a minute he spoke again: 'Now, you see, if I was trying to get to the K Club, I wouldn't be starting from here.'

And that was it. No directions, no sense of where on earth we should be starting from, just a shrug of the shoulders and a smile. He ground his cigarette into the pavement and turned.

Being polite, I said earnestly, 'Understood. Thank you for your time.'

Alice and I waited for him to go into the pub. We looked at each other and exploded with laughter. I wondered if there were other walks we shouldn't be starting from here.

I checked my phone again and found the flicker of a signal, enough to show us a map. We had turned right when we should've turned left and gone a mile in the wrong direction. Once I'd worked out a return route, it didn't take long and we were back in the comfort of the hotel, where they treated us like royalty.

They love their horses in Ireland, and they embrace anyone who seems to know something about them. Walking through Dublin Airport, I am greeted by cheery faces and the inevitable question, 'So, Clare, who do you fancy for the Champion Hurdle / Gold Cup / Derby / Grand National?'

They want to know if I'm going to the Dublin Horse Show – which I haven't yet attended but will do one day – or if I'm over for the races. Usually, I'm en route to filming with a trainer or, in the old days, I would be covering a big race day for the BBC.

The audiences are different, too. Back in about 2001, I was working with Willie Carson at the Curragh for the Irish Derby and a crowd had gathered around us. Their stage-whispered comments reached our ears.

'Bejasus, it's true, so it is!' a woman said to her friend.

'Would you look at that?' A father to his son.

'I always wondered whether he'd grown, but not many people have a growth spurt in their fifties.' An older gentleman with a pint of Guinness in his hand.

'He does stand on a box!' they chorused.

It was always the biggest talking point of our fourteen-year on-air partnership. Did Willie Carson stand on a box? People would ask me every day of the week, and I wondered why it caused such fascination. If they watched the racing for any length of time they would see us move into the paddock, roaming through the assembled trainers and jockeys or standing up close to the horses. I wondered how they never noticed that Willie's height would suddenly drop when we were out of the studio (it being impractical for him to carry a box around with him).

Of course he stood on a box.

For the benefit of the Curragh crowd, Willie reached down and picked up the magic box. It was a rather smart mini-pedestal, designed to bring his eye level up to mine. I am not, as Wikipedia insists, 6 foot 4 – I am 5 foot 7; but that's still seven inches taller than Willie. The idea was that he should remain shorter than me but that we wouldn't be quite so mismatched.

He turned the box over to reveal the plaque underneath. Then he read it out to the crowd: 'Dear Mr Carson, here's the extra six inches you asked for.' He cackled loudly. 'Makes all the difference!' he shouted.

I loved working with Willie. He has an infectious enthusiasm for life and a sharp understanding of top-class racing. Willie rode hatfuls of Group 1 winners, won the Derby four times, was Champion Jockey five times, made winning moves at the top level and made mistakes, too. He understands what it is like to operate under pressure, what it feels like to ride a brilliant horse and how things can go wrong. The most important thing is that he can communicate all that to people watching at home.

Lester Piggott may have been more successful, but with the best will in the world, he is not a born conversationalist. Until Frankie Dettori retires from the saddle, I doubt there will be anyone who can bring the world of flat racing alive the way Willie did on TV.

Coincidentally, Willie's wife, Elaine, was one of the many nannies charged with the task of trying to control my brother and me when we were little. Andrew and I were mad keen on riding, but only one of us believed in stable management. Andrew didn't have a clue.

'Turn your pony out when you finish,' Elaine said.

So Andrew took her at her word and turned his iron-grey fireball

Raffles out in the little paddock at the stud. The only problem was that he had neglected to take his tack off first.

'You didn't tell me to,' he said to Elaine. She hadn't told him to, but she had assumed he might have the intelligence to work it out.

It was hard to understand what, if anything, was going on in my brother's brain. He had been told to groom his pony, so he did so, reluctantly, but he didn't fancy carrying the grooming kit back to the tack room. Instead, he put the brown bag around Polly the lurcher's neck to see if she would carry it for him. Polly wasn't a donkey and neither was she brave – in fact, she was probably the wettest dog we ever had – but she was very affectionate. The grooming kit started to swing beneath her neck and the drawstring spun round, tightening all the time. Polly yelped and started to panic. The kit tightened again, and she took fright, turning round and running back to the house.

Andrew's eyes widened as he realized that Dad would discover his idiocy. He sprinted under the archway of the entrance to the stud, up the gravel path past the loading ramp, and into the yard. I had never seen him move so fast, but his chubby little legs were no match for a lean lurcher: by the time he got to the back door of the house, Polly was already there, quivering and whimpering. I arrived not far behind.

Dad was crouched down beside Polly, trying to untangle the grooming kit. He was stroking her head and soothing her as he did so. Andrew stopped a few feet away, trying to figure out what to do. The grooming kit came off and Polly disappeared into the house, her tail clamped down between her legs and her neck bruised. Dad lifted the grooming kit off the ground.

'Whose is this?'

In the same situation, I would have pretended it wasn't mine. But it had 'Andrew' emblazoned on the side of it, so that wasn't an option for my backward little brother. His face was crimson with fear and athletic effort, and his mouth was opening and closing like that of a fish. My father was white with rage. Cruelty to animals was a sin above all others in his eyes. Even my kleptomania, which got me suspended from school, was not as bad as this.

Andrew was still speechless, so I stepped in front of him.

'It wasn't his fault,' I said. 'He didn't mean to hurt her. He just wanted her to carry his bag. Didn't you?'

I looked round at Andrew, whose mouth was still silently open-ing and shutting. He nodded his head and burst into tears.

'Well, next time, carry your own bloody bag,' my father said, as angry as I'd ever seen him. 'Now get to your room, and stay there.'

An hour later, I went up to check on Andrew. He was lying in bed, his face buried in the pillow. I took Polly with me. She wagged her tail and pushed her long nose under his chin. She had forgiven him, and that was all that mattered. My father told Elaine to keep an eye on Andrew.

'He's either stupid or lazy, or both,' he pronounced. 'Gormless boy.'

'Gormless' was my father's favourite word for Andrew. Once, when we were skiing in Zermatt, in the shadow of the Matterhorn, we christened Andrew 'The Mattergorm'. I think that would be quite a good name for a racehorse.

I doubt that looking after us was Elaine's most beloved job, but by the time she married Willie Carson she seemed to have forgiven us the sins we had committed. Willie was always Andrew's favourite jockey, and he would try to imitate the head-down, arms-pumping style of his hero. His attempts were very realistic, but the downside was that he could never see where he was going.

'*Get back on the gallop!*' Dad would shout, as Andrew careered off track at a 45-degree angle.

Willie's last Derby win, on Erhaab in 1994, was the very first I covered for the then nascent BBC Radio 5 Live. It was a sensa-tional ride: he forged a path through on the rail to make ground late and fast then switched to the middle of the course to come round Colonel Collins and King's Theatre and arrived there with so much momentum he could afford to ease up in the last couple of strides.

He had won the Derby at the age of fifty-one, and I honestly believe that his confidence in the horse and his knowledge of the crazy undulations of Epsom racecourse made all the difference.

I remember him running towards me screaming, as I held my BBC microphone out.

'Yeaaahhh!' he shouted. 'Wasn't that brilliant?'

He was so high on elation that he rattled on for five minutes without drawing breath. It was one of the best winning interviews I have ever done and I barely had to ask a question.

Two years later, in September 1996, Willie got kicked horribly as he was trying to get on a horse in the paddock at Newbury. He was thrown fifteen feet and suffered lacerations to his liver. He made a full recovery but, in the following spring, he announced his retirement from race riding, at the age of fifty-four. Julian Wilson, who presented the BBC's racing coverage, was quick off the mark in persuading Willie that a career in television would suit him. He had been a captain on *Question of Sport* in the 1980s and was one of the few racing faces recognized by people in the street. It was an inspired appointment, and when Julian retired in 1998 Willie and I became the BBC's racing double act.

I enjoyed the unpredictability of working with Willie. I had to concentrate extra hard to ensure that if he made a mistake I knew enough to correct it, and I loved the strange nature of our on-air partnership. You don't often get a male–female combination in which the younger woman is leading the presentation, and rarely do they have as much fun as we did. We laughed all the time, on air and off.

Willie's talent was not appreciated enough by the racing press. Yes, he may have lacked a little microphone discipline and occasionally got his words jumbled up, but he could leap through the screen into the viewer's home and make them feel involved. That is a rare skill.

I loved covering racing and I had adored growing up in a racing yard but, as I reached my thirties, I was starting to realize how small my world had been. The key to broadening my horizons was walking.

My knowledge of Ireland and Northern Ireland had been limited to Leopardstown, the Curragh, the K Club and Down Royal in the north until I started walking there. What an experience! From the Giant's Causeway, to the Mountains of Mourne in Northern Ireland, to the Wicklow Mountains, Mullaghmore Head in County Sligo and the Ballybunion Cliff Walk in County Kerry, there are a multitude of exhilarating paths to choose.

There is a quality of green in Ireland that you don't see in other countries – the benefit, I suppose, of an annual rainfall that averages at 100cm – deep, lush, verdant grass and hedgerows brimming over with growth. That grass is one of the reasons there are so many good horses bred in Ireland.

In January 2012 I joined what has become Northern Ireland's biggest walking group, the Wee Binnians. There was a frost painting the ground with a layer of icing sugar, the skies were clear and the air was crisp. It was the perfect day for a bracing walk (or scramble) up the side of Slieve Binnian, in County Down.

C. S. Lewis had visited the area, and the Kingdom of Mourne, as it's known, was apparently the inspiration for Narnia. It's a mystical, timeless landscape in which you can be utterly lost, with no view of civilization or modernity.

The Wee Binnians group had been set up in 1987 by Veronica McCann, and now had over 250 members. Wee Binnian is one of the smallest peaks in the Mountains of Mourne and, as many of the walkers were beginners, Veronica felt the name accurately reflected their lowly aspirations. The point of the group was, and still is, to welcome walkers of all levels, so there are different grades of walks according to difficulty. But, as seems always to happen with my walks, we hadn't selected the easy option.

Veronica showed me on the map where we would be walking, and said, in an entirely straightforward manner, 'Actually, this is going to be my final resting place, so that'll be my last walk in my life, up here.' I looked at her to confirm that she was talking about her own death. 'I'm a strategic woman and, at my time in life, you have to keep making plans. This is where I want my ashes scattered, and Gráinne here is in charge because she's a fair bit younger than me. Also, I'll be making sure that my grandchildren stay fit by clambering up here to talk to me.'

We climbed up the steep, stony path and, with the help of the group, who kept me chatting, I reached the top about an hour later. I realized then how desperately unfit I was. Veronica, seventy-two, was sprinting ahead of me like a mountain goat and was already sitting against a rock with her tea, sandwiches and, crucially, hot port.

From the top, we could see miles to the west and north to Northern Ireland, south along the coast of Ireland and, to the east, all the way across to the Isle of Man in the Irish Sea. I told Veronica she'd picked a fine resting place. One of the group started singing 'Lily of the West', and the others told me how they'd joined up, where they'd walked, the friendships they'd made and the romances that had formed. A few couples had ended up marrying each other, and 'Baby Binnians' had been born. They told me how Veronica had inspired them with her determination and her ability to make everyone feel welcome.

'With my working life, it was essential for me to come out walking,' Veronica said. 'Once I'm in the hills, I feel I have space to have fun and space to think. It's amazing to have been involved with the club for twenty-five years.'

I had assumed that the descent from Slieve Binnian would be easier than the ascent. After I'd fallen over twice and picked up boggy smears all over my backside, I realized my error. One of the members gave me two poles and told me to slow down. He walked in front of me and suggested I follow in his footsteps. I slipped a few times more, but I didn't fall again.

I understood then the spirit of the group. They look out for each other, and they look forward to their ascents every week and cover each other's backsides on their descents. I rang home and told Alice I wanted to live in the Kingdom of Mourne.

'It sounds lovely,' she said. 'When's your flight home?'

I've had many memorable walks in Ireland, with many great people, but the best walking companion in the land has to be the botanist and broadcaster Éanna Ní Lamhna.

The first time we met she promised me a 6- or 7-mile walk in the Wicklow Mountains. She lied about the distance (it was at least double that) and told me that all the climbing was at the beginning, which was also a complete lie. But the experience was one I will never forget.

'It's a lovely circular walk that'll take us three hours,' she said. 'Or four . . . or five, or six, depending on how we're going.'

I thought she was joking.

Éanna talked with rattling rapidity, spraying information with energy and enthusiasm, words tumbling out of her faster than water from the cascade ahead of us. As we set out from Glendalough ('Glen of the Two Loughs'), towards the Poulanass Waterfall, Éanna directed me towards the railway sleepers forming a staircase up into the Wicklow Mountains.

'These are the easy steps, don't you worry,' she said. 'There are only about two hundred here by the side of the lake, and then we've got a thousand at least to come. I've never counted them all because it would just be disheartening and I don't like to be disheartened.'

I was breathing heavily and my thighs started to ache, so I kidded myself into a state of masochistic meditation. I tried to enjoy the pain, knowing it would be worth it for the view.

Pain is all about mindset. There's a part of every top sportsman or sportswoman that actually enjoys pain – they learn to like it because they know that by punishing their body they are working towards the ultimate reward. They know they will have enjoyed it when it is over, if you know what I mean. I thought of Chris Hoy,

AP McCoy and Katherine Grainger as I climbed the wooded sleeper steps, dreaming of my gold-medal or Grand National moment.

Éanna (who is twenty-one years older than me) was springing up the steps, chattering about bell heather, ling heather, hazelnuts, pine cones, bogs, rock formations and mining.

'The main thrust of the climb is yet to come,' she promised, as she nibbled on a hazelnut. 'We were just warming you up.'

Finally, an element of reward – the view. We looked down into the U-shaped valley and the rippling black waters of the Lower Lough, with a sixth-century monastic site just visible. The light was mottled, with shafts of sunlight falling down on to the dark rocks below and illuminating a lone tree.

There was something biblical about the scene. People had been looking at this same view for thousands of years.

Sometimes when I'm walking, the emotion of it all gets too much. Generally, the tears do not flow because I'm tired or upset but because it's so beautiful. I also had a moment like that in Northern Ireland in the Mountains of Mourne: the morning sun came flooding across Carlingford Lough, turning the water pink. It was stunning before we even started.

A year later, when a horse called Carlingford Lough won the Galway Plate for AP McCoy, I could picture the place it had been named after. On one side of the lough stands the ruins of a castle and, call me one-track minded, but I was quite proud that I had also heard of Carlingford Castle – he'd finished second to Teenoso in the 1983 Derby, and gave Mick Kinane his first ride in the race.

As the miles and hours passed and we walked up the ridge known as the spine, Éanna revealed more of her knowledge and more of herself. Having told me the climb was over and the rest of the walk was 'pure enjoyment', I kept wondering if she was a compulsive liar. As the rain battered us, she baffled me with the logic that 'Irish miles are longer than English miles'.

'I had forgotten it was quite so steep up here, but you're meant to be distracted by the views and the light,' Éanna said. 'If we went up any further we'd be in heaven, so don't you worry, it'll be flat and downhill from now. We didn't walk into a bog hole, we've got good boots, the rain will pass and we haven't broken anything, so things could be worse!'

She was a natural optimist, and her energy was contagious. She taught me about glacial valleys, acidic soil, edible hedgerow berries, wild flowers and plants, fungi, waterfalls . . . and also revealed how she had fallen in love with the man who became her husband.

'I wasn't a strong walker as a child,' she said, 'but when I went to university in Dublin I met this gorgeous hunk of a man and he loved to walk in the mountains, so it was a case of "love your man, love your mountains". In an effort to persuade him that I was fierce interested in all that he was, I would follow him up into the mountains and pretend that I liked it.

'We came up here one Sunday. There were four or five of us, and one of the girls decided that she wanted to cross the waterfall – mad thing to do – so of course she slipped and fell in. And there she was, clinging to a rock and screaming for help, and my beloved leaps in to save her. And I got this St Paul on the road to Damascus feeling: "Ooh, if he gets out alive I'll never be nasty to him again."

'So we formed a chain and we hauled them both out, and subsequently we got married and had three children, and we are still together. I can tell you, we give waterfalls a wide berth.'

Ten years later, in 2012, I met up with Éanna and her husband, John, to walk in Dublin Bay. By then, they had been married for thirty-five years. John was much quieter than Éanna (but if I'm being honest, that's not difficult) and seemed silently to absorb the information that his wife delivered at breakneck pace, occasionally adding a detail or two of his own.

Éanna can't walk on a beach without diving off to collect shells or look for lugworms. It was like taking a puppy for a walk. I thought she was beside me, and then she wasn't and I'd see her frantically digging into the sand with her bare hands.

She burst into song about cockles and mussels and told me how Molly Malone (of the song) died of typhoid. Then she told me about lugworms and their predators, curlews, who have nerve endings at the end of their big, long bills to help them find their breakfast in the sand.

She did all this without seeming to take a breath. It was a staggering display of non-stop, information-laden, one-way conversation. John stood there, listening to it all as if he'd never heard it before, smiling. He had retired earlier that year, so Éanna, in a flash of inspiration, had decided that they should climb all twenty-six of the highest peaks in Ireland and Northern Ireland. They did them all and got a certificate from the Mountaineering Association for their trouble, which was lovely – but not enough for Éanna, who decided they would go further afield and climb Mount Snowdon. So they did that. And then she thought they should do Ben Nevis. So they did that, too.

Bear in mind that they have both long since celebrated their sixtieth birthdays. And the woman who had initially traipsed along to try to show interest was now suggesting mountain climbs for the two of them. As for John, 'I'm charged with what's called the "mountain foreplay",' he explained. 'That consists of studying maps, books, the Internet and coming up with the plan. Éanna just turns up, and I tell her where to park the car and where we're going. Then off we go, and it's lovely. She tends to slow down a bit in terms of the chat when she's with me because she's so used to me, so I do get a little bit of peace and quiet when we're out in the mountains.'

'Believe me,' chuckled Éanna, 'you can't chat much when you're clambering up Ben Nevis.'

Éanna had a Mary Poppins umbrella that she didn't use for protecting herself from the rain or for flying but to open and turn upside down under a tree. She then shook the tree and watched the creepy crawlies fall into the umbrella. It's a great way for a botanist to examine spiders, earwigs and the like – but not so good if you've borrowed your husband's golf umbrella and not told him.

'John has got used to opening his brolly on the course and finding a few spiders falling on to his head,' she said.

'By the way, have a look at this earwig. Now, of course, people think they're called earwigs because they drill a hole through your ear and eat your brain, but they don't. They eat flower petals. And, in fact, their original name was "arsewig". God knows what people would think they did if they were still called that.'

Laughter filled the air in Dublin Bay, and we walked on, looking at plants and animals, learning about history and geology and biology. It was like going back to school with all the fun of lessons and none of the trauma of taking exams. A butterfly fluttered beside us, then suddenly a dragonfly called a red-veined darter landed on Éanna's hand, just as she was talking about the wonders of the outdoor world.

She has a touch of magic about her, and it's not just the Mary Poppins umbrella. Éanna Ní Lamhna could give an hour's lecture on mud and it would be fascinating. She has that rare gift of eternal enthusiasm, and it's impossible not to be swept along by it. John is her foil, a solid, steady presence who went back to get the car for us to rescue us from the rain, because that's the kind of man he is. She fell in love with him for rescuing a woman from a waterfall, and he's still doing it today.

'I want to live in Ireland,' I said to Alice when I got home.

She looked up briefly.

'Of course you do, darling,' she said, and carried on reading Twitter.

4

Barefoot and Backwards

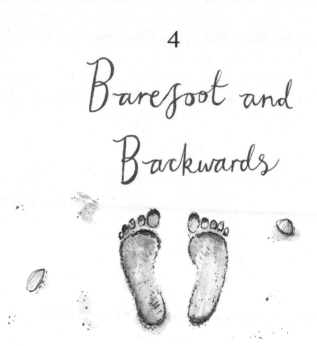

Aside from naked rambling, I am fairly happy to try anything once. So when I got a four-page handwritten letter suggesting I should walk barefoot, I thought, 'Well, why not?'

Michael Weltike first tried barefoot walking in the 1980s, almost by accident. 'I used to go hiking with my brother and sister and sleep out on the hills,' he explained. 'On one occasion, my brother and I decided to walk up a mountain adjacent to Ben Nevis carrying our boots rather than wearing them. It was a revelation to feel the texture and temperature as we walked. When we got to the summit, we didn't feel tired at all, but energized and refreshed. I didn't think any more of it for a while . . .'

We were meeting on the western edge of the Mendip Hills in Somerset, on an overcast day in February. Michael wore a red-and-yellow hand-knitted hat, green trousers and fur-lined boots. I looked at his feet, and he must have detected the disappointment in my eyes.

'Don't worry.' He smiled. 'They'll be coming off as soon as we get off the road.'

We walked away from the medieval church in Compton Bishop and gradually gained some height, but I starting fretting about the sky. Why couldn't we have a clear day so I could enjoy the views from the Mendips? Why did it have to be cloudy and grey? It was the sort of sky that gives you nothing – no colour, no warmth, no detail.

The sky dictates my mood more strongly than anything else. My brain clouds over when the sky does and, equally, it brightens with the light. I remembered how distressed I was when I had to work in an office with no windows and no natural light. Now, with the prospect of walking barefoot with Michael, I had an alternative mood measurer. I had a chance to change my focus and look to the ground instead.

'Normally,' Michael said, taking long strides beside me, 'we're insulated from the ground by our boots and by concrete flooring in houses. By making contact with natural materials, you can earth yourself through them. We've evolved over millions of years as barefoot beings and then we were wearing animal skins on our feet. It's only recently that all these artificial materials have come in that have cut us off, in a way.'

He stopped and smiled as he bent down to untie his laces. We had reached the close-cropped grass of the Mendips and it was time to 'strip off'.

The Mendips are a range of hills south of Bristol, running from Weston-super-Mare to Frome. You can see the start of them from the M5, their limestone largesse dominating the landscape. In the south of the area is Cheddar Gorge, the deepest ravine in the country and our own version of the Grand Canyon. The Mendips are pockmarked with caves, including the spectacular Wookey Hole, and in 1903 made headlines around the world when a complete skeleton, thought to be nine thousand years old, was discovered. The skeleton was known as Cheddar Man. Another good name for a horse. ('Cheddar Man comes to Tattenham Corner and is still hard on the bridle . . . Cheddar Man goes a length up with a furlong to run . . . *Cheddar Man* has won the Derby!' Oh yes, it works.)

The Mendips look over land famous for cheese, strawberries and ice cream. They provide the gradients for fell runners, hill walkers, rock climbers, abseilers and, in our case, barefoot walkers.

As soon as I had peeled off my first sock I could feel a strange sensation, and it wasn't just the cold of the earth. As we walked, the mud squelched between my toes as I slipped through it and every time I hit a patch of moss it was warm and soft. It was thrilling, as if I'd suddenly been 'plugged in'.

Michael's feet were long and thin, with toe bones that seemed super-humanly strong. I don't really like feet and, to be totally honest, have a bit of a phobia about hairy ones. Luckily, his were smooth and hairless, and they were soon coated in thin, teak-brown mud, which meant I could pretend they weren't really feet at all. We bounced along on short, sheep-grazed turf, the land that gave this area its medieval affluence from the wool trade. I felt even more springy and positive than usual.

'There's an energy exchange between you and the earth going on now,' Michael explained. 'We're all electromagnetic beings and so is the earth, and if we can make that connection it can have profound benefits on our well-being.'

When I'm walking with someone I try to let their experience become my experience. Where, normally, I might suspect something or someone of being eccentric or even a tiny bit unhinged, I go with the flow and buy into their world. So I tried to ignore the cold, the wet, the rabbit poo and the sheep droppings that decorated the hills and started to feel surges from my feet. I used to run around a lot with bare feet when I was young but, as an adult, I really only do it on holiday on a beach. This was the first time I could remember walking on grass on a winter's day, not worrying about staying clean.

I was aware of my toes and how they help to balance my body, of the changing temperature of the earth and the delight of soft, short grass. Some dog walkers passed us and exclaimed in surprise and perhaps a little in fear when they saw our bare feet. I felt even more excited that I was doing something so innocent but which seemed to create such a reaction. How strange that we have become suspicious of anything that is different, even something that harks back to our natural beginnings.

After half an hour I decided that the benefit of barefoot walking was about to be outweighed by the gradual freezing of my toes. I grabbed Michael's towel and wiped off the soles of my feet. As I pulled my socks back on I appreciated them more than I ever had before. It was like climbing under a warm duvet on a cold night. My feet were tingling and they felt more alive than they had in a long while. Maybe I've been hard on feet all these years. They're still funny-looking, but I guess we need them.

My feet were grateful to be wrapped up warmly, but I promised them that, come the spring, they would be let loose again. It's such a simple pleasure, and I wonder whether it allows us to connect with our distant past in a way that, most of the time, modern life prevents.

For Michael, barefoot walking was not just a passing pleasure, it had become a necessity. He had suffered from depression and, while in hospital, had started walking barefoot through the grounds.

'I strongly feel that it helped me out of the situation,' he said. 'The doctor couldn't believe how quickly I had slipped into depression and then how quickly I had come out of it. I thought I had to investigate it further and try to walk as often as I could barefoot, especially in wild places. I feel reconnected with life and I would recommend it to anyone as therapy.'

Michael felt more sensitive and centred because of walking barefoot. After I'd put my boots back on (my feet were cold, dirty and getting shredded), he carried on barefoot for another two hours – splashing through puddles, skipping over rocks, padding on tarmac. He washed in a stream when we got back to Compton Bishop, dried his feet and put his boots back on. His face was glowing and he looked barely half his fifty-eight years. I told him that he would probably live to be two hundred at this rate. He looked genuinely thrilled.

There are so many ways of walking to stay healthy. One that has a strong following is walking *backwards*.

I was filming pandas in China recently and, as we left the hotel at the crack of dawn, we nearly knocked over a woman who was walking backwards up the road. All the way along the steep path, people were walking backwards up the hill. It was four in the morning and there they were – men and women in their forties, fifties, sixties walking backwards up a hill. It was like a scene from a zombie movie.

The theory is that walking backwards exercises muscles that do not ordinarily get used and increases the heart rate, making it a more energetic workout. They say a hundred steps backwards is the equivalent of a thousand forwards, which is a good job, as you're going to get wherever you're going about ten times more slowly.

Since then, I have been trying the backward-walking thing around London. It's useful because, if Archie gets behind on the walk, I can keep an eye on him and pretend to other normal, front-walking folks that I am just a responsible dog owner.

'I'm just watching out for my dog!' I try to explain, as they frown and take their child's hand. Then I stumble backwards into a speed ramp and swear loudly. Alice is usually yards ahead by the time this happens, quickening her step and pretending she doesn't know me.

'For God's sake, turn around,' she whispers. 'People will think you're weird.'

'Good,' I reply. 'I thought we didn't care what other people think.'

'Oh, do grow up. You know what I mean.'

I carry on walking backwards, just to prove the point.

Walking backwards increases the metabolic rate. Because it's a new and unfamiliar exercise to most of us, it improves balance and coordination, helps the circulation, gives relief from lumbago and is good for the knees, but most important of all – and this is possibly the reason that the Chinese are so committed to their daily routine of early-morning suicidal backward locomotion – it sharpens the brain.

Yes, yes, I know. That sounds bonkers, but the idea is that, because all five senses are involved in making sure you don't walk straight into a tree, your brain activity is increased, you concentrate harder, you become more aware and, in some cases, happier. Some Chinese also believe that walking backwards means they can correct sins or mistakes they have made. The obvious drawback is that, if one is even vaguely unbalanced, one will fall over and break many bones, rendering the improvement to one's brain and/or muscles a little unnecessary. But I don't want to rain on their retro-walking parade.

I have some sympathy for them searching for a way in which to improve their mental state, because being in a Chinese city for any length of time can be a depressing experience. Not because of the people or the food, or even the attitude of some hotels that having cockroaches sharing your bathroom is perfectly acceptable. These things are all manageable, but what I can't live with is the fact that there is no sky. Seriously, there is no sky over Chengdu, the fastest-expanding city in the world. Instead, there is a depth of cloud that takes five or ten minutes for the plane to fly through. You don't see sunrise or sunset; it just gets light and then gets dark. There is no blue, no white clouds shaped like bunny rabbits, no pink haze. And no views.

Fourteen million people live and work in a haze of fug, that combination of smog, fog and mugginess. It minimizes the world and makes it feel as if it is shrinking in around you. We went up into the hills to film the pandas at the Wolong National Natural Reserve, and I could barely see beyond the tops of the trees. I knew we were up in the mountains with valleys down below because we'd climbed up and up in the car, but there was no view at all, no sense of distance or perspective. It was claustrophobic and depressing.

I was allowed to cuddle baby pandas and feed the toddlers, which was one of the highlights of my life, but I will never forget that fug. No wonder the locals get up early to walk backwards up a hill.

The best thing about walking is that you can find a space where all around you is sky. You have to climb to get there, but that's part of the deal.

'Are you all ready? Right, let's go.' The Grand Walking Officer was directing the troops out of the car park from the village of Exford in Somerset. He had a stick in his hand, a map around his neck and a rucksack on his back.

Lucy had picked me up at Tiverton Parkway (again) and I had driven (of course) through the narrow lanes of Bampton and Dulverton towards Exmoor National Park. Two thirds of the park lies in Somerset, one third in Devon, but although we were on the Somerset side, we were meeting a group that came from North Devon.

In this group, mostly made up of people who had now retired, there were fourteen of them with two dogs. I would hazard the average age (not including the dogs) was sixty-five. They meet every Tuesday to walk, their only rule being that the walk must end at a pub.

The weather was warm enough for some to wear shorts, although as Janet, a retired teacher, told me, 'We always wear shorts in Somerset. You have to.'

We set out along the River Exe, which glittered between the leaves of the trees to our right. The river burbled, and so did the group as we forked up on to the moor. There was a marked lack of arable farming in the area, with the vast majority of fields given over to grass so that sheep and cows can rule the domain. As we climbed higher, the vegetation became sparser, but a strong, thick beech hedge defied the wind, its leaves rustling loudly in the breeze, yet its branches remained unbending.

We stopped to admire the view across the fields to Exmouth, the church steeple standing proud in the middle of the village. Looking east to Dunkery Beacon, the highest point on Exmoor, you could fully appreciate the gentle nature of this moorland. It didn't feel hostile or barren but gave that precious sense of space and freedom.

We had sky all around, the air was clean and pure, the sun was out and someone else was doing the map reading. All was well in my world.

Although there are many advantages of walking with a group – the variety of voices and experiences, collective humour and natural bonhomie – one of the drawbacks is that I can't talk to everyone. We have to be selective, and Lucy has perfected the art of shepherding, with me as her barking sheepdog. She whistles, and I peel one or two individuals from the group to walk with us at the back, away from the hubbub.

Soon I was picking up tips on how to plan for retirement. Everyone concurred that you had to have a diary full of events to look forward to.

One of the women recalled the day her husband stopped work. 'He said, "What are we going to do today?" So I said, "Well, I'm going to carry on doing all the things I've been doing for the last thirty years of our marriage and you can join in or not. It's up to you."

'I think it was the first time he realized that the house hadn't run itself all those years. We had to find a new rhythm and find things we both wanted to do. It was a bit stressful to begin with, but now I really enjoy it and we're learning not to irritate each other.'

We were in single file, shuffling down shale steps that looked as if they'd been through a bread slicer set to 'super thin'. If you looked at a vertical cross section of the steps, they were made up of layer upon layer of thin, dark-grey rock.

Mary, who had two poles, was fairly skipping down them, in the manner of a mountain goat. My progress was more like one of Hannibal's elephants. My step has never been light. The Grand Walking Officer was leading the way as we followed obediently behind, making our way through a tunnel of trees like a snake of schoolchildren.

I heard the rustling of beech leaves as we came back towards the banks of the River Exe. They make a particular kind of music as they gossip with each other in the wind. The trees were coated with a thick layer of lichen, a testament to the purity of the air.

Members of the group were laughing with each other and teasing Patrick, who is ex-army, challenging him to balance on a slippery log to cross the river. Patrick was tall and wiry, with muscular legs. He was wearing a navy-blue polo shirt tucked into khaki shorts, his belt carrying what looked like a walkie-talkie and a pen-knife. He was like a grown-up Boy Scout, and he would be able, I am sure, to negotiate the log if he wanted to. It had no ropes or anything on it to save a brave or daft person from falling into the water from it.

The two dogs that came with us, a Labrador and a collie cross, were chasing sticks into the water. Patrick gave the impression that he was perfectly capable and brave enough to cross the log, but his wife, Sarah, interjected with a brilliant piece of logic.

'It's very overgrown at the end,' she loudly declared. 'And he's got no dry clothing,' she added quietly.

'That's what one does,' she confided in me later. 'Saves one's other half!'

There was a perfectly safe bridge, which the rest of us crossed, followed by a reluctant Patrick. The group was discussing Pilates, bridge, holidays, future walks, and the other things they do to keep their bodies and minds active. They were full of energy, willing to explore something new, appreciative of the landscape around them.

Getting to know this group makes me realize that I've been afraid of stopping and looking behind me. My life is so varied, so full of adrenalin highs, changing subjects and remarkable people that I worry I will turn into apple crumble the day I call it quits. After meeting this group, I feel differently: I'm full of hope and excitement.

Of course, this may wear off – Lucy will tell you that I am a very impressionable individual. I'll come back from walks wanting to convert to Buddhism or deciding that I'm going to be a poet, an artist or a taxidermist.

We paused to look backwards at the steep slope of a lime-green hill leading down to a wall of trees.

'Sometimes you have to turn around,' said the Grand Walking Officer. 'If you keep just looking forward, you miss the best views.'

5

Urban Renewal

My mother is under the impression that living in a city is inherently less healthy than living in the countryside. But the statistics tell another story: people in cities tend to walk more each day than their rural counterparts, who often drive to work, to see friends and to the shops.

I enjoy walking in cities. It's the only way to really appreciate them. London's boroughs whizz by in the car or from a bus, whereas on foot you discover that the character of each area is distinct. You take in the street names and wonder at the past happenings in Bleeding Heart Yard, Knightrider Street or Petty France. There is a personality to our street names that New York, for all its efficiency, will never achieve with its grid system.

Who wants to meet at First and 14th when you can come out of the Tube at Mansion House, turn right on to Cannon Street, left up Walbrook, left at the top along Poultry (before it becomes Cheapside) and rendezvous in Old Jewry, not far from Ironmonger Lane?

There are people and stories and centuries in those names. Although you'll get hopelessly lost, you know you do so in the footsteps of millions before you.

I recently walked from a meeting near St Paul's to another near Buckingham Palace. By underground or car, they'd always seemed opposite ends of the city. In fact, the route is less than three miles, and it takes in the river, Trafalgar Square and St James's Park. It took less than an hour and I didn't even get lost.

Charles Dickens walked between ten and fifteen miles every day, and when he was in London the city would have been choked with fog and pungent with the stench of human sewage and horse droppings. For all that modern London is busy with cars and people, it may actually be more pleasant to walk around in 2014 than it was in 1840.

The paths along the Thames and the vast expanses of parkland make London a walkers' paradise. It's easy to get to Hampstead Heath, or Epping Forest, or Richmond Park and, as a country girl, I am always amazed to discover so many open spaces in the capital. As my ramblings have taken me around the UK, I've discovered that London is not alone: Manchester has Heaton Park, Liverpool has Newsham, Stanley and Sefton parks, Birmingham has Aston Park, Leeds has Roundhay Park (at more than 700 acres, one of the largest city parks in Europe), part of Sheffield lies within the Peak District National Park, and Glasgow has some ninety parks and public gardens, including the magnificent Necropolis.

It's all there if you're willing to look for it. The mistake I made when I first came to London was that I didn't know I would have to do the legwork myself. I thought the city would come to me. I assumed I'd be busy every night, either working on shift at BBC Radio Sport, or out on the town. My diary would be effortlessly packed and life would be a non-stop whirl of different faces and conversations. In reality, London can be the loneliest place in the world. Yes, there are lots of different faces, but if you don't know any of them all they do is swirl around you, sending you dizzy with confusion.

Everyone seemed to be on the way to something or someone, and I was going nowhere. I remember sitting in my top-floor flat in

Parsons Green, staring at the phone and willing it to ring, hoping for an invitation to something. I didn't realize that London doesn't happen for you without a bit of effort. I learned to suggest outings or to invite myself to things, just to avoid endless nights watching TV and eating pasta with pesto sauce.

Back then, I wasn't into walking, otherwise I'm sure life would have been different. I could have joined a walking book-club, or I could have been part of the many walking networks that suggest routes every weekend in or out of London.

It wouldn't take much to get the whole of London walking further and doing so more regularly. These days I speak to a lot of big businesses: along with suggesting that they might like to sponsor women's sport, I always ask if they have a walking group. I tend to get a few baffled looks, but I'm deadly serious.

Imagine how many boardroom meetings would be better taken as a circular four-mile walk. More fun, more energy, more creativity and no risk of people falling asleep or mucking about on Facebook while someone else is speaking. Everyone would share the same experience but in a different way, they would talk to different people, and by the time they got back to the office they'd be flushed with excitement and ideas.

Few cities can top London for a combination of architecture, culture, thriving community and walking options. One that can is Edinburgh.

Most people enjoy walking because they enjoy the feeling of escape. Well, there is simply nothing like walking out of a humming Waverley Station, rejecting Princes Street and heading for Holyrood Park instead. An hour or so later, having clambered up the path that runs parallel to the basalt cliffs called Salisbury Crags, you can be standing on top of a volcano, looking down at the castle and the city from Arthur's Seat. Now that is a true escape. You may have been overtaken by barefoot fell runners en route and you will probably not be alone at the top, but it's a thrilling feeling to stare down at the teeming streets below while the wind whistles around your ears and the sky stretches out before you.

I climbed up to Arthur's Seat on a late summer's day and looked across the city to the Firth of Forth, the red Forth railway bridge glinting in the sunlight, the road bridge alongside it dancing with cars. I could see up the Fife coast and imagined golfers thwacking balls on links courses all the way along it. Turning around to the south-west, the view was dominated by the grass- and heather-clad Pentland Hills – the 'hills of home', according to Robert Louis Stevenson. I walked there once and got hopelessly lost, but that's nothing new.

I used to spend New Year's Eve in Edinburgh, with my university friends. One of them – a tall, handsome historian with floppy black hair called Rob Fell – annually abused his mother's good nature by inviting us all to stay in her Georgian terraced flat. It was on one of those gorgeous crescents in Edinburgh and was impeccably kept. That was until about 4 p.m. on 31 December, when it would be covered in clothes, half-eaten packets of biscuits, sleeping bags and empty wine bottles.

By the third year of our Hogmanay adventures, Mrs Fell had decided to move out of the flat for the week. Luckily, I had broken my ribs falling off a horse in a daft drag-hunt race – he had stopped at a double of hedges and I had been shoulder first into the ground. Then he'd trodden on me, just for good measure. You may think that is *unlucky*, but when there's only one decent bed on offer, having broken ribs is the trump card.

'Clare should have my bed,' announced Mrs Fell as she departed with her overnight case. 'She's broken her ribs, for God's sake. She can't sleep on the floor.'

I dumped my bag on her enormous double bed and said, calmly, 'I suppose I'd better do what your mother says, Rob.'

I managed to delay my manic grin until I'd shut the door and disappeared into the en-suite bathroom. There I flushed the loo to disguise the noise of me shouting, 'Result!'

Our Hogmanay festivities consisted of many things I don't clearly remember, but I do know they involved a lot of alcohol and that at about 11 p.m. we would head out into Princes Street to try to get a decent position for the fireworks. It was always very cold. I mean really, bitterly cold, which made it tricky to look vaguely trendy (although I had no idea what this meant – as far as I was concerned, you couldn't go wrong with a pair of green jeans and a polka-dot polo-neck body). My solution was to wear the polo-neck body, tie a jumper around my waist and take my super-thick puffa jacket. I may have looked like a walking Michelin man, but at least I wasn't going to get frostbite.

One year, I had had a few drinks and was feeling full of love for the world so I decided I'd start kissing boys. There was no selection policy involved: anyone would do. I skipped up to a policeman and asked him if I could kiss him.

'That's nae strictly allow—' he started to say as I stood on tiptoes and planted my lips on his '—ed'.

'Happy New Year!' I said as I ran away.

I remember standing between Rob and my best friend, Mike, as we watched the fireworks cascading out of Edinburgh Castle. Mike and I had been friends since the day I arrived at Cambridge. He was ridiculously tall, but gentle and polite. I had an army officer boyfriend during my first two years at university, so with Mike there was never any of that sexual awkwardness that so often hampers a male–female friendship. Mind you, that Hogmanay I was pretty determined that I was going to kiss him.

'Come on,' I begged him. 'I've got nine so far and you'd round it off to a perfect ten.'

I tugged at his jacket, trying to bring his face down to my level. Mike had been drinking, too, but he never lost his innate sense of decency. He looked down at me, pity in his eyes.

'I'm sorry, Clare,' he intoned, 'but I will not be a number.'

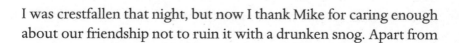

I was crestfallen that night, but now I thank Mike for caring enough about our friendship not to ruin it with a drunken snog. Apart from

Louise, who was my closest friend from Newnham College, my university friends were nearly all male, and they are all still friends today. They know my schoolfriends well, because they've all been coming to the same parties for the last twenty years. I do love a party, and I always try to celebrate my birthday, because it's at the end of January, and I figure that everyone needs a get-together at the end of January.

I turned forty in January 2011 and was determined to welcome the landmark in style.

My father knew it was my birthday because I'd been banging on about it for months and because I'd asked him to my party. Dad loves a party, too. He doesn't like organizing them, and he moans like hell about going to them but, once he's there, he always enjoys himself. His favourite parties are his own ('because those are the only ones where I like nearly everyone in the room'), or mine, because he adores my schoolfriends. It's amazing how well he remembers all their names when he can barely recall mine.

In fact, he once said to me, in all seriousness, 'You came to our wedding, didn't you?'

'No, Dad, I didn't. But I'm sure it was lovely.'

'You didn't come? Why not? I'm sure we would have invited you.' He looked genuinely puzzled and seemed upset that I'd snubbed him, until I explained that I hadn't yet been born and, if I had, I may not have been the star guest – certainly not in my grandmother's eyes.

Of course, I'd asked my mother to my party as well, but she knows when my birthday is, partly because she'd spent hours in labour bringing me into the world and partly because it is the day after hers. I must've seriously ruined her twenty-second birthday, and I've never really said sorry for that. Sorry, Mum.

Alice and I organized my fortieth to take place at Les Ambassadeurs in Mayfair. The theme was red and black, the intention signalled on the invitation by a brilliant graphic designer friend of ours that showed a roulette wheel with the little white ball falling in an added '40' slot. I wore a black and red dress.

My schoolfriends, university friends and workmates came, and I tried to ignore my father dancing with most of them. We drank Bellinis, ate 'substantial canapés' and danced until the early hours. I was tiddly to the point of being relaxed but not pie-eyed. I couldn't allow myself to get stupidly drunk because I had an important filming commitment the next day.

James Corden had written a sketch for Comic Relief and asked me to be a part of it. I had one line but, essentially, my job was to sit next to Paul McCartney.

That's Paul McCartney of The Beatles. Paul McCartney of Wings. The recently ennobled Sir Paul McCartney.

'Can you come in on Sunday 30 January? It's the only day Paul can do and I want you to sit next to him,' James had asked me.

I took about a tenth of a second to respond in the affirmative. I'd done a few things with James, including an edition of *A League of Their Own* in which we had invented Mo Farah's celebration gesture. James had decided he needed something to rival Usain Bolt's 'Lightning Bolt', and we were throwing around suggestions.

'Ooh, ooh! I know!' I'd said, like a twelve-year-old child in class who thinks they have the answer.

I put my arms up with my hands on my head to form an 'M'.

'What about this? You know, like the "M" in "YMCA" . . .'

An idea is only a good idea when other people agree it is. For a long second I wondered whether they would all dismiss me as a fool.

'That's brilliant,' James pronounced. 'Let's call it the Mobot.'

If you have ever seen Mo Farah in action, you'll know it caught on.

So there I was in Make-up the day after my fortieth birthday when Sir Paul McCartney walked in with a friend. He was wearing jeans and a donkey jacket. He looked casually cool.

'Hey, team,' said the voice that had sung 'Hey Jude' a million times. 'How's it going?'

I swivelled my chair round, my hair looking particularly attractive in kirby grips.

'Hi, Paul,' I said, thrusting out my hand. 'I'm Clare.'

'Yeah,' he said. 'I know who you are. I watch you and Willie on the racing. Nice to meet you.'

He shook my hand, and my mouth made a goldfish shape and I started to move it up and down, no words coming out. Paul told me how way back when The Beatles had just made it big and he had money for the first time in his life, he'd bought his dad a racehorse. They'd gone evening racing at Aintree, when the course still held flat meetings, and this horse had won.

'It wasn't a big race, ya'know.' He was smiling at the memory. 'But it was one of those times with my dad that I just really enjoyed. I could be there, he loved it and the horse won at our local track.'

He sat next to me to have a bit of powder put on his face and we chatted away like old friends. No entourage, no demands for special treatment, no sign of being one of the wealthiest and most success-ful artists in the history of music.

James came over to say hello and talk us through our roles. The concept was a huge round-table meeting with James as 'Smithy' at the centre of it, discussing who should go to Africa on a Comic Relief mission. James has never been restrained in his imagination for these sketches, and I am firmly of the opinion that he sits in the 'genius' folder of the broadcasting filing cabinet. He can make people do and say anything and, crucially, help them enjoy taking the mickey out of themselves.

Dermot O'Leary sat to the right of James, plus a couple of the boys from JLS. Paul was on my right, and Rio Ferdinand on my left. When the sketch was broadcast, the table also included David Beck-ham, Tom Daley in his diving trunks, Gordon Brown, Keira Knightley and a late appearance from George Michael. It was clev-erly directed to make it look as if everyone was together, whereas we filmed on different days.

James had sent me my line in advance, with a note saying, 'Of course, if you don't want to say it, that's fine, but I really hope it's OK.'

The joke was that Keira Knightley would be selected to go to Africa and the men around the table were falling over themselves to go with her. Then I put my hand up and say, 'I'll go' – the gag being that everyone knows I'm gay.

The key to being accepted by society for being who you are is being confident and publicly proud, so I was only too happy to play along. My only request was that I didn't want to say it in a leering, lechy way, partly because I thought it was funnier to play innocent and partly because I don't want to contribute to the historic image of lesbians as predatory.

The whole thing was done in about half an hour. Richard Curtis came in to thank us for our time and said to Paul, 'It was Clare's birthday yesterday. Her fortieth.'

Paul looked at me and started singing. He sang me my own personal, unaccompanied 'Happy Birthday'. I thought I was having some kind of strange hallucination.

When he finished, I didn't really know what to say, so I did that thing of trying to overcompensate.

'Thank you so much, that was wonderful,' I said. I should have stopped there. But of course I didn't. 'You know, if you ever want to come to Aintree again, I can get you badges.'

I said it because it was the only thing I could think of that I could do for him. What didn't occur to my slightly fuddled brain was that he's *Paul McCartney*. He's one of the four most famous Liverpudlians ever. If he wants a badge for Aintree, it's pretty certain that he can a) get one, b) doesn't need a freebie from me and c) would probably book himself a box.

He didn't laugh in my face. Instead he said, 'Oh, that would be great. Cheers.'

And off he went with his mate, who was wearing matching faded jeans.

I'm still half hoping that, if I meet Paul again, he'll say, 'I've been thinking about coming to Aintree again. I might just take you up on that offer of a couple of badges . . .'

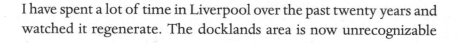

I have spent a lot of time in Liverpool over the past twenty years and watched it regenerate. The docklands area is now unrecognizable compared to 1997, when a bomb scare at Aintree meant I had a little more time in the city than I was planning.

I was working for 5 Live as a junior reporter, my main responsibility being to update listeners on the betting. As the fire alarm went off in the grandstand, I desperately pressed the talkback button to get the attention of the editor of *Sport on 5* (now *5 Live Sport*). He thought I had a breaking betting story but, instead, I announced on air that the alarm was going off and we were being told to evacuate the stand. I thought there was a fire somewhere.

None of us had any idea what was happening or how long it would be before we might be allowed back. I remember being worried that I'd left the phone line open to the Press Association, who provided us with the betting information, and that it might cost the BBC a lot of money. Other people had more urgent concerns, such as the Tote operators, who had thousands of pounds in cash to protect.

The phone signals were blocked by the police as the security cordon tightened, so nobody could get in touch with anyone else. They had received a coded warning from the IRA that there was a bomb somewhere on the racecourse. None of us knew this, so everyone was chatting and wondering how long the Grand National might be delayed.

I thought it was a good idea to go to the working men's social club opposite the horsebox entrance to the course, now part of the owners' and trainers' car park. I sat drinking tea with the trainer Charlie Brooks and his jockey Jamie Osborne, who were responsible for the second-favourite, Suny Bay. I figured that, at the very least, I would know if the race was going to be run that evening, because the authorities would have to let the trainers and jockeys know.

Just before 4.15 p.m. we heard that the meeting had been abandoned, and then we heard two loud bangs. The police had carried out two controlled explosions. No one panicked. I think we carried on drinking tea and Charlie may have ordered a proper drink once he realized he wasn't going to be saddling a Grand National runner that day. No one was scared and I never once felt in danger. Most people were just a bit cross that their big day had been ruined.

I tried unsuccessfully to contact my brother, who was due to ride in the Amateur Race after the Grand National. He left the weighing room, as all the jockeys did, in his breeches and boots, with nothing more than a thin white under-shirt on his top half. I think he ended up in a house on the Melling Road until he worked out a way back to the city centre.

He may have been cold, but his unusual clothes turned out to be a winning move, because all the jockeys were offered accommodation in the Adelphi Hotel. They shared a massive dormitory but, before any of them went to bed, they made the most of Liverpool hospitality, as they were bought drinks by fellow guests at the hotel bar.

The actress Martine McCutcheon, who at the time was a big star on *EastEnders*, was there. My brother asked her to sign his shirt and, when she asked who he was, he replied, 'My name's Tony McCoy. I'm the champion jockey.'

She was suitably impressed and Andrew still has the autographed shirt with 'To Tony, love, Martine McCutcheon' written on it.

I went back to the Atlantic Hotel, near the docklands, where the BBC had managed to keep the rooms they had booked the night before. I had no washbag or change of clothes, as they were in my car, which was impounded at the racecourse, but at least I had a room for the night.

At a press conference the next day it was announced that the Grand National would be run on the Monday evening at five fifteen. Peter O'Sullevan, who was in his final year as BBC Television's lead commentator, called home Lord Gyllene as the winner, beating Suny Bay by twenty-five lengths. The rescheduled race was watched by 15.1 million people on television, making it the most popular sporting event of the year. Millions more listened on the radio.

I stood up in the commentary position with Peter Bromley, giving betting updates and doing Peter's 'You said' cards, which required me to write down exactly the finishing order he had given.

'Even if you think I've got it wrong,' he said to me sternly, 'you write down what I said. Not what you think. I can cope with my own mistakes, but I can't cope with yours.'

I concentrated very hard, because I never wanted to let Peter down. He came across as a gruff, stern military man, but he was always very kind to me. One day, when I had a sore throat, he offered me a swig of his cough mixture. It tasted like firewater, but the deadly mixture did the trick. I certainly didn't cough again that day, or even that month.

Standing with Bromley gave me the best view in the house, but 1997 was my final Grand National for 5 Live. The following year, I became a fully fledged member of the TV team, working with Des Lynam, Richard Pitman and Peter Scudamore.

I enjoyed the unscheduled stop in Liverpool and used it to explore the city on foot. I have walked there a couple of times since, and it is remarkable to see the effects of investment and development, the success of which helped earn Liverpool the right to be European Capital of Culture in 2008.

Similarly honoured in 1990, and also recovering its identity in the aftermath of a molten shipbuilding industry, Glasgow is a good example of a city that reveals itself only when you start looking a little closer, on foot.

Glasgow was known as the second city of the Empire in Victorian times and was once the fourth-biggest city in Europe, behind London, Berlin and Paris. The River Clyde provided it with a huge, gaping mouth through which the city was fed by trade and shipbuilding. Since then, Glasgow has been through torrid times, suffering huge unemployment, poor health and low life expectancy, but hosting the Commonwealth Games allowed it a chance to celebrate its twenty-first-century regeneration.

In autumn 2010 I headed into the city centre to meet a group of historians from the Glasgow Women's Library. One of them,

Christine, is a 'history detective'. I was rather taken with the idea of being a spy of the past, if a little disappointed that she wasn't wearing a cape and a deerstalker. We walked north from the pink sandstone blocks of their building.

'Look up!' she cried. 'You must look up if you want to really appreciate these buildings.'

There on the corner of what used to be a bank was a skull staring out from the stonework. Gargoyles laughed at us from on high, macabre monuments crafted by long-dead stonemasons.

Revving engines and whining sirens formed the background music of our early steps as we walked east, away from George Square and its impressive, grey stone City Chambers and pink square. George Square is marked in history as the only place where tanks have ever been deployed on mainland Britain against the country's own people. It happened on 1 February 1919, after sixty thousand striking shipbuilders and engineers had demonstrated for a forty-hour working week; the tanks that had made their debut in the First World War were used to contain the demonstration (eventually, a compromise was reached and the working week was reduced from fifty-seven to forty-seven hours).

There are buildings all over the city that are worth examining in closer detail – the Central Hotel, Central Station, the Glasgow School of Art (currently being restored after a major fire), the Royal Exchange (now the Museum of Modern Art), the Mitchell Library and St Aloysius Church, which was the home of the Jesuit order in Glasgow – but we were heading not to a place or a building but to a space of commemoration. We walked past the University of Strathclyde towards the Necropolis, the city of the dead.

You might think it depressing to want to walk around a massive graveyard, but Glasgow's Necropolis is magnificent and majestic, rather than macabre. It contains around fifty thousand graves, three and a half thousand of which have monuments or mausoleums. The different hues of sandstone give it either a pink tinge or a warm, yellowy-brown glow. Originally a park full of fir trees called – yes, you've guessed it, Fir Park – the Necropolis was conceived in

1832 to contain the city's expanding numbers of dead. The fir trees didn't appreciate the fumes of industry spewing forth from the city and started to fade, to be replaced by ash trees and willow. Consequently, the place has a softer, less threatening feel to it than some graveyards.

'This feels like crossing a drawbridge into a fort,' I said, as we walked over the Bridge of Sighs on to an island of green patterned with grey slabs and square tombs, an occasional obelisk rising up into the sky. We were passing 'to the other side'.

It's an enormous space – some thirty-seven acres in total – and the suggested walk around the Necropolis takes at least two hours, longer if you pause to read inscriptions and investigate families. An army of schoolchildren were running round the lower section, their faces glowing with exertion as a teacher with a clipboard waited for them at the iron gates.

Christine told me that until the 1950s women were not allowed to attend a funeral. They could follow the coffin and come to the gates but they could not enter the Necropolis or witness the burial. So, even when a woman was buried, her daughter, sister or mother could not be by the graveside. Instead, they would turn back at the gates and head off to prepare the feast for the wake. Christine had discovered the Necropolis when she was working nearby and used to come for a walk at lunchtime. She started to get more and more interested in the place and its people and pointed out interesting memorials.

'That's Corlinda Lee,' she said, indicating a tall monument with a pointed top. The stone was tinted green with lichen and the relief of Corlinda's face had worn away, the original bronze portrait having been stolen aeons ago. 'She was queen of the gypsies. She married George Smith, uniting two influential gypsy families in the nineteenth century.'

George Smith was a wily old fox and had come up with the ingenious idea of taking his extended family on a grand tour of Great Britain and Ireland, showing people how real Romany gypsies lived and staging a 'Gypsy Ball' in every city they visited. It was the nineteenth-century equivalent of Channel 4 filming a fly-on-the-wall documentary, and it caused quite a stir. Even Queen Victoria paid a visit to their encampment in Dunbar in 1878, and some stories suggest that she had her palm read by Corlinda Lee.

We walked on upwards, climbing through foliage and up uneven steps, turning to look down on the city. It was a clear day, and we could see for some forty miles to the south and east, as far as Tinto Hill, one of the highest peaks of the Southern Uplands. The columns of smoke rising from the chimneys near the River Clyde represented a mere fraction of the industry that would once have turned the skies grey with smog.

The name 'Glasgow' means 'beloved green place', and from the height of the Necropolis you can see that the city is built in the river valley, which would once have been green and fertile. The locals told me that when you drive to Glasgow at night and see its lights twinkling in the darkness, you can still get that sense of it being in a hollow.

Daniel Defoe, the author of *Robinson Crusoe*, visited in 1707, and described Glasgow in his book *A Tour through the Whole Island of Great Britain*:

> Glasgow is, indeed, a very fine city; the four principal streets are the fairest for breadth, and the finest built that I have ever seen in one city together. The houses are all of stone, and generally equal and uniform in height, as well as in front; the lower storey generally stands on vast square dorick [Doric] columns, not round pillars, and arches between give passage into the shops, adding to the strength as well as beauty of the building; in a word, 'tis the cleanest and beautifullest, and best built city in Britain, London excepted.

As we walked, I asked questions about the families buried there. Christine, the 'history detective', had most of the answers. She was a good snooper. She also told me that ivy, so often found in graveyards, represents eternal life (because it's evergreen) and friendship.

'It's a pretty clingy kind of friendship,' I said.

She added that the best time to see the Necropolis was at dawn or dusk, because the light was so different; in the winter months when the sun stays low, it throws its beams on to inscriptions that you would never otherwise see. She is always discovering something new.

Our climb finished at the spot where the grim-faced John Knox, leader of the Protestant Reformation, stands on his plinth. He would have disapproved of Corlinda Lee's acceptance into Glasgow society, as he had declared war on gypsies, calling them 'devil worshippers'. Mind you, he'd have disapproved of most things – especially a group of female historians from the Glasgow Women's Library. The women were kinder to him than the author of that 1558 classic of misogyny *The First Blast of the Trumpet against the Monstrous Regiment of Women* would ever have been to them. Knox lived through the reigns of five queens of Scotland and England, was a permanent opponent of Mary, Queen of Scots, and her mother, Mary of Guise, and antagonized Elizabeth I enough for her to deny him safe passage through England.

My group of historians explained that different generations of academics have had alternative views on John Knox. In the nineteenth century, he was treated with enormous respect as the man who founded the Scottish Presbyterian Church, and praised for his bravery and integrity. In the twentieth century, historians highlighted his miserable nature, the fact that he hated people having fun, that he was a woman-hating bigot and that he ruined the arts in Scotland with his narrow Calvinist views. In the twenty-first century, historians are looking at him again: who knows what they'll conclude.

While Knox has a statue here in the Glasgow Necropolis, he is buried in Edinburgh, at St Giles' Cathedral, where he used to deliver his sermons. The cemetery has long since disappeared under a car park, and Christine told me that his grave is somewhere under stall number 23.

'I hope a lot of female drivers reverse into that spot,' I said, somewhat uncharitably.

The joy of walking in a city, whether it be London, Glasgow, Paris or Rome, is in finding the hidden gems. I love the contrast between the bustle of the urban population going about their working lives, the historical significance of the buildings, the traffic, the noise and the oasis of calm that you will always find, if you look hard enough.

As part of the build-up to the Commonwealth Games in Glasgow, I was asked what I liked most about the city. 'The Necropolis,' I replied. Some people thought I was joking or somehow mocking the city, but I was absolutely serious. I know a graveyard isn't everyone's idea of a major tourist attraction but, believe me, this one is worth taking the time to explore.

Inkpen Beacon–Ashmansworth

What had begun as a three-day adventure with my brother covering seventy miles of the Wayfarer's Walk turned into one day of walking home. Admittedly, we covered nineteen miles in that day, which is no mean feat, but I wanted to do more. So the next morning I thought we'd start at the beginning – Inkpen Beacon – and walk home with my mother and Alice.

It's about thirteen miles. I guessed it would take us between three and four hours, a little longer if we stopped off for a coffee.

I had asked both of my parents if they wanted to walk with me, but Dad 'didn't much fancy it'. Walking isn't fast or dangerous enough for him. Secretly, my mother and I are relieved. It would have turned into an extreme sport with him constantly asking whether we were going the right way and trying to cut

Wayfarer's Walk

corners across private land. (Like my brother, he doesn't really understand the concept that trespassing is illegal.)

I am also secretly thrilled that Mum has decided to come. I don't tell her, of course. That would be too close to being emotional, or even 'soppy', and she might think I am going to give her a hug or something awful. She brings Boris the boxer with her and we bring Archie. Anna Lisa drives us to Inkpen.

As we hurtle down narrow country lanes by car, Alice says, 'Is it really this far?'

And fifteen minutes later: 'Really? Are we walking this far?'

'It's much more direct when you walk it,' I say, in my most confident voice. 'We're wiggling around here, but the path goes right across the top of the ridge and it's straight as an arrow. Don't worry.'

We start a few yards from Combe Gibbet, a double hangman's cross standing some twenty-five feet high on top of a Neolithic long barrow that marks the border between the parishes of Combe and Inkpen. Here, in 1676, the bodies of lovers George Bromham (or Broomham) and Dorothy Newman were hung.

They had been found guilty of the murder of George's wife, Martha, and son, Robert, and were publicly hanged in Winchester. Their bodies were brought back to the place where they conceived the murder and displayed in chains, suspended from the gibbet as a lesson to all. The gibbet was used only once and has been replaced several times, most recently in 1992.

Reports differ as to whether Bromham and Newman murdered his wife and son by beating them to death with a stick, and then disposed of the bodies in a nearby dew pond, or whether (and this is particularly gruesome) Bromham took his wife to Newbury market and on the way there asked her whether she'd ever seen a hornets' nest, because he knew of one just off the path. He then held her head in the nest until she was stung to death. He killed his son because he had discovered George Bromham's affair and overheard him talking to Dorothy about the plot.

The story achieved cult status because it was the subject of a student film made by John Schlesinger in 1948, *Black Legend*. Schlesinger went on to win an Oscar for *Midnight Cowboy*, but credited *Black Legend* as his first success.

With the grisly landmark of Combe Gibbet behind us, we set off across the top of Walbury Hill, with West Woodhay Down to our left. The weather forecast is fine and the dogs are raring to go. Boris is Mum's latest boxer, and he is, as Jamie Mackinnon had pointed out, 'A bit of a handful for you, Mrs B.'

He is now heavier and considerably stronger than when Jamie made that comment.

Imagine, if you will, tying a rope around a car and then trying to control it while it drives forward, bouncing from side to side if it sees a pheasant, or a rabbit, or a paper bag. (Not that a car would think much of a pheasant or a rabbit, or indeed a paper bag, but it's the strength I'm looking for in that analogy, not the motivation.) So Mum has Boris on a lead, and he duly tugs her forward and from side to side.

'Why don't you let him off the lead?' I say helpfully, as we set

Wayfarer's Walk

out on a wide grassy track with wheatfields to our left, a small wood to our right and the road nowhere in sight. 'He doesn't know where he is so he can't run off home, and there's no one around.'

'No,' my mother says through pursed lips as he tows her along. 'It's fine. I want to preserve his energy, otherwise he won't make it home.'

I have to stifle a laugh at the idea of a young, energetic, fit and healthy dog needing his energy preserved while a woman in her sixties who has just told me she has never walked this far in her life has her arms pulled out of their sockets.

Archie, meanwhile, trots along merrily off the lead, behaving like an angel. If I sound like a proud parent, I assure you, it is a rare occurrence.

Archie gets a bad press in my family. He is, according to my mother, 'a typical only child' – by which she means he is spoilt. It's quite unfair on single children and on our dog, who, I admit, does sleep on the bed, gets on the sofa, sits wherever he feels like in the car and demands his tea at four o'clock on the dot by sitting and staring at whichever one of us is at home. If we ignore him, he raises a paw and bashes us gently but insistently on the knee until he gets what he wants.

He is a Tibetan terrier and has non-shedding hair, so every six weeks or so he has to have a haircut. Alice brushes him and quite often gives him a bath. He doesn't really like early mornings and won't ask to go out until about ten o'clock.

This tests my parents' idea of a dog to the limit. He stayed with them when he was much younger, and when Dad tried to force him out of bed at 6 a.m. Archie growled at him.

I will confess his faults straight up – he doesn't react well to discipline and isn't good inside with other dogs or with very young children, because he doesn't understand them. Outside is a different story. He comes when he's called, doesn't chase every living animal on the planet, doesn't bark incessantly and doesn't pull on the lead – all of which I would say scores him quite well compared to other dogs in the family, if we happened to be getting competitive. Neither does he sit at the dining-room table, which Boris has taken to doing – whether or not there is a person already in the chair.

I have tried to point out that Tibetan terriers, as the name would suggest, come from *Tibet*, so they're quite hardy and were used for herding and guarding, as well as being holy dogs in the temples. My father won't have it. He also cannot under-stand that Archie will look larger when his hair is long than when it's just been cut.

'He's getting fat, your dog.'

'He's not, Dad. He's just fluffy. Look, feel his ribs. He's not fat.'

Dad harrumphed. He is horribly fattist. A week later, I came home with Archie freshly shaven.

'He's lost weight, your dog. Looks very fit,' he said. 'Well done, Archie.'

I can never be bothered to go through it all again.

Archie is a great walking companion. He never gets too far behind or ahead and he has absolutely no idea what to do if he

Wayfarer's Walk

sees a rabbit, apart from squeak. A cat is a different matter – but you don't get many of those out in the fields of Hampshire.

'Oh, Archie, are you enjoying being a country dog?' My mother is talking to me through the dog. Don't pretend you haven't done it. We all have. 'Big, wide open spaces, no pavements, and no one has to follow you with a plastic bag.'

'Luckily enough, he can do London and the country,' I say cheerily. 'He really doesn't mind where he is, as long as he gets fed and has a walk.'

It's true, he doesn't mind and, more to the point – he's *a dog*. His life is not full of choices, responsibilities and worries. When I die, I want to come back as a dog, and if I had to pick a dog I'd want to be, I'd be Archie. He has life pretty well sewn up and, if he gets a little snappy with dogs who invade his personal space, well, I'd probably do that, too.

'Seriously, Mum,' I say, 'why don't you let Boris off the lead? He'll stay with Archie and it'll be good for him.'

She looks tempted but says I am unaware of the daily struggles at home of trying to keep Boris anywhere near – and, of course, this is 'the perfect opportunity for lead training'. So I give up: if my mother is happy to be dragged along for four hours, who am I to question her?

I relax and fall into easy chat with Alice as we admire the views. Mum is a few strides behind, persuading Boris to walk at her pace and gradually winning the battle.

A tree is down across the path, forcing us to detour into the woods. We can't get round it, but it is easy enough to scramble underneath its trunk. Boris tries to help by pulling Mum through the gap, a little faster than she would have liked.

We have seen a Huf Haus from the road and within a mile or two it appears on our right. Alice and I have always fancied the idea of an energy-friendly house made of wood, steel and glass that is built in a factory, arrives in flat-pack form and goes up in weeks rather than months. This one is in a perfect location – perched high on a hill with green fields and trees all around. It's not my mother's thing at all, which she makes very clear, so we agree to disagree and plough onwards, towards Pilot Hill.

Alice and I walk efficiently but not particularly fast, which is a relief to my mother. She is terrified that we'll leave her lagging, or that we won't stop to admire a view, but I am very firmly of the opinion that walking is about taking it all in, bending down to look at flowers, staring into the distance and looking up at trees.

I spent an hour once with a group of artists; we lay on our backs in the snow, staring up at branches. We'd had to delay the walk a day or two because my car had been snowed in at the Mill in Kingsclere (which I was renting from Uncle Willie). The seven hills of Stroud were under a blanket of cold, wet snow and my bottom got very wet, but I came away with a much better appreciation of the filigree of leafless tree branches.

That walk got a bit weird when the leader asked us all to hug a tree and then quizzed us on what it made us feel. I made up something that wasn't true but sounded good. I'm afraid that, as hard as I tried, all I could hear was the song from *A Chorus Line*:

Wayfarer's Walk

'And I dug right down to the bottom of my soul, To see what I had inside . . . Nothing, I'm feeling nothing.'

Our walk leader also made me draw left-handed, which just annoyed me. I'm bad enough at drawing right-handed, without being made to look like a complete idiot. There was a lot of talk about enjoying the process rather than the outcome. I wasn't sure I quite understood. Neither did Lucy, who watched me trying to draw an iron gate.

'It looks like a rabbit,' she guffawed.

At one point our leader asked me and Lucy what we were up to. Lucy was recording as I described the scenery. I explained that I needed to give the listener a clear idea of location and conditions, and he sniffed as he said, 'Oh well, I suppose there's an art to it somewhere.'

Lucy raised her eyebrows and I tried to force a smile, as if he'd made a joke.

On the plus side, our snowy walk in Stroud did make me think I should lie on my back and stare at trees more often. We all should. Although preferably on dry ground, or at least on a waterproof sheet.

Mum's youngest brother, John, and his wife, Sophie, live in Ashmansworth, which is just under two hours into our walk. The perfect time to stop for coffee and go to the loo, I suggest. Mum phones Sophie, who is going to yoga at 10.45 but would love to see us if we can make it before then. I look at my watch and pick up the pace. It's 10 a.m.

'We'll never make it,' says Mum.

My brain has already summoned the smell of coffee, and I need a pee, so I will make sure we do make it. I ignore the view, the primroses to the side of the path, the moss-covered bark on the trees around us – things I would normally enjoy – because the lure of coffee and nice loo paper is just too much.

We knock on the door at 10.35 and Sophie greets us warmly. 'John's up in London, but I've got coffee and hot-cross buns,' she says.

We tie the dogs up to separate benches outside and take them some water. I ease off my Internet-bargain maroon boots, which have by now worn in rather well and don't press on the same toes which my trainers demolished the day before.

On the kitchen table is a steaming jug of fresh coffee, some milk, sugar and mugs, plus some plates. I can see hot-cross buns by the toaster. Oh yes, we have landed in walkers' heaven! The best thing about trekking a long way is that you feel as if you can eat anything and everything. All you need is someone else to provide for you.

We haven't had any breakfast, so Alice and I descend on the buns like hungry caterpillars. I have some of Uncle Gub's home-made jam, which appals Sophie, who thinks hot-cross buns should be eaten just with butter. Alice and Mum are on her side, but I am too busy licking damson jam from the corners of my lips to care.

Wayfarer's Walk

It's amazing how an injection of caffeine and a hot-cross bun or three can pick you up of a morning. We are revived and rejuvenated and ready for the second half of our adventure. Sophie says the next section, from Ashmansworth to the A34, is beautiful, so we verily skip out of her garden and back up the road to rejoin the Wayfarer's Walk.

6

Inner Hope

I love the idea of beginning a walk at a place called Inner Hope. It's right next to Outer Hope. And it marks the start of the most spectacular section of the South-west Coast Path, to Salcombe.

I would happily live in either Inner Hope or Outer Hope, just to have that address. The walk itself sounds like an Enid Blyton adventure, as it takes you up on to Bolberry Down, above Slippery Point, with a view of Lantern Rock, past Cathole Cliff, up to the Warren, around Bolt Head and into Salcombe Bay. I had imaginary cucumber sandwiches and lashings of ginger beer in my rucksack – sadly, not the real thing, because I always forget I need sustenance.

This is as close to a perfect walk as you can get – just under eight miles in distance, not too many tricky down and ups on rocky paths and a near-constant view of the sea, with waves crashing into the rocks below. It's a walk that makes you feel fresh, alive, energized and gloriously, wonderfully happy. Think how much you'd pay to get that in a bottle, and here it is, in return for a little bit of effort – basically, for free.

The South-west Coast Path is 630 miles in total, starting in Minehead on the edge of Exmoor and taking you right round the north side of Somerset, Devon, Cornwall and then back again on the bottom edge to Poole Harbour. I have walked or cycled various sections of it, but have not yet covered the whole thing.

Heading to Inner Hope to record *Ramblings*, we got lucky with a perfect September day: blue skies, a slight breeze and a warming sun on our faces. I was walking with a couple called Gordon and Caroline Luff and their son, Sam. Gordon had written into the programme when he heard we were doing a series of 'Listener's Walks'. They were keen *Ramblings* fans and wanted to share their story. Caroline was recovering from breast cancer and serious back surgery. All through her recovery she had dreamt of walking again, with the ultimate aim of climbing Cader Idris in Snowdonia. This walk in Devon was an important step as Caroline rebuilt her strength and her confidence.

They are both very active people, and walking is their passion. Caroline could not bear to be incapacitated as she recovered from her back surgery. She treated cancer as a passing phase – a double mastectomy and she says she was right as rain. The back, however, was a different issue and the pain had been getting progressively worse.

'After three years, the surgeon said, "You have only one option left." He told me that if it went wrong I could be paralysed but, luckily, it worked, and here I am. Walking is the only therapy for me, because I love it so much. I was very despondent, and Gordon thought I would never be going out on walks like this again.'

In the early stages after the operation Caroline hadn't even been able to get out of bed to go to the loo. But her fitness from years of walking meant that her muscles were strong and, with a heavy dose of Inner Hope, she started to fight back.

I think walking together is crucial to a relationship and a way of spending valuable time together. It's uncomplicated and fluid, unlike driving. Especially unlike driving.

When I'm in the car with Alice and she's driving, she gets unaccountably cross with me for pointing to the other lane of the motorway, clicking as I would to a horse to speed it up, or telling her to overtake. Early in our relationship she pulled over and turned the engine off. Using the calm, controlled voice of the shipping-forecast announcer, she said, 'This is very simple. Either I drive and you shut up, or you drive. Which would you rather?'

I got the point. In contrast, walking together isn't stressful at all, apart from keeping an eye on Archie to check he's not having a stand-up row with a dog he's decided to dislike. He does let himself down sometimes, which is why he's only allowed to come with me on special occasions.

I didn't have Archie to worry about as I soaked in the fresh air and the freedom of the cliffs above Hope Cove. Gordon was in shorts and a sleeveless top, with a long walking staff in his hand. On visual impressions alone, he is a tough, confident, practical man but, as I have discovered over the years, our eyes are the least trustworthy of our senses in terms of judging character.

I despair that so much is made of the way people look, what they wear, how they do their hair. Women are constantly judged (in the media and therefore, by extension, in society) in terms of how they look. I walked once with a blind man called David and asked him if he ever wondered what his guide looked like. He replied, 'You live in a visual world, so you would ask whether I wonder what my guide looks like. I don't live in that world and I find it much more honest to assess character in other ways.'

I try to remember David's words if I catch myself judging someone from afar, or when I look at yet another newspaper article about a woman who has lost or gained weight, dyed her hair, cut her hair, let it grow, worn a short skirt, a maxi dress or no dress, is in a bikini or a coat. It drives me *nuts*.

What would the world be like if men were constantly judged by what they are wearing, or how their hair is styled, or how much their waistline has expanded? It would stop working, that's what would happen. This obsession with the visual reduces women to objects to be admired or rejected at auction. It's pathetic.

Gordon was not a man who would judge a woman just by how she looked. He was thoughtful, kind and open about living through his wife's trauma.

'We've been married now for twenty-eight years, and it's been very tough to see Caroline in pain,' he said. 'I shed a few tears, privately. The cancer really took me by surprise, because we were the "action couple". That just floored me completely. The back operation crept up on us more. She'd always had minor niggles with her back and it just got worse and worse.'

This was the first time they had attempted a walk of any length or difficulty since Caroline had broken down in tears on the path just before Salcombe because she was in so much pain. She was convinced then that she would never again be able to walk properly.

We were walking ahead of Caroline and Sam at this point and Gordon kept glancing backwards to check she was OK. We had covered about a mile and everything seemed to be fine, which in itself was a miracle, as he explained.

'The walking truly ended the year before last. I'd decided we probably could do the Thames Path, because it's all flat and we could do it in bite-sized chunks. We got as far as Oxford, and Caroline's back was getting worse and worse so we had to stop. I knew then something had to be done, because the Thames Path was about the easiest long-distance walk I could think of.'

This touched me, because Gordon had thought so carefully about a walk that wouldn't cause Caroline any pain – yet even that was too much. Now they were back in the place where she had broken down, and here she was, doing that thing that we all take for granted – putting one foot in front of the other.

The footpath swept on a right-hand curve and, when we stopped to look back, we could see the line where so many boots had trodden cutting through the low heather bushes, the line that showed the

Lucy and me with the furry microphone on the Firth of Forth

Walking on the shifting landscape of the Sands of Forvie in need of a 'chittery bite'.
With Elizabeth Hay, Ellie Ingram, Lucy and Annabel Drysdale

With Pete and the Monday Walkers, stopping for whisky in Perthshire.
That's me in the fetching hat

Archie, wet and muddy

Alice looking for trout in
the River Teign

Willie and me on our last
day together at Ascot

The Mountains of Mourne.
'Can we live here?'

Sky, hills, river valley. Space to breathe

Eanna and John
on Dublin Bay.
'Love your man,
love your mountain'

With Patrick Gale
in Cornwall

Gordon Luff:
Inner Hope

With Anna Maria Murphy in Polperro, notebook in hand

Cool, calm Karen, who produces *Ramblings*

A Devon pony says hello
to the microphone

Devon, South-west Coast Path

distance we had already covered. Caroline was smiling. She was back in a place she loved, with people she loved, and she wasn't in pain.

We walked down a wide, grassy path towards the sea. There is a tiny beach, no more than a hundred yards wide, called Soar Mill Cove. The water looked so inviting I couldn't help but zip off the bottoms of my trousers to reveal my lily-white legs. I took off my shoes and socks and, with a rush of childlike vigour, bounced off towards the English Channel.

I screamed as soon as my toes hit the ice-cold water, but kept on running. The smell of seaweed filled my nostrils and the shock of the temperature change sent an electric charge through my body. It felt as if I'd plugged into an energy surge. Gordon and Caroline followed me in at a more sedate pace, holding hands. Sam was the only sensible one, staying on dry land, taking photos of his parents.

Sam was a reluctant contributor to the conversation but, once we'd dried our feet off and climbed up from Soar Mill Cove, he appeared alongside me. I asked him about his university course and what he wanted to do with his life. Then I asked about his mother.

'I always remember the day that Mum and Dad told us that Mum had breast cancer,' he said quietly. 'My attitude was: "They can cure that, so it's not a problem." I always knew she'd get through it. I never doubted her.'

As he was talking to me, I realized that Sam had probably never had this conversation with his parents. There are some things that are just easier to say to a stranger. I wondered why he had been so sure.

'I have a very positive outlook on life,' Sam replied, 'and I just knew that she would be able to walk again, and if she just started with walking down the road she'd go further and further and she'd be OK.'

We walked on together, into a field of wild ponies, who came up to investigate the microphone. We had been told that we couldn't get lost if we kept the sea on our right and just followed our noses. This was an instruction even I couldn't fail to follow. We puffed and panted up the steep climb to the Warren. The last time she did this,

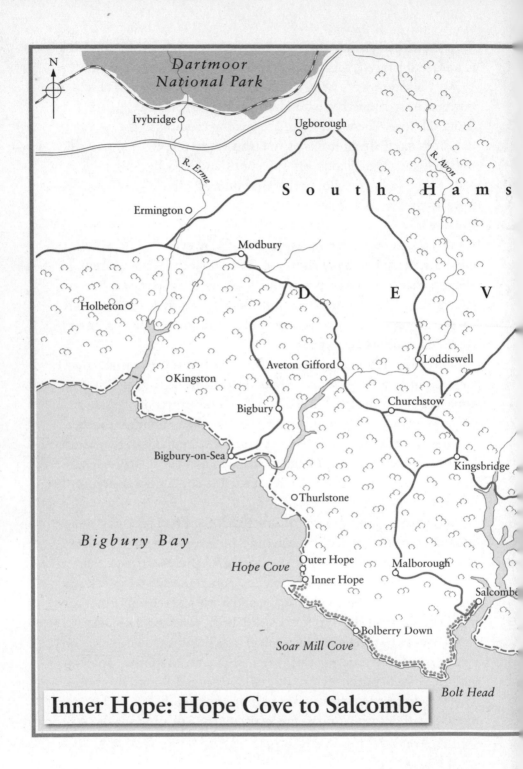

N

Dartmoor National Park

Ivybridge ○

Ugborough ○

R. Erme

R. Avon

S o u t h   H a m s

Ermington ○

Modbury ○

D   E   V

Holbeton ○

Loddiswell ○

○ Kingston

Aveton Gifford ○

Churchstow ○

Bigbury ○

Kingsbridge ○

Bigbury-on-Sea ○

○ Thurlstone

Bigbury Bay

Hope Cove   ○ Outer Hope   Malborough ○

○ Inner Hope

Salcombe

○ Bolberry Down

Soar Mill Cove

Bolt Head

Inner Hope: Hope Cove to Salcombe

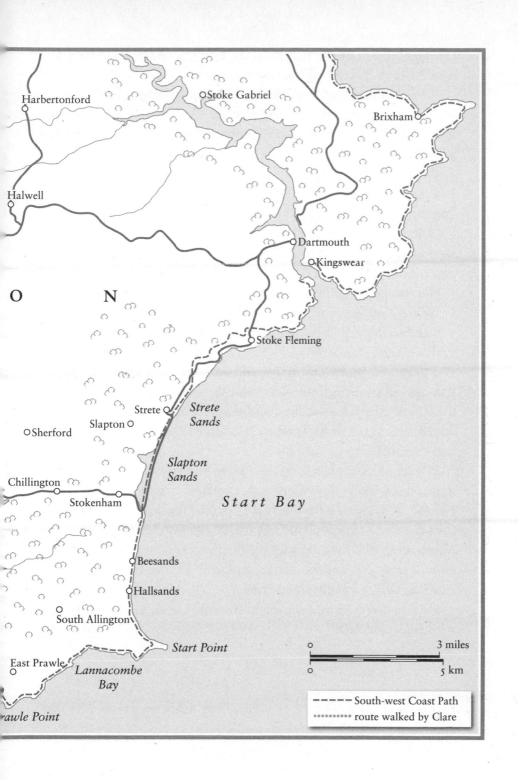

Harbertonford

Stoke Gabriel

Brixham

Halwell

Dartmouth

Kingswear

O

N

Stoke Fleming

Strete

Strete Sands

Slapton

Sherford

Slapton Sands

Chillington

Stokenham

Start Bay

Beesands

Hallsands

South Allington

Start Point

3 miles

5 km

East Prawle

Lannacombe Bay

awle Point

— — — South-west Coast Path

· · · · · · · route walked by Clare

Caroline admitted she had been in 'excruciating pain'. This time, nothing hurt that wasn't also hurting on the rest of us.

We could all see the confidence flooding back through Caroline's brain as her body did what she wanted it to do. Gordon explained that not being able to walk had 'challenged her security', and I knew what he meant.

We had laughed and chatted for about two hours by the time we had reached Bolt Head for the last section into Salcombe Bay. Caroline stopped and looked at her husband and son.

'The last time we came,' she said, 'I couldn't walk down this final section because my balance wouldn't allow it and I was in so much pain. So we stopped here.'

She started to lead us down the path towards Salcombe.

'When you get used to living with constant pain, people don't realize the stress that causes. It's so nice to do this walk and not be in that situation.'

She smiled, and Gordon grinned back. For him, the feeling was the same. Last time, both of them had been carrying a rucksack of lead. Now the pain had lifted and they could enjoy the walk. They held hands again and I dropped back to let them walk into the village together.

In high season, Salcombe is so busy you constantly have to step aside on the footpath to allow other walkers to pass. Off season, it's blissful. The locals have the place back to themselves and the visitors are a welcome revenue stream. It was warm enough for an ice cream and, while we sat waiting for the ferry, Gordon said, 'She's come a long way, from a very dark place. Now we can do the things together that we really enjoy doing.'

He reached over and squeezed his wife's arm, a gesture infused with pride and relief.

People fall in love while they walk. They fall in love with their surroundings, with the sound of their footsteps and with each other.

When Alfred Wainwright first set foot on the fells of the Lake District, the emotion that washed over him changed his life and set him on a career of mapping and writing about walking:

> The sun was shining, the birds singing. We went on, climbing steadily under a canopy of foliage, the path becoming rougher, and then, quite suddenly, we emerged from the shadows of the trees and were on a bare headland, and, as though a curtain had dramatically been torn aside, beheld a truly magnificent view. It was a moment of magic, a revelation so unexpected that I stood transfixed, unable to believe my eyes. (*Ex-Fellwanderer: A Thanksgiving*, 1987)

That's love at first sight, that is. I can imagine his heart rate quickening and his tummy flipping the way it does when you fall in love. For Wainwright, discovering the Lakelands was a spiritual as well as an emotional experience:

> I saw mountain ranges, one after another, the nearer starkly etched, those beyond fading into the blue distance. Rich woodlands, emerald pastures and the shimmering waters of the lake below added to a pageant of loveliness, a glorious panorama that held me enthralled. I had seen landscapes of rural beauty pictured in the local art gallery, but here was no painted canvas: this was real. This was truth. God was in his heaven that day and I a humble worshipper.

Mind you, Wainwright was a famously grumpy walker, unwilling to talk to strangers. And the last person on earth he would ever have walked with was Ruth, his first wife, who seems to have got the raw end of the deal. He *did* walk with his beloved Betty (who became his second wife) . . . on the condition that she didn't talk.

What Wordsworth did for the Lakes in the nineteenth century, Wainwright did in the twentieth. His 'pictorial guides' mapped the Lakeland Fells with pencil drawings showing the heights of the climbs, marking boulders and giving advice on where to proceed with care and which routes to avoid in bad weather. Wainwright wanted to stretch the legs and warm the soul.

He managed to turn a map into a magical tour of a place you wanted to discover. You could read it without being there, and you could dream of one day seeing and experiencing the real thing.

Ramblings aims to be the aural version of that idea – a vicarious experience for people listening at home. It makes me stop and look more closely when I try to explain what's around me and share the experience of scrambling down a slope, splashing through a river or puffing up a hill. Even when I'm walking alone I find myself slipping into description mode, wondering what I would say about the scenery around me, the weather or the atmosphere that it creates.

In a way, doing the programme for so long has probably taught me a version of mindfulness, a way of staying in the moment and making the most of every step. People tell me that they often regard *Ramblings* as their exercise for the day. I'm not sure I can promise they will burn any calories by listening, but they will be able to escape from the general traffic of life for half an hour.

Lucy says that a good *Ramblings* has three essential ingredients – a varied walk, described and shared clearly, a decent guest who can tell their story in a natural and original way, and finally, a bit of magic, that moment you can only get by being where you are in the very instant you are there. It never happens if you push too hard, and neither of us can explain how or why those moments occur. But they definitely happen, and when they do we look at each other and smile.

Seconds later, I will invariably say, 'You *were* recording, weren't you?'

Lucy always gives me one of her special withering looks.

7

Stories and Spirits

I'm in London, sitting at my desk, and I'm staring at a large photograph of waves crashing into the rocks, foaming as they hit an immovable object and fly backwards on themselves. It's called *Sea Shuffle*, and I found it in a hotel in Cornwall. You know those hotels where they hang artwork and photographs on the wall, with price tags? And you wonder who on earth buys them? I buy them.

'Oh no, not another picture,' Alice says when I come home with a square parcel tucked under my arm. 'You know we haven't got room for another picture. What have you got this time?'

I knew exactly where *Sea Shuffle* was going to go. I wanted to look at it for creative inspiration, so it would be facing my desk. My desk and Alice's sit opposite each other, and poor Alice has to look at a very angry painting that I bought by mistake at a charity silent auction. I hadn't realized the bidding was about to close when I upped the previous bid by £500. Oh well, it was in a good cause . . . and it's behind my back.

So, I'm looking at *Sea Shuffle* and remembering when I bought it. I was with Lucy, in Penzance, and I kept going on about the photo.

'Just go ahead and buy it,' she finally said. 'You can easily carry it on the train and, if not, I'll take it in the car and give it to you next time. You'll only regret it if you don't.'

She was right. I would have regretted it if I hadn't bought it. I like to have a reminder of the places I have walked and, despite visiting Cornwall many times, I hadn't bought anything that really captures the spirit of the place. This photograph of frothing waves gave me a slice of Cornish wildness to stare at every day. Even Alice has come round to it, I think.

Getting to Cornwall is the tricky part. By car, the journey is interminable. By train, it's beautiful, and fast to Exeter, but then rather slow. I once took a sleeper to Penzance, and it wasn't an experience I'd care to repeat. I got on some time after midnight at Reading, found my little cabin, changed into my pyjamas and spent the rest of the night terrified of going to the loo in case I bumped into a strange man, also in pyjamas. What would we say to each other?

So I drifted in and out of disturbed sleep, desperate for a pee, waking up each time the train lurched forward from one of its resting points. I had imagined the sleeper train chugged slowly through the night, arrived at Penzance and then sat there until its passengers gently woke up and disembarked. There would be a cut-off point, at 7 a.m., when an alarm would sound and everyone would have to leave.

That's how I thought it worked. It doesn't. Instead, it goes along steadily, stops at Taunton at 2.30 a.m., Exeter St David's at 3.06 a.m., then it pulls over for the driver to have a kip before it starts stopping at every station you can think of between Newton Abbot and Penzance. I mean, *every* station – Totnes, Ivybridge, Plymouth, Saltash, St Germans, Liskeard, Bodmin Parkway, Par, St Austell, Truro, Redruth, Camborne, Hayle and St Erth – before, finally, it gets into Penzance, just before 8 a.m. If anyone ever gets off at Par or St Erth, I will happily pay the driver £50. I presume he just stops there for fun.

It all adds up to a rather fitful night for driver and passengers. I was also disorientated in my bunk bed because I couldn't work out if I was facing forwards or backwards, and that bothered me. The answer was neither, because the beds are at 90 degrees to the movement of the train. Which is plain confusing.

Lucy met me at Penzance Station, and at least when she said, 'Christ, you look tired. Are you tired?', I could answer honestly, 'Yes. I'm knackered.'

The good news is that Cornwall is always worth the effort it takes to get there. And the fact that it isn't easy means that those looking for a quick getaway avoid the kingdom of Kernow.

For the walker, Cornwall is paradise. There are over 2,400 miles of paths inland and along the coast, ensuring that you will never, ever, run out of options.

My favourite time to walk the coastal paths is January and February. There is hardly anyone else around, the skies are usually clear and crisp and the morning frosts give the grass and bare branches a thin powdering of white. Incomers to Cornwall are known as 'blow-ins', which I rather like as a term. It's not hostile, but it reflects the tidal nature of tourism. If the locals are being slightly ruder, they call them 'emmets', after the lizards that come out for the sunshine and then disappear again.

There are a sizable number who started as blow-ins or emmets but would now happily never again go east of the River Tamar. Cornwall is a magnet for writers, artists, carpenters and craftsmen. Anyone with a heart and an art is welcome. Looking at a map, you'd think from the place names that it is overrun with saints – St Ives, St Austell, St Agnes, St Stephen, St Mawes, St Michael's Mount – but it is also the land of Merlin, of fairies, witches, ley lines and legends. It is rich with character, myth and mystery. Perfect for a nosy parker like me.

One of the most popular walks on the south coast is from Looe to Polperro and beyond to Fowey. If you like a rugged coastal walk in the ghostly light of a pale winter sun, this is ideal. Starting in the shelter of the woodland alongside the river, the route emerges through the postage-stamp fields to the coastal path for a full-faced assault on the senses. The footpath is well marked and the undulations are enough to ensure a decent workout, without leaving the body in bits.

There have been people living in Looe since 1000BC. It was once one of Cornwall's busiest ports, with exports of tin, granite and arsenic, as well as being a centre for fishing and shipbuilding.

I've decided I'd quite like to spend New Year's Eve in Looe, because they wear fancy dress, have fireworks off the pier and everyone goes for a swim in the sea on New Year's Day. Alice isn't so keen. There's a statue down by the harbour of Nelson. Not Viscount Nelson, the naval hero, but Nelson the grey seal. Like his namesake, Nelson the seal had one eye but, unlike his namesake, he was unmoved by approaching naval forces, preferring to scoff fish and bask in the sun on Pennyland Rocks. His bronze lies, fat and wrinkled, his front flippers splayed across a rock, at the entrance to Looe Harbour, above an inscription describing him as 'A Grand Old Man of the Sea' and 'a splendid ambassador for his species'.

The bronze was unveiled in May 2008 by sailor Sir Robin Knox-Johnston CBE, who was first to complete a single-handed non-stop circumnavigation of the globe. If that wasn't honour enough, the official inauguration of Nelson the seal's statue was also given a fly-past by 849 Naval Air Squadron. I think the ceremony and the grand monument to a one-eyed seal sum up the delightful daftness of our nation. I like to imagine that it gives us character, rather than making us look silly. It's a marvellous statue, by the way. Very seal-like.

The hairdresser's in Looe is called 'Village Gossip' and was full of customers doing just that. (It makes a change from 'Live and Let

Dye' or 'British Hairways', neither of which is as clever as our local dry cleaner's on Turnham Green: 'Turn 'em Clean'.)

I was meeting a writer in Looe called Anna Maria Murphy. She writes poems, short stories and plays which tell of lost love, un-requited love, lifelong love and the wrong love. For her theatre company's thirtieth birthday, Anna Maria decided to walk the foot-paths of Cornwall in search of people and their real life stories.

Her inspiration was Mary Kelynack, a Newlyn fishwife whose descendants still live in Cornwall today. In 1851, at the age of eighty-four, Mary decided she wanted to meet Queen Victoria and see the Great Exhibition. So she walked to London. It took her five weeks, and when she arrived she saw the Great Exhibition and met Queen Victoria. She went to Mansion House and had tea with the Lord Mayor, who gave her a sovereign. Mary promptly burst into tears, thanked him and said, 'Now I shall be able to get back.' I hope she didn't take the sleeper train.

Anna Maria Murphy thought the tale of this 84-year-old woman walking three hundred miles was inspirational. Although she didn't want to go to London, she thought she would walk for twenty days along the footpaths of Cornwall, meeting people as she went and discovering their stories. She turned it into a work called *Roads Less Travelled*.

We were meeting in the car park on the outskirts of Looe Har-bour, on the edge of Kilminorth Woods. It was a damp, misty morning that demanded many layers. I thought I may strip off later, but I wanted to be sure I was warm enough, particularly in the woods, which looked forbidding. Anna promised to lead me on a walk and, while I had no clue about the route or the people we might meet, I knew enough from reading her work to expect the unexpected. Her stories are always based on truth, and it seems that people tell her their innermost secrets; it's as if she charms them into a sort of spell, from which she creates a fact-based fiction. Her work has that elusive ring of authenticity.

We headed off on a Victorian promenade through Kilminorth

Woods and within minutes were far away from the busy village, surrounded by moss- and lichen-laden trees. A woman came towards us with two little dogs, and I thought I would run an experiment to see if Anna was just lucky or whether she really had a knack for getting people to tell her things.

I started jabbering on about the woman's dogs and correctly identified them as Papillons (ten years of presenting Crufts means I've picked up more than I realize). The woman told me one was a rescue dog and was still adjusting to life in a happy home, learning gradually how to live rather than existing under the shadow of fear and uncertainty.

Anna was taking notes in her notebook, which was full of names, sketches and little maps. She asked the woman where she had come from originally, because her accent was interesting. I thought she might be Belgian, but it turned out she came from Newcastle. (Scoff all you like, but mix Geordie with a bit of Cornish and, I'm telling you, it sounds like Belgian.) From this encounter, and this Papillon owner, Anna had the makings of a story about a woman who rescued dogs.

The path was wide and laden with rotting leaves, cushioning our steps and silencing our progress. The whisper of the ancient oaks hid its wildlife from view. A wooden fence to the right gave us some support and protection from tumbling down into the River Looe below. The path narrowed and the trees closed in overhead, creating a dark, dank atmosphere as we approached a set of steep steps heading up into the ether. The promise of light ahead led us on as we panted our way up what they call the Devil's Wall.

After I got my breath back, I quizzed Anna about her own story. She was born in Polperro, above a fish market. A childhood living with the stench of fish guts and imagining herself haunted by the spirits of conger eels and lobsters means that she doesn't much like fish now. She told me that people in Cornwall are very adaptable because they're used to changing jobs according to demand, and that the flow of people in and out creates a fascinating backwash.

'We should be grateful for the families who save up all year to come here and be by the sea. Their stories are our flotsam and jetsam.'

It was a wild day. As we came out of the woods, we saw the sea for the first time, with the white horses prancing, looking flighty and fractious. A grey sky above was brewing a storm that we hoped might hold off until we got to Polperro. We passed a wooden sign that read 'Jack the Giant having nothing to do, built a hedge from Lerryn to Looe.'

It marked a near-ten-mile-long Cornish hedge that had been built to protect the coastal villages from invasion and which stretches from the Fowey to the Looe estuary. The barrier had once stood seven feet high and twenty feet wide. It dates back to the Dark Ages and probably marked the edge of an ancient kingdom. For all our ability to fly across the world or connect with people online, my imagination takes me further when I feel linked to primeval history. I love walking through woodland that has stood for centuries, or thinking of those who would have walked this way in years gone by.

As we walked towards Talland Bay, I thought of the book I have on the myths and legends of Britain. It tells the tale of Parson Dodge, an eighteenth-century vicar of Talland. He was an exorcist of such renown that people were frightened to go near Talland Church at night in case they bumped into him chasing out evil spirits. There is, however, a rumour that Parson Dodge was in cahoots with the smugglers and encouraged the tales to keep locals away while the stolen goods were being moved.

Even today, vicars are called upon to rid houses of poltergeists and ghosts. When I first met the Archbishop of Canterbury, Justin Welby, I talked to him about living in Lambeth Palace.

'Is it haunted?' I asked.

'What?' he said. 'With all us archbishops having lived there? Of course not.'

I asked him what he meant, and he told me that it was well known that all men of the cloth have powers to rid places of ghosts and poltergeists. When he was a vicar in Liverpool, he would often receive requests from his parishioners to rid their house of an evil spirit. The person in question may not have been a regular church-goer or believe in God, but they believed in their vicar's ability to chase out ghosts. Welby didn't disappoint them.

In Talland Bay, there was no sign of evil spirits. But there in the pink bay with pink shale stone was a woman dressed entirely in pink. She was packing up her car when Anna started chatting to her.

It turned out that the lady in pink had a near-death experience ten years ago and can now communicate with dead people. I asked all the scientific questions about what happened with her illness and how she recovered, but Anna was more interested in the visions.

'I was walking through Looe, and a great big angel turned up,' the lady said. 'I was in a bookshop at the time, and my vision was taken up with this huge, fiery figure. The bookshop owner saw me go a bit funny and said, "Are you all right, duck?" So I went into that little angel shop that used to be there and I asked them about it. That was the beginning – after that, it was constant.'

The lady in pink said it was like having a new boss that she had to answer every time he came calling. I felt a bit sorry for her, to be honest. What with fiery red angels appearing at all hours and con-versations with dead people she'd never met, it must be exhausting. She explained that she had come to Talland Bay because the Mary line runs through there.

I knew a bit about the Michael line, which is a ley line believed to run from St Michael's Mount to Hopton in Norfolk, via Glaston-bury Tor, the Avebury stones and Bury St Edmunds. The Mary line intersects it at various points and aligns the water points and holy wells, while Michael hits the high spots, such as tors and church spires.

Once I walked near Llanthony Priory in the Black Mountains with a ley-line hunter who had a group of dedicated female follow-ers. They would sleep under the stars and hunt for ley lines with divining rods. It turned out that on several of these trips he had taken the opportunity for – let's put it this way – a little extra warmth from his female followers. All of them seemed very happy with the arrangement and I'm sure it benefited his energy levels in one way or another.

Back in Talland Bay, Anna was fizzing with excitement. As we walked on, she said, 'That is pure story gold. "The Lady in the Pink Coat".'

While she jotted down notes in her hardback notebook, I had to stop. My foot had been bothering me for the last mile or so, and I was convinced my walking boots had shrunk. I stuck on a blister plaster, which did the trick. I wondered if it was the energy from the Mary line making my feet expand.

We climbed up on to the cliff path that leads to Polperro, past a First World War memorial. It's a narrow, exposed path that gives you a blasting from the Channel: a natural facial that would cost a fortune in a spa. There was no one around, and I was in my own little world, thinking of what it would be like to be haunted by angels, while Anna was busy composing her story.

Walking towards us very fast was a tall, slim figure. His hair was blowing in the wind and he had a newspaper under his arm. He saw the microphone and stopped to say hello. 'Where are the cameras?' he asked.

It was Richard Madeley. Richard Madeley off the telly. He and his wife, Judy Finnigan, live in Talland Bay, and they were both down for the winter, writing and reading books. He walks to Polperro every morning to get his newspaper.

I explained that this was radio, not television, and he congratulated us for coming in the off-season.

'Best time to be here,' he said. 'We love it.' And he bounded off in the direction from which we had just come.

A Belgian-sounding Geordie who rescued dogs, a woman in pink who saw angels, and Richard Madeley off the telly. This walk was getting weirder and weirder.

We rounded the bay alongside a walled garden into the busy harbour of Polperro. The tide was out and the boats were balancing precariously on the dry bay. Walking into Polperro is the only way to get there, because the streets aren't wide enough for cars. The

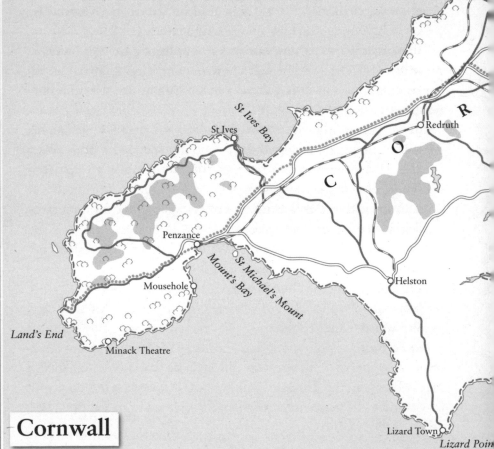

N

ATLANTIC OCEAN

Perranporth

C O R

Redruth

St Ives Bay

St Ives

C

Penzance

Mousehole

St Michael's Mount

Mount's Bay

Helston

Land's End

Minack Theatre

Lizard Town

Lizard Poin

Cornwall

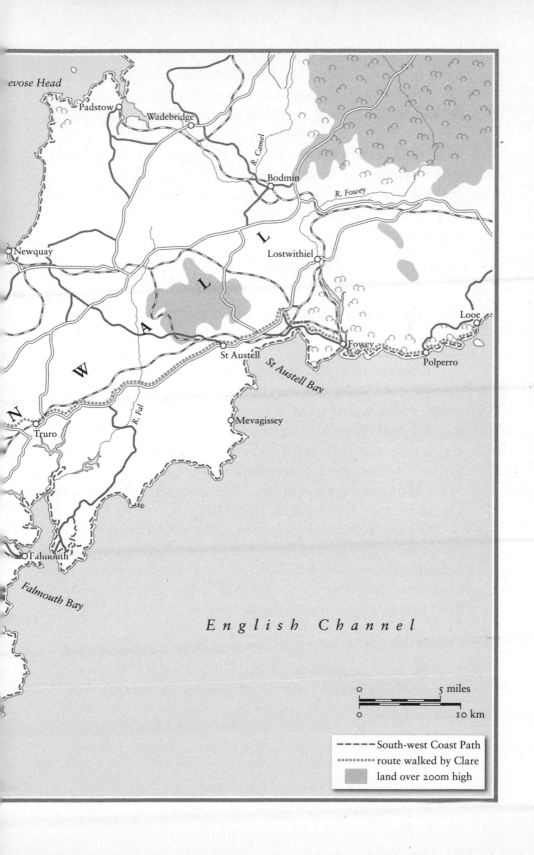

evose Head

Padstow

Wadebridge

R. Camel

Bodmin

R. Fowey

L

Lostwithiel

Newquay

L

A

Looe

St Austell

Fowey

Polperro

N

St Austell Bay

W

R. Fal

Mevagissey

N

Truro

Falmouth

Falmouth Bay

English Channel

o   5 miles
o   10 km

–––– South-west Coast Path
•••••• route walked by Clare
land over 200m high

houses are crowded on top of each other into the tiny space of a cliff ravine, each one with its own tale to tell. One has its outer walls entirely covered in shells; another is grey with white windows. Anna told me it had been the doctor's house.

On dark nights, they say you can hear the cries of Willy Wilcox in the caves under the western side of the harbour. He was a fisherman who went exploring and got lost in the maze of tunnels under what is now known as Willy Wilcox's Hole. Apparently, he is still looking for a way out.

I left Anna in Polperro to write up her stories, and continued to Fowey – the home of another writer, the novelist Daphne du Maurier.

Du Maurier first came to Cornwall as a child, and stayed in a blue-shuttered white house on the Fowey estuary where the ferry crosses to Polruan. It is called Ferryside, and her son, Kits Browning, still lives there. Walking the paths around Fowey, she came across a dilapidated, secluded house in the woods called Menabilly. She became enchanted, obsessed even, with the place and dreamt of restoring it to some sort of glory. She wrote *Rebecca* in 1938, using Menabilly as the inspiration for Manderley.

'Last night I dreamt I went to Manderley again' is one of the best-known openings to a novel, but it is the sense of place as well as the haunting nature of the dream that puts the reader right there, staring at that same view. Manderley itself is as strong a character as Mrs Danvers, Rebecca or Maxim de Winter:

There was Manderley, our Manderley, secretive and silent as it had always been, the grey stone shining in the moonlight of my dream, the mullioned windows reflecting the green lawns and the terrace. Time could not wreck the perfect symmetry of those walls, nor the site itself, a jewel in the hollow of a hand. The terrace sloped to the lawns, and the lawns stretched to the sea, and turning I could see the sheet of silver lying placid under the moon, like a lake undisturbed by wind or storm. No waves would come to ruffle this dream water, and no bulk of cloud, wind-driven from the west, obscure the clarity of this pale sky.

I turned again to the house, and though it stood inviolate, untouched, as though we ourselves had left but yesterday, I saw that the garden had obeyed the jungle law, even as the woods had done. The rhododendrons stood fifty feet high, twisted and entwined with bracken, and they had entered into alien marriage with a host of nameless shrubs, poor, bastard things that clung about their roots as though conscious of their spurious origin . . .

Moonlight can play odd tricks upon the fancy, even upon a dreamer's fancy. As I stood there, hushed and still, I could swear that the house was not an empty shell but lived and breathed as it had lived before.

Light came from the windows, the curtains blew softly in the night air, and there, in the library, the door would stand half open as we had left it, with my handkerchief on the table beside the bowl of autumn roses.

Du Maurier wrote all this before she ever lived in Menabilly. Then, in 1942, she rented it from the Rashleigh family and stayed there with her family for twenty-six years. She loved the sights and the scent of Cornwall, the industry of the harbour and the freedom of the cliffs with their unlimited view across the ocean. In *Vanishing Cornwall,* she writes:

There was a smell in the air of tar and rope and rusted chain, a smell of tidal water. Down harbour, around the point, was the open sea. Here was the freedom I desired, long sought for, not yet known. Freedom to write, to walk, to wander, freedom to climb hills, to pull a boat, to be alone.

Walking around Fowey, you cannot fail to be infused with the spirit of Daphne du Maurier. I visited Lanteglos Church, where she married Major Frederick Browning, known as Tommy, in June 1932. There is no village, just a farmhouse and the church. It has a wild, slightly drunken graveyard where yellow lichen gives the gravestones a Jackson Pollock effect: they look as if they have been splashed with paint.

Du Maurier walked incessantly, as many writers do, looking for characters, or places, or happenings that would turn into a story. 'I walked this land with a dreamer's freedom and with a waking man's perception,' she told an interviewer. 'Places, houses whispered to me their secrets and shared with me their sorrows and their joys. And in return I gave them something of myself, a few of my novels passing into the folklore of this ancient place.'

Jamaica Inn is based on Cornish wreckers and smugglers, and a pub of that name on Bodmin Moor. Her short story 'The Birds', which became an Alfred Hitchcock thriller, apparently came to her when she was walking from Menabilly to Polridmouth and saw a tractor ploughing a field, pursued by a giant flock of seagulls.

Du Maurier wrote menace so well, and the landscape in which she chose to immerse herself suited her perfectly. She fell in love with Fowey, saying, 'This for me and me for this.' Her daily walks fuelled her writing and her mind.

I could see why. The freshness of the air, the ease with which you can walk a couple of miles and escape the crowds, with their ice creams and Cornish pasties; the changing scenery and the shifting weather patterns. It is invigorating, inspiring, challenging.

When you're high above the harbour, you realize how much sound travels in this environment. I could hear laughter and screams from down in the streets. It is no place for keeping secrets, which of course makes it perfect for a writer.

We passed a man with a dog.

'That's Spam Miller,' said the du Maurier expert with whom I was walking. 'His dog is called Dog. So was his last one, and the one before that.'

A man called Spam with a dog called Dog. Yup, that's Cornwall for you.

The verges smelt rich with wild garlic. A local woman told me how she and her sister used to be responsible for bringing the cows in from the pasture for milking. They had to keep them moving, because otherwise the cows would stop and munch on the wild garlic, which they loved. If they ate too much, the garlic came through in the milk. I don't know about you, but garlic milk on my cereal doesn't really appeal.

I looked down into the harbour, to see the Troys. They were heading out for their weekly races, their huge, coloured sails billowing out like pregnant elephants. The Troy-class boats are unique to Fowey; there are only twenty-nine built in the same mould, with lead keels and huge sails, harking back to an earlier age of super-fast schooners. Many of them race on Wednesdays and Saturdays, picking up serious speed, the sails flinging over to be nearly horizontal as they tack.

Risk-takers tend to love Cornwall, because there is always something vaguely hazardous to do. But there is also food for the thoughtful, with any number of literary festivals, music nights, art galleries and theatres. The most dramatic setting for any play is the Minack Theatre, just south of Porthcurno, between Land's End and Penzance.

At the same time as Daphne du Maurier was marrying 'Tommy' Browning in Fowey, a group of actors led by Rowena Cade were staging *The Tempest* in the open-air amphitheatre created by the gully above the Minack Rock, with the Atlantic Ocean as its backdrop. That performance in 1932 saw the creation of the Minack Theatre, and over the next decade Rowena Cade herself, along with her gardener and a friend of his, built the mosaic stage floor, the columns, the arches, the stone steps and the seating area. They broke up granite, heaved timber into place and carefully placed stones so that the theatre looks as if it must be thousands of years old. In fact, it is not even a hundred years since it was covered in grass and gorse.

I never went there as a child, but having walked Cornwall's coastal paths, its moorland and its wooded lanes I have to admit that the area has a real claim on my soul. I once walked from the Minack Theatre to Land's End with the novelist Patrick Gale. It was a stormy Daphne day, evidence of how the wind and the waves had buffeted the rocks into Barbara Hepworth-style sculptures. The sea was throwing spray up on to the cliffs, where it would stay for a second and then be sucked back again. Patrick was brought up on the Isle of Wight, but now Cornwall is his home.

'You have a landscape you were raised by and a landscape you marry,' he said. 'I was raised by the landscapes of Hampshire, but I was betrothed to Cornwall as a seven-year-old, when I first came here, and moved here as soon as I could.'

Patrick looked like an MI6 spy. He was wearing a beige canvas trench coat, turned up at the collar to meet his silvering hair, and he had a notepad in the giant pocket in case an idea should come to mind.

'I'm a restless person and I do a lot of writing in my head when I'm walking, so it's very much part of my routine. There's something very enabling about leaving your manuscript behind, and sometimes I find I've been wrestling with a plot point and it'll be while on a walk that I have that eureka moment.'

We battled through the wind to reach the ancient hamlet of St Levan, named after the priest who banned anyone called Joanna from being baptised in his chapel. He did it because he was cross with one particular woman called Joanna who told him off for fishing on a Sunday; the ban stands to this day. St Levan's Well has three enormous stones above it, and one below to kneel on. Patrick told me that it was a good place for dogs to have a drink, although he'd left his ageing wolfhound and lurcher at home.

We had a mutual rant about the tendency of dog walkers to leave poo bags tied to hedges or fences.

'I mean, for God's sake, do they think there's a poo fairy who will come along and pick them all up?' I was shouting, partly because of the wind and partly in anger. 'It's just so stupid. Either kick it out of the path or pick it up and put it in a bin, but don't do *this!*'

I flicked at a loaded poo bag hanging from a hawthorn branch. It fell down, so I picked it up and carried it for the next five miles, fuming at the idiocy of the dog owner and secretly wondering if picking up alien poo, albeit in a bag, was an act of piety likely to score points with the saintly community.

Land's End is different from the rest of the Cornish coast. There is heather and bracken and gorse, but no trees – nothing over about five foot in height, apart from the occasional palm tree. Chunks of granite emerge from the soil like teeth, pushing their way up to the surface. Cornwall was peri-glacial, so it went through a period of freezing, then melting, freezing, then melting. This meant that granite was shifted by the muddy, melted flow of mush and was randomly scattered over the land, leaving it looking as if a team of giants has been playing football on it.

We walked through an alley of hedgerow and flowers, Patrick stopping to nibble on things and smell them. He and his partner, Aidan, often go for an evening dip in the sea, once the tourists have disappeared.

'It's a very exciting swim here, a bit like swimming in a washing machine.'

Patrick schooled me more in the pagan traditions. The local hospital is the only one in the country (possibly in the world) to have a white witch on hand as well as a Catholic and Protestant priest.

As we walked towards the sunset I had that feeling of being right at the end of the line, at the furthest point west one could be. There was horizon all around us, the cliffs making face-like shapes. No wonder they have been given names such as the Armed Knight, Dr Johnson's Head and Dr Syntax's Head. The landscape sings with the songs of ancient souls, and yet it is also an area of thriving technology. Not long ago, it was highly industrial.

Patrick recommended the Porthcurno Telegraph Museum if you wanted to learn more about how the UK was linked by cables to the rest of the Empire. This was where those submarine cables came ashore, and Porthcurno was, for a hundred years, the largest cable station in the world. Without the cable and wireless technology they pioneered, we would have no transatlantic phone calls, no faxes and, probably, no Internet.

I was interested in the technology, but I was even more interested in the cabling inside Patrick Gale's head. It seemed that walking was absolutely essential to him to create, that he was as much a product of his environment as Daphne du Maurier or Anna Maria Murphy.

'I worry about my characters as if they were real friends having a bad time, which I think is a healthy sign, but it can get very peculiar when I've been writing for hours. So walking is a very nice airlock between writing the novel and heading back home.'

We ended our walk just short of his house, looking at a family of seals poking their heads above the frothy waves. My cheeks tightened and exfoliated by the wind – a free 'Cornish facelift' – I left Patrick to his characters and his plots.

The north coast of Cornwall is equally thrilling and gives more of a sense of the rich industrial history of the area. You will stumble across ruined engine rooms and the wonderfully named 'buddles' that were used to separate and clean the tin that came from the mines. Once, the area was busy with buildings, machinery, pools and hundreds of people mining tin. The noise of industry has been replaced by the loud call of the stonechat, which sounds like pebbles being knocked together, or the descant song of the willow warbler. The colours of the workers' clothes have been replaced by the pink sprays of thrift or the bell-like bulbs of sea campion, mottled with pink veins and emanating white flowers, and the bright yellow of the gorse.

The gorse flower is supposed to help those who have lost belief or hope. I'd suggest a bracing walk along the North Cornwall cliffs would be the remedy for most things, especially on a stormy day. There's no point just seeing Cornwall in its benign state. You need to see it in all weathers and all times of year to appreciate its vitality and to let it inside you. Once it gets there, it will always be a part of you.

I am looking again at the photograph on the wall opposite my desk. Alice has just come in with a cup of tea, and I've asked her if we can go and live in Cornwall.

'No, darling. We live here. But you can go walking there again if you like. Any time.'

She smiles at me indulgently, ruffles my hair and heads out again. 'Archie will need another walk in half an hour, so get on with your writing.'

She leaves me my cup of tea and softly closes the door.

8

Walking Rubbish

'What a lovely day,' I said.

'Yes,' agreed my walking companion. 'Perfect weather to see every bottle cap, every cigarette pack, every tin can.'

On a bright and relatively warm April afternoon I was with the author and comedian David Sedaris. We were in West Sussex, heading across the A283 to Broomers Hill Lane, a typical hedge-lined country road that went uphill from Pulborough to nowhere in particular.

Usually, I'd be soaking up the best of the trees, the birdsong, the sheep dotting the distance like cotton-wool buds. But now my eyes were fixed to the ground just in front of me, with occasional darting glances to each side.

This walk was different. This was about a microscopic vision, digging into the underbelly of the landscape, searching for the ugliness. We were rubbish collecting.

It's funny how people with a passion see the world through a prism that is tilted the way they need it to be. The light comes in the same way for all of us, but it bounces off in the direction we choose.

When he is not touring America or selling books across Europe, David Sedaris goes out each day to collect litter.

On Broomers Hill Lane, David was immediately in action, stooping down to pluck bottles and cans from the banks.

'It's the same stuff over and over,' he said, as his bin liner filled. 'This is not abnormal in any way. This is completely unremarkable.

'I have this crazy belief that tomorrow people are going to stop doing it. So I can clean up today, because tomorrow all of this is going to change. And I know how insane that is, but if I didn't believe that I would just focus on how futile it is.'

I started reading David's books when I was writing *My Animals and Other Family*. I wanted to see how he'd described his own family in a way that, to quote a literary critic, was 'warped, without being bitter'. I devoured *Naked*, *Me Talk Pretty One Day* and *Dress Your Family in Corduroy and Denim*. He was so rude and so funny, always going further or being more outrageous than I would dare.

He grew up in America, but now lives in Britain. Karen Gregor, who shares the production of *Ramblings* with Lucy, had heard that he was avid about picking up litter, and we thought he'd fit as part of a series about self-improvement: someone trying to improve their environment by cleaning it up. Alice was free that day and I wanted her to meet David, so we both got on the train and headed south.

I wouldn't recommend the Southern Railway as Britain's finest mode of transport. The trains are invariably late and, in our case, don't always stop at the advertised stations. The panic spread at Clapham Junction as it was announced that nearly every train to

Gatwick Airport or beyond was delayed or cancelled. One poor group of tourists, who had a plane to catch, rushed off to the taxi rank. Five minutes later, a train that was going to Gatwick stopped at our platform. I hate to guess what their taxi fare came to and how long it took them to get there. I suspect they missed their flight.

We got on the train, which slowed down at Pulborough, where we wanted to get out. But it didn't stop. I rang Karen.

'The bloody train won't stop. No, I don't know why. We may end up in Bognor at this rate, but if it stops before then we'll get out and take one back again.'

Karen never panics and never gets cross with me. She has two small boys, and I think she has learned patience through them. She rang David and his boyfriend, Hugh, who were picking us up from the station. They said it happens all the time.

Half an hour later, having negotiated a swift change in trains at Amberley, we met in Pulborough, West Sussex. I knew of the village as the place where the brilliant Dancing Brave was trained by Guy Harwood. In the summer of 1986 he won the 2000 Guineas, the Eclipse and the Arc de Triomphe. He should have won the Derby as well but was given too much ground to make up and finished second to Shahrastani. It is one of the most famous defeats in Epsom history.

So, in my mind, Pulborough was all about Dancing Brave. It's a classically beautiful part of the British countryside, with fertile emerald fields on the floodplain of the River Arun, thick hedgerows and views across to the South Downs. Every year they stage a twelve-hour lawnmower race and, on the August bank holiday, a charity duck race. I suspect the lawnmowers are easier to control than the ducks.

Hugh dropped us off in a car park and headed home.

'Have fun, and make sure you come back for lunch,' he said. 'I'm cooking a pie.'

David is a slight man, with brown-rimmed glasses. From a distance, you might mistake him for a younger Woody Allen. He was wearing a blue jacket over a white hooded sweatshirt and khaki trousers. All his clothes looked slightly too big for him. He is not naturally gregarious, but when he gets a subject he wants to talk about his energy and intensity come to the surface.

His favourite subject is litter. I say 'favourite', but it's only in a negative way. He is obsessive about litter.

'I live for litter,' he told me.

My Uncle Willie would approve. He doesn't like Christmas much and does his best to avoid us all, sometimes by going to Tot Hill Services to pick up litter. It's his way of changing the world – and of getting out of a family gathering.

'I filled three bags and I put them outside the entrance to McDonald's,' Uncle Willie told me proudly one year. 'It was mostly their stuff anyway.'

Uncle Willie's full name is William Edward Robin Hood Hastings-Bass, 17th Earl of Huntingdon.

'He's not like a normal Earl,' say my nephews. They're right, he's not, although I'm not sure how many Earls they have met.

Uncle Willie likes to wear cut-off cargo pants and a rugby shirt or jeans with frayed rips that he's bought from TK Maxx. He goes to the gym regularly and favours the aerobic classes, in which he is thrilled to say that he is the only man. He reads widely, watches films and goes to concerts and plays – which he then summarizes, to save you the cost of a ticket. He is interested in what other people are up to and loves to help restructure their lives, but always gives the impression that he has somewhere else that he has to be. At nearly sixty-five, he prefers to 'hang out' with people half his age. They rejuvenate him. He loves the Internet and spends his mornings hooked up to the other side of the world – doing what, I am never quite sure.

He used to be a racehorse trainer and won the Gold Cup at Royal Ascot three years in a row. He trained in Australia for a while and got his brass four-poster bed shipped out on a cargo ship. They called him Bill Bass, and he loved it, but he came back to train in England, then suddenly gave up when he couldn't make the numbers work. Nor did he like dressing up, and he would refuse to wear a morning suit to go into the Royal Enclosure at Ascot, preferring a long waterproof Driza-Bone jacket or a grey suit and to be in the general enclosure. He may be an Earl, but he's descended from Robin Hood, and as such is a man of the people.

Uncle Willie's mobile phone is always buzzing with messages or calls, because people love to talk to him and seek his advice. He's very good at giving it – even if you may not have asked for his input.

'What have you been up to?' I ask, with genuine interest, as I have no idea what he actually does on a daily basis.

'Oh, you know, a million things,' he says. 'I've been up since six. Very busy. Got to go now. Pop by if you can, but I may not be there.'

Uncle Willie does a bit of buying and selling of horses and goes to the yearling sales in France, Germany and Australia. He doesn't like paying for hotels so will stay with friends or pitch a tent nearby. He once managed to persuade a hotel in Deauville to let him put his tent up in their garden, so he got access to their pool and gym. He's quite resourceful in his quest to save money.

His latest venture is to open and run a bed and breakfast in Grandma's old house. He has got a good deal on a new carpet and he's patched up the kitchen, but he refuses to update the bathrooms. He is convinced that an avocado bathroom suite is a historically important period design feature. Alice and I have tried to point out that the house was built in a bloody awful period and guests will not be impressed with shocking decor and a headache-inducing shade of green.

I've given him a WiFi extender for the guest rooms, because the one thing I know people can't abide is a poor Internet connection. He will offer them his home-made granola for breakfast, and fresh fruit.

'The best bit,' I tell him, 'is that they will get life coaching and career advice as well as breakfast – and they won't even have to pay extra for it!'

'Quite right,' says Uncle Willie. 'They don't know how lucky they are.'

Back in the car park in Pulborough, David Sedaris insisted that I don the uniform that might save my life. It was a fluorescent jacket with 'Horsham District Council' written on it. He also handed me a bin bag with a metal hoop and one of those mechanical fingers that means you can pick things up quickly, as long as you are accurate. I hadn't seen one since I was a child, so I practised in the car park on a crisp packet. (We may just have found Uncle Willie's next Christmas present.)

Alice took a bin bag and a metal hoop, too. She wasn't just coming along for the ride. My family say I am competitive – which is true: I would rather win a game than lose it. But Alice is in a whole different league. She is determined to do not just her best but better than anyone else. She played lacrosse as a teenager and made it on to the Junior England squad before she got sidetracked into acting and reading the news on the radio. She has a winner's mentality.

I was shocked at how much litter you see as soon as you stop to look.

There seemed to be a pattern to the discarded pieces of people's lives. They either throw out the packaging for things that are unhealthy and are perhaps being consumed in secret (beer cans, bottles, cigarette packets), or things that we think of as disposable (ketchup packets, fast-food containers, sandwich wrappers).

There is a whole world you can invent for the people driving along hurling things out of their cars: perhaps they are unhappy at home, secret alcoholics, binge eaters who stuff a burger in their face before going home for a roast dinner, stressed executives who puff away on a fag before arriving home to a house full of kids.

David said that quite often he finds a doughnut box with one doughnut left in it, or a vodka bottle half full, or a cigarette packet with cigarettes still in it. His theory is that the person is in denial and wants to get rid of the evidence of eating, drinking or smoking as fast as possible: if it's no longer in the car, he or she can't be guilty.

One can make up all these storylines, but it still doesn't excuse the fact that these people are wilfully throwing rubbish out of their cars into the hedgerows of Pulborough, confident that someone else will pick it up, or perhaps simply not caring whether they do or not.

That 'someone else' was us. Instead of raging against the machine, or despairing at the horror of it all, David was engrossed. This is his exercise and his therapy.

'It's not a bad hobby for me,' he explained. 'I do it every day and it's especially good for me if I'm studying. I'm going to Poland, and I've been listening to this audio programme in Polish. So I just walk along, pick up other people's garbage and prepare. Then I go to another country and notice how much rubbish they either have, or don't have.

'I'm completely doing it for me. It gives me a feeling of accomplishment and, more than that, we bought a house here and this is where I live, so I want it to be clean.'

I couldn't quite share his acceptance of the situation. As cars flew by, I willed one of them to throw something out of the window so that we could put a face to at least one of the villains and challenge them to a fight. I would swing my loaded bin liner at them or pour the contents into their car.

Alice did this a couple of years ago. We had gone to see her parents in Esher but had come from different places, so we were in two cars. I was following her back to London in crawling bank-holiday traffic when I saw her get out of her car just before Hampton Court. She went to the window of the car in front and had a quick conversation, then got back in her car and slammed the door. She looked quite cross.

Of course, I phoned her straightaway.

'What was that all about?'

'I was giving him back a bottle he'd thrown out,' she said in a terse voice.

Alice can sound quite terrifying when she is cross. I always make her do the tricky phone call when we need to complain about a leaky boiler or question a bill. She's better at it. I would end up making friends with them and asking them round for dinner; Alice will negotiate a free service or a refund.

'But anyone could have been in that car. They could have attacked you, or thrown it back at you, or –'

'Don't be ridiculous,' she interrupted. 'You were right behind me, there are people all around and it just made me furious. How dare they?'

'What did they say?'

'Nothing much. They looked a bit shocked. They were young, perfectly nice-looking, and I suppose they just thought it was all right to throw a bottle out of the window. Well, it's not.'

We were relatively new to Twitter at the time of the bottle incident, so we didn't anticipate the way a story can sometimes take off. Alice tweeted that she had thrown litter back into a car, and she received over a hundred responses. The *Evening Standard* called me and asked to talk to her.

'I wasn't brave,' she told them. 'I was just cross.'

They ran an article calling her a 'litter crusader'. I misread it as 'little crusader' and wondered how they knew that she's not very tall. The next day the *Daily Mail* printed a full-page piece with the headline 'BBC NEWSREADER TAKES ON LITTER LOUT' and called her 'a national heroine'. When she got in to work to read the news, she opened her emails to find dozens more requests for interviews or columns. On Radio 2, Vanessa Feltz hosted a phone-in with the question 'Would you do an Alice Arnold?'

Alice was rather discombobulated by the attention, but the issue certainly chimed with people. It also coincided with the spring-cleaning season. Sadly, it didn't make a lasting change to the attitude of those who litter.

Back on Broomers Hill Lane, David was telling me about the things he had picked up.

'I've found loaded diapers. My mother had six children – she might have thrown a child out of a car window but never a diaper.

'Hugh found twenty pounds the other day. I mean, I've been picking up litter every day for years and I've never found money, but he does it one time and finds twenty pounds! Huh.'

David has always been a tidier. He told me that his bedroom as a child was always spotless and he wouldn't let his sisters over the threshold 'because I didn't want them to befoul what was really the only clean room in the house'. Now, he thinks of the outside area near his home in the same way he used to think of his bedroom. He's taking on a big cause.

Did you know that slugs love beer? Nor did I until I picked up bottle after bottle containing drunken slugs wallowing in the remainders of pale ale. They stank: a really rancid stench. One bottle was sealed. I delicately opened it to smell the contents.

'I think it's wine,' I said. 'A whole bottle of wine. Or maybe it's elderflower. I can't tell.'

David was laughing. 'I wouldn't sip it if I were you,' he said. 'I've found plenty of bottles of urine along here.'

I dropped the bottle in disgust. Wishing I had worn gloves, I poured it out and put the empty bottle in the bag that was resting on its hoop on my hip. We were now on to our third bags.

It was ridiculous. Here we were in one of the prettiest villages in England and I felt that it was ruined. The beauty of the cottages and the lanes was a sham because under the surface was evil waste, deliberately chucked by people with no sense of responsibility or concern.

I'm a solutions kind of a person. I read some self-help book once that told me to look at the solution, not the problem, so I'm always looking for the magic answer.

'I know,' I said, in one of my eureka moments. 'We need to make it fun to dispose of litter. What about a drive-through dump? You don't have to get out of the car – you just throw your litter into skips and score points. If you get a certain number of points, you win!'

I thought it was brilliant. Recycling centres always have long queues at weekends. This way, it wouldn't waste your time, or involve stepping out of the car, and you could win a prize.

It was one of my best ideas ever. Even better than the Mobot, or making every business conduct at least one meeting a day while walking, or even having a dog on my lap while I presented Crufts.

Karen, Alice and David weren't so sure. They pointed out that it would mean a series of ugly skips by the side of the road and that it rewarded people for doing what they should do naturally – getting rid of their rubbish.

A car came towards us rather fast and slowed down, its driver no doubt curious about the three people with bin liners. I stared at her. We are used to calling people who don't dispose of their rubbish carefully 'litter louts', which could give a false impression that they are slovenly youths. This was a middle-aged woman with mousy-brown, shoulder-length hair, both hands on the steering wheel and a look of panic on her face.

I tried to do a Sherlock-style deduction. Could she be an offender? My instincts were that she wasn't, but I knew Benedict Cumberbatch would examine her more closely, work out her daily routine and probably consider her a suspect.

'The trouble is,' said David, who has far more experience in this field than me, 'you just don't know. She could be a chucker, but I've never actually seen anyone do it. I sometimes think I should hide here in the hedgerow and wait until I see someone throwing something, and then I could pursue them and arrest them.'

I found the day rather fascinating, but also terribly sad. So I cheered myself up by thinking about all the exercise we were taking, constantly bending down and up again, a form of standing sit-ups. I came up with the slogan for a fitness campaign: 'Get Fitter with Litter'. My second brilliant idea of the day. This was good for my brain, as well as my abdominal muscles.

Looking at the positives, we were also halfway towards building a car. We'd found a hubcap, a rear-view mirror and a number plate. I was sure there would be a tyre or two if we looked hard enough. Perhaps we'd find one before we headed back to the house to sample Hugh's pie.

When we got to the top of the hill I dragged David into the driveway of a house. A footpath goes across the fields there, and it had a beautiful vantage point across to the South Downs, beyond which I knew you could see the Channel. It was what they call 'the quintessential British vista' and, yes, you got rolling uplands, fertile river plain, hedgerows dividing fields into envelope-sized rectangles, a grey church spire and villages that you knew had at least two pubs, a post office, a duck pond and a village green where cricket is played in the summer. They would have cherry trees heavy with blossom, wisteria dangling from cottage windows, a thatched roof or two, box hedges and rose gardens, red-brick walls and wooden benches, oak trees and copper beech. I imagined teashops full of retired couples, children playing Pooh Sticks on a stone bridge, polo fields in the distance and the mustard windowframes and doors of the Cowdray Estate.

I asked David what he could see.

'To tell you the truth,' he said, staring into the distance with a look of a crusader aching for a foreign war, 'I see all the rubbish that we're not seeing right now.'

'What, from here to Bognor Regis, you look at that view and all you can see is hidden rubbish?' I was amazed that his enjoyment of the countryside could be so ruined by having spent so much time clearing it up.

'Yes. I feel that people are looking too much at the long view, and they say, "Oh, it's so beautiful." They're not looking down at the ground, which is covered with rubbish, so they don't see the problem.'

It's amazing that David even wants to live in the English countryside now he knows the ugly truth. It would be like finding out that the love of your life was having an affair: soul-destroying. Yet he soldiers on, trying to plaster the wound by picking up all the rubbish he can find, tying it into black bags and taking them to the dump. By the end of our short walk, we had amassed ten bin liners full of rubbish. Alice had four to my three. You might think this wasn't a victory to celebrate or that she wouldn't be in any way triumphalist. You'd be wrong.

It was exhausting, not because of the physical exercise but

because of the concentration. At one point, David disappeared up the bank into the hedge. He'd caught a glimpse of a can reflecting in the sunshine and was determined to dig it out.

I asked him if there was one thing that he would really, really like to find.

'Yes,' he said, with certainty. He had thought about this before. 'A dead body.'

Ashmansworth–Highclere

Buoyed by coffee and hot-cross buns, we rejoin the Wayfarer's Walk. Spring is in the air and the splendour of the Hampshire countryside folds out before us. The fragrance of new growth fills us with optimism, and the fragrance of something else powers Boris the boxer forward and, of course, sideways.

We cross a main road, past a former pub called the Three-Legged Cross, where walkers who have taken the bus from Newbury can hop off and explore west or east. It's now home to a rather glamorous furniture-design company. On another day, I would have spent at least an hour in there examining coffee tables, but the Wayfarer's Walk pulls us forward.

The next section is familiar territory, although I have ridden rather than walked it. We come into the Highclere Estate and, through the trees, get our first glimpse of Highclere Castle.

Wayfarer's Walk

'Look, there's the castle,' I say, pointing into the distance.

'Where?' asks Alice.

'Over there!' I jab excitedly – you know, how you do when you're trying to show someone a dot in the distance. Alice is quite blind, so this is never easy.

She thinks she has face blindness, a rare affliction that means she can't remember what anyone looks like. I spend my time at any party whispering names in her ear. Even people she knows well and really likes are strangers in her fuzzy vision. Anna Watkins, who won an Olympic gold medal in the double sculls with Katherine Grainger, is a case in point. Alice loves Anna and has had many good chats with her about broadcasting, sport and whether Alice could've made it as a cox (she's quite small, as I may have mentioned before). You'd hope a seven months pregnant, six-foot-tall woman whom she admires and likes would be memorable.

At the BT Sport launch party in the summer of 2013, I didn't even bother doing the usual memo – 'Anna Watkins, Olympic gold medallist, you sat next to her last week' – because I was sure Alice would see her and give her a big hug. Mortifyingly, I saw Alice looking confused and heard Anna saying, 'It's Anna Watkins. We've met before.'

Oh God.

I'm lucky that she recognizes *me* most of the time. One day, I'll get back from filming with dolphins in Japan or rhinos in South Africa, walk through the front door and find Alice on the phone to the police reporting an intruder.

So pointing out Highclere Castle in the distance is a fruitless task even if Alice does follow the line of my finger to the third tree on the right, then come down a bit . . . *there*!

Thanks to the ITV series *Downton Abbey*, the castle is now famous on both sides of the Atlantic as home to the Earl and Countess of Grantham. What the scriptwriters invent, though, isn't nearly as dramatic as the real history of the place and the people who have lived in it.

The grand Gothic castle that stands proud in the centre of the estate was designed in 1838 by Sir Charles Barry, on the instruction of the 3rd Earl of Carnarvon. Barry had just finished building the Houses of Parliament, and you can see the similarities in the intricate stonework, narrow towers and turrets. It was a Victorian version of the Jacobean style, described by Barry as 'Anglo-Italian'.

During our childhood we never went inside the castle, but we saw it often enough from a distance when Dad was playing cricket on the estate, when we went drag hunting there or rode round the cross-country course. Dad trained horses for the Queen and therefore had plenty of dealings with Her Majesty's racing manager Lord Porchester, who would become the 7th Earl of Carnarvon. He never lived in the castle and regarded it as an impossibly expensive place to maintain, but his eldest son, Geordie, has taken a very different view since he ascended to the Earldom.

The castle is now open to the public and is used as a wedding venue – infamously, for one of Katie Price's marriages: a

Wayfarer's Walk

Cinderella-themed one, I believe, with Peter Andre as the pumpkin. Snobs suggested that Highclere had gone downmarket, but I just see it as part of its transformation into a modern, money-making estate. You've got to make a few mistakes to find out what works and, anyway, if a woman wants to dress as something out of a fairy tale and arrive in a pink carriage covered by a sheet because *Wotcha!* magazine has bought the exclusive, who are we to judge?

Downton Abbey has taken Highclere into a different league of financial security, and its owners should now be able to keep the castle from crumbling for generations to come.

The castle may get all the headlines, but the grounds are magnificent. The park was designed in the eighteenth century for the 1st Earl by Capability Brown and has more than fifty Lebanon cedars, planted for maximum architectural effect and still standing proud nearly three hundred years later. Lime trees, ancient oak, copper beech and silver birch mark our way as we tentatively skirt the estate. Even though it's a public right of way, it feels odd to be walking across the estate of someone you know without having told them you're coming. I know Mum is worrying that it isn't really allowed.

The most renowned Earl was the 5th, who was keen on the then newly invented automobile (he suffered a nasty car accident in Germany in 1901 which left him very weak), racehorses (he founded Highclere Stud in 1902) and Egyptology (he started going to Egypt after his car accident, in search of warmer weather). He was also quite keen on spending money but, rather fortunately, he had married the illegitimate daughter of Edward de Rothschild, who came with an enormous dowry and an annual allowance for her husband.

Spending it wasn't difficult for the 5th Earl. Cars and race-horses are not cheap hobbies, but even more expensive was his new passion. While in Egypt, he met a young archaeologist called Howard Carter, who persuaded him to provide the backing for his digs. They had mixed success, put the archaeology on hold during the First World War, then went back to excavate what they could in the Valley of the Kings, which was assumed by most to have been plundered dry.

Having spent the modern equivalent of £10 million financing Carter for over a decade, Lord Carnarvon was running out of patience and money. During a house party for Newbury Races in 1922, he told Carter it had to end. By now, they were searching for the elusive tomb of Tutankhamun, the boy king who had died or been murdered around 1223BC. Carter was desperate, and declared he would finance his last season himself. Carnarvon relented and in November 1922 received a telegram from Carter saying: 'At last have made wonderful discovery in the Valley. A magnificent tomb with seals intact. Re-covered same for your arrival. Congratulations.'

They had struck gold, and a heap of other treasures besides. Carnarvon travelled to Luxor to share the joy of uncovering the greatest ancient find of the twentieth century. Four antechambers were packed full of artefacts and, when they finally reached the sarcophagus, Carter found the only mummified Egyptian

Wayfarer's Walk

pharaoh that hadn't been disturbed and ruined by robbers. It took him and his team ten years to classify and clear the contents of the tomb.

Sadly, the 5th Earl of Carnarvon didn't live to enjoy the fruits of his investment. Four months after descending the stairs into the tomb he died from an infected mosquito bite. The 'Curse of Tutankhamun' was born. Legend has it that at the moment he died in hospital, his dog let out a howl and dropped down dead at home.

As we walk, we can see his burial place to our left on the top of Beacon Hill – his tomb stands upright on the site of an ancient hill fort. My grandmother told us that he had asked to be buried standing up, so that he could keep an eye on the place. I find the whole thing rather spooky, and I remember the first exhibition they had at the castle, when we were allowed to see the artefacts from Tutankhamun's tomb. I was frightened to be in the same room as them in case I got cursed.

Feeling the 5th Earl's eyes upon us, we progress along a wide path through a copse until we come to a flint roundhouse that looks like a medieval castle. I have since discovered that it's called Grotto Lodge and was built in Victorian times as a gatehouse to the estate. It has cross-shaped arrow slits that suggest trespassers won't be given a cup of tea and a slice of cake. Mum and Alice turn left towards the gate to examine the sign. Mum's eyes aren't very good either, but when they get closer they see it says: 'KEEP OUT'.

'Ah, it must be the other path,' says my mother.

So we keep Grotto Lodge on our left and wander deeper into the woods, eventually emerging into the light of Sidown Hill. Mum gets excited because she can see Highclere Stud down in the valley on our left. I realize from this angle how wonderfully protected their paddocks are and what a benefit it is to bring up young thoroughbreds on the undulations of rich, chalky downland turf that's never been ploughed and is protected from the wind by the soft curves of the hills around.

'If we go directly towards Beacon Hill, it will be much quicker,' observes my mother.

That's the trouble with knowing your local landscape too well. You know the quickest route. The way the Wayfarer's Walk has been negotiated is not the most direct, but it is pretty.

Harold the tractor driver is working the field to our right. I know Harold because of some filming we did around here the previous summer; Highclere Estates had promised to give me some feed for a charity project I was working on for the Riding for the Disabled Association (RDA), but in return I had to cut some corn on the combine harvester. And be filmed while doing so.

'So, if you can just talk Clare through the controls,' Tim, the director, had said. 'Then she can take over.'

A combine harvester is a beast of a machine. I had never been in the cab of anything so big in my life and I certainly wasn't about to drive it solo.

'Harold will be in the cab with me, won't he?' I asked.

Wayfarer's Walk

Answer came there none.

Harold showed me how to steer, which seemed quite straightforward; how to turn the machine on – again, quite straightforward; and then suggested that I just slip it into neutral when I wanted to come to a halt so that it came to a nice steady stop. Fine. Tim was filming all of this, but it was very cramped in the cab, so he said, 'Harold, do you mind if you leave us in here, and I'll just get Clare to do a bit on her own?'

Harold made the fatal error of agreeing. I started the engine, clunked the lever down into drive and started singing to myself as we chugged up the hill, 'I'm driving a combine harvester, oh yes I am.' *Ping!* went the machine. A bale popped out the back.

'I'm making straw, oh yes I am. I'm making straw on my comb-eye-ine . . .'

I thought how proud my nephews would be. I was high up in my engine, queen of all I surveyed, doing something practical and feeling like a land girl. Five bales had popped out and I'd reached the crest of the hill, so I kept my line and said to Tim, 'Have you got enough now, because I should probably stop?'

I slipped the lever into neutral, but the combine didn't stop. In fact, it picked up speed. We had gone over the hill and were heading down the other side, getting faster all the time.

I'd love to pretend I remained calm and analytical, but I didn't. I nearly wet myself with panic.

'Tim! Tim! It's not stopping! What am I going to do? This is all your fault. Oh God. There's a hedge ahead of us. *Oh God . . .'*

I swore. A lot. I thought of Harold, and James Phillips, the estate manager, and how cross they'd be. I thought of my nephews and how disappointed they would be and then I thought of the insurance forms and whether or not I had signed something that said I was liable for any damage I might cause.

The combine harvester was picking up speed. I thought there was a pedal that looked like a brake, but Harold hadn't told me to touch anything other than the lever I'd put into neutral, so I didn't dare step on it.

Instead, I had a flash of inspiration. I decided to treat the combine harvester like a runaway horse and turn it into the middle of the field. I did so quite smoothly and gently, talking to it all the while: 'Whoa, boy, whoa there. That's it.'

The pace started to slacken and, although it felt like minutes, it was probably only seconds later that the combine harvester came to a halt, sideways across the field, leaving a stream of curving bales behind it. I swore at Tim. I was shaking with fear and rage. It takes a lot to scare me, but I had been out of control in a 30-ton combine harvester that costs more than the average house. I could see Harold and James running across the field, and I considered crying, just to make sure they wouldn't shout at me.

I opened the door and fell down the steps. James caught me as my legs gave way.

'I could see you heading off towards the end of the field,' he said. 'And all I could think was "There's a drop the other side of that hedge of about twenty feet on to a railway line. *Don't go straight on!*"'

Then he laughed.

Wayfarer's Walk

Harold looked very concerned. For his combine.

'I thought you were only going to the top of the hill,' he said. 'When you went over the other side I thought, "Don't put it in neutral now." But you did. Oh, well. Lucky it didn't explode, with the bales coming out that quick.'

He looked at his beloved combine and patted it on the side. 'Could've been worse, I s'pose.'

I apologized to Harold and James, plus the combine harvester, which I also patted. It seemed the right thing to do. I told Tim I hated him and would never do anything for him ever again.

An hour later, we arrived at a Retraining of Racehorses centre, trying to find a horse for the RDA. Tim was attempting to convince me that the runaway combine harvester would be the funniest bit of the whole film. I wasn't so sure.

When I wave at Harold on his tractor, he doesn't seem to see me.

Barefoot walking
with Michael

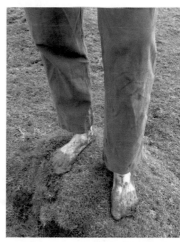

Michael's feet with a
coating of mud

Werca's Folk singing by the River Coquet, with Sandra Kerr conducting

'Which way's the pub?'

Percy and stuffed toy.
Spot the difference

With retired
walkers on
Exmoor,
feeling free

Lucy with the tiny
recording bit of
the big mic

With Jonno, Toby and the Olympic torch. I'm trying not to cry

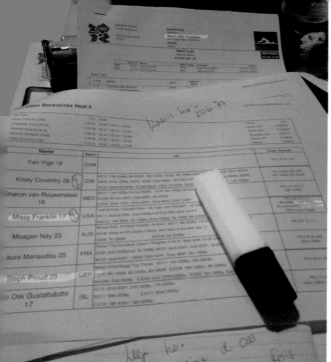

My Olympic swimming
notes and famous
highlighter pen

With Bert Le Clos and the lovely Mark Foster at the Aquatics Centre. 'Unbelievable!'

Me and Mo doing the Mobot

Ask Ade at the Paralympics

With the Games Makers by Greenwich Observatory on the last night of the Olympics

We arrive at Deane. Andrew insists we can walk through the flood

Nearly home as the sun sets

Near Inkpen: Mum is dragged under a tree by Boris

Me, Mum and Alice in Team Blue

9

The Walking Cure

Lucy met me at the station in a hire car.

'Keys,' I said, and put my hand out.

'Hello, Lucy, how are you? Kids all right?' she said, raising an eyebrow.

'Yes, yes, all of that,' I replied. 'After you've given me the car keys.'

The only trouble with me insisting that I drive is that it means Lucy has to map read. This is never a straightforward affair.

'Wait, wait,' she said, fumbling with the pages of an OS map. 'I have to work out which way we need to leave the station.'

'Haven't you got a road map?' I asked. Of course she didn't.

'Here, put the postcode into my phone, that'll work best.'

I threw my phone into her lap, then thought better of it and pulled over to do it myself.

Lucy now has a satnav and knows how to work it. Consequently, our journeys are now shorter, happier and more accurate – as long as her battery lasts and she puts in Newport, Isle of Wight, rather than Newport, Wales, or Newcastle-under-Lyme rather than New-castle upon Tyne.

We were heading to the Severn Hospice in Bicton Heath, just on the north-west side of Shrewsbury, to meet a bereavement walking group. It was founded by a Radio 4 listener called Caroline Clegg after hearing an episode of *Ramblings* featuring a mental-health walking group (of which more later).

We arrived at the hospice to find a crowd gathered in reception. It was a cold January day, and one of the women, Maggie, who worked there had knitted me a pair of gloves and a scarf.

'It's a birthday present,' she said.

I had no idea that they knew it was my birthday the next day. I was touched.

Caroline told us that the Strollers group was run by volunteers. What had started as a nice idea – to support the recently bereaved – became something that really worked and mattered to the people who needed it most.

One of my challenges when we are walking with a large group is to remember everybody's name, but this was easy in the Strollers because everyone wears a name badge. It removes any awkward-ness over forgetting a name or nerves about starting a conversation with a stranger. One man I spoke to had joined when his wife died and then trained as a counsellor so that he could help those more recently bereaved on what he calls their 'grief path'.

'This is a bridge between dealing with your grief and trying to deal with the new tomorrow,' he said. 'You want to be back there in the past, which you can't be, and you don't want to be in the future, because that's a bit intimidating. This starts to move people into a more social lifestyle, with the safety of knowing that those around them have been through a similar experience.'

The literal movement of walking forwards, clambering over stiles, getting stuck in the mud and asking each other for a helping hand seems to aid the journey from the darkness of grief into a place where the sun shines, at least some of the time.

We headed out across a busy road, through a gap in the hawthorn hedge and into a field. We were following a section of the Severn Way and within a few minutes we were squelching through the fields, chatting about this and that. After about half an hour a man called Alan offered me a mint. He wanted to say hello and then we started talking about his wife, who had died a few months before.

'This Christmas has been awful,' he said, 'and I had an eightieth birthday when I didn't want to do anything at all. I found it was very hard. We were married fifty-five years, so there was always someone there, and then, suddenly, nothing. It was very difficult to start mixing again. But this is a lovely walk, isn't it?' He offered me another mint.

He had said enough, and it was as if he was giving himself permission to enjoy the views, the company and the exercise.

The River Severn curled its lazy way through the meadows down to our right, and we ogled a very smart manor house on the other side. We headed up the slope towards an oak coppice, snowdrops shyly revealing themselves, and crossed a stile into the woods. Coming out the other side, it was clear there would be options depending on how far people wanted to walk. Some could take the shorter route back to the hospice, others could come with us and walk a little further via Rossall Grange and Udlington. They weren't walking for fitness, or necessarily for the view, but the walk was taking them away from the feeling of isolated grief, and the medicine of fresh air and exercise seemed to be working.

Standing on a wide path by the side of a farm, another walker, who had also 'graduated' from being bereaved to becoming a bereavement counsellor, told me, 'It's wonderful to be with people who have a bond because of a similar experience, to hear other people confirm some of the feelings you have, especially when you think you're going a bit doolally with your thoughts. And you make such good friends. It becomes like a bit of a self-help group, because those who are further down the line in bereavement are then passing on their experience.'

Most of the members are pensioners, and they have more time than they want or need to think about the loved ones they have lost. They told me how good it was to be outside, to have a purpose, to have company, without the pressure of answering the inevitable question, 'Are you all right?'

It's easier to share feelings when there is no pressure of eye contact or long silences in a room. For men in particular, who find unburdening a burden, doing something active while talking is more natural. Walking helps you to get over the shock, to mix gently with others, and to continue to talk about your grief years after your loss with people who understand.

The group offers fellowship, companionship and practical guidance. I am prouder of that group being set up because of *Ramblings* than anything else I've ever done. It's important to me that things like the Strollers exist, because it makes me feel that I've actually contributed something.

It's easy sometimes to fall into the trap of doing one job after another without thinking about it, without creating anything that lasts.

I take on a lot of work and, although I enjoy it hugely, I'm aware that I am probably the worst kind of person to be freelance. I'm always terrified that if I say no to the job I'm offered today, I won't be offered one tomorrow. If I take a day off, I will be considered lazy or unambitious; and if I turn down charity requests, I will be labelled 'mean'. Being a freelance is an uncertain existence, because no one pays you when you're ill or have time off. There are plenty of people in the same boat – writers, actors, anyone who is self-employed – and I suspect we all share the dread that comes with insecurity.

On the plus side, the life of a freelance is a constant surprise, full of jobs you never thought you'd do, places you never imagined you'd visit, people you would never otherwise have met. I am making the most of being fit and healthy by having as many different experiences and adventures as I can. Consequently, I don't have much time off.

I cope with it pretty well, and Alice insists that we book holidays (left to my own devices, I might forget), but there are times in life and times of year when stress weighs a little heavier. I feel it in the winter months, whether or not I am busy, just because the days are short and the skies are grey. One way of relieving it is to walk.

The combination of winter months and being away from home is not a good one for me, and I used to suffer badly from homesickness. I first started to use walking as a remedy in Melbourne in 2006. I was there for the Commonwealth Games, doing the night-shift Australia-time for programmes that would go out late afternoon or early evening here in the UK. It meant that I had to try to sleep during the day, but no matter how often I told Housekeeping that I didn't want to be disturbed, they would knock on my door or ring the room to double-check. It made me quite grumpy so, when I woke up at about four in the afternoon, I headed out for a walk. I would do a circuit down one side of the Yarra River, over the bridge at Flinders Street and back the other side. It was probably only a couple of miles, but it set me up for my night shift, through to six o'clock the next morning.

When I was in Russia for the Winter Olympics in February 2014, I walked every morning for at least an hour along the promenade. I watched the fishermen casting their lines into the Black Sea, and one morning I saw a pod of dolphins playing in the waves. It was the warmest Winter Olympics host city ever, and most days I didn't need a jacket. But I wasn't walking to get a suntan: I was walking because it helped me survive.

My shifts were early afternoon until midnight, so I could have a late breakfast and then head off for my walk along the Black Sea.

By day twelve (of seventeen) most people at the Games were flagging. It's a long haul, and everyone gets a bit tetchy, sniffly, and desperate for a decent cup of tea. I am normally counting down the days to going home, but this time I was fine. It's not that I didn't miss Alice – I did – but I could handle it. For the first time I felt really strong throughout, and I'm sure it was because of my morning walks. The programme flourished because of it, and the evening highlights took on a life of their own, with a shopping trolley (our floor manager Mat Wayne had 'borrowed' it from a local supermarket and refashioned it with compartments, a screen and even a plastic holder for the microphone) becoming the biggest hit of all.

Alice had given me a Jawbone UP for my birthday – a wristband that monitors movement – so I was using it to count my steps and record my sleep pattern. Every day, I made sure I hit my minimum target of ten thousand steps. Poor Sue Barker, with whom I had breakfast most mornings, must have been fed up with me banging on about hours of deep sleep enjoyed and numbers of steps taken.

Some days, by the time I'd done my morning walk, then crossed Olympic Park to the International Broadcast Centre where broadcasters from all over the world were based, come back to the studio for make-up then walked all over the park presenting, I logged over twenty thousand steps (about ten miles). I finished the Games in rude health, thrilled to be back in the BBC fold. I was embarrassingly upbeat, singing when I went into the office and generally behaving like Tigger.

Digital communications help. Covering previous Winter Olympics, I racked up horrendous phone bills trying to keep in touch with friends and family back home and was emotionally exhausted by the final week. For Atlanta in 1996, the Internet barely existed and you couldn't take a photo with your phone, let alone instantly send it home.

In Sochi, video calling was a revelation. From your mobile phone, you can see home, eat supper with your partner, talk to the children (or, in our case, the dog) and just be in the same room, for hours if you want, all for free. Cricketers tell me it's the only way they can survive long tours, and I know it's a lifesaver for athletes like Mo Farah with training camps abroad. My nephews and niece love it; I took them on a virtual trip through Olympic Park, and Toby told his schoolteacher the next day that he'd 'been to the Winter Olympics'.

The downside of mass communication is that everyone can talk to you, and not all of what they want to say is very nice or helpful. I was getting grief from a small group of vocal people who believed I should boycott the Sochi Olympics because of Russia's stance on the 'non-promotion' of homosexuality to minors.

I had thought long and hard about going, and decided that I was not there to defend or promote Russia, I was there to do my job, which was to cover the Winter Olympics as well as I could.

I believe in the freedom to pursue your career without fear of prejudice on the basis of race, religion, gender or sexuality. It seemed to me hypocritical and counter-productive not to accept the role as the lead presenter in Sochi *because* I am gay – that would be playing into the hands of the homophobes who want to judge gay people as lesser human beings. I felt the whole point was to show Russia that being gay or straight is no more relevant than being left- or right-handed, blonde or brunette.

Also, I thought that if we, as a nation, were going to boycott Russia on the basis of human rights, we should *all* boycott it – it wasn't just up to one openly gay presenter. The LGBT community in Russia had made it clear they didn't want a boycott. The athletes weren't boycotting, the BBC wasn't boycotting, Channel 4 wasn't boycotting. So what would a one-woman boycott achieve? Nothing – apart from making me look like I thought I was more important than the Olympics themselves.

The Olympic Movement has its faults, but its aim is to take sport around the world, to encourage people to compete well, but within the rules, and to improve access to sport for all communities. By hosting the Winter Olympics in Sochi, President Putin was put under the media spotlight and was asked questions about his attitude to what he calls 'non-traditional' relationships. Most countries who get away with reprehensible behaviour do so because they are not challenged by the outside world. Russia was being challenged and could be in no doubt that its attitude was considered backward.

It's worth remembering that it was only ten years ago in the UK that the armed forces lifted their ban on homosexuality and that, until 2003, Section 28 prevented schools and institutions from 'promoting' homosexuality. That created a culture of shame and encouraged teachers to hide their own relationships. Now, equal marriage is a reality and hundreds of out, proud, gay people show it's possible to have a successful career without the need to lie and deny. We've come a long way.

I was heartened by the opening-ceremony speech from the International Olympic Committee chairman, Thomas Bach, who openly acknowledged Russia's bigotry and pointed the way forward:

'This is the Olympic message the athletes spread to the host country and to the whole world. Yes, it is possible to strive even for the greatest victory with respect for the dignity of your competitors. Yes, yes, it is possible – even as competitors – to live together under one roof in harmony, with tolerance and without any form of discrimination for whatever reason. Yes, it is possible – even as competitors – to listen, to understand and to give an example for a peaceful society.'

So all the political issues were swirling in my head, as well as the rules on interference in short-track speed-skating, the sweeping technique in curling, the judging system in slopestyle, the story behind the first individual Japanese figure-skating gold medallist and the pronunciation of the names of the Korean speed skaters and Norwegian cross-country skiers.

Yet I stayed as Happy as the Pharrell Williams track that became our anthem. And if I could attribute the delight of that trip to any one thing, it would be my morning walks.

I hope viewers felt something of that, too. In a dark February, it's uplifting to see snow-covered mountains and bright-blue skies.

Even more uplifting is seeing medals being won – Jenny Jones, Lizzy Yarnold and the men's and women's curling teams made it the most successful Winter Olympics for a British team since 1924.

Even events which we did not win were compelling: most memorably, the short-track speed-skating, where poor Elise Christie got disqualified three times.

And, as with the Summer Games, the female members of Team GB led the way. Yet more proof that when women's sport gets funding and media attention, it can be box office.

The winter athletes are refreshingly enthusiastic about media coverage – partly because they get so little of it – so they were happy to come to our makeshift studio at nearly midnight and chat away about the day's events. The four-man-bob team, led by John Jackson, was the last to compete at the Games. By the time they made it down the mountain, having finished fifth, the closing ceremony was about to start. They gave a brilliant interview but, as they had arrived late at the Games and had been following it from afar, all they really wanted to do was pose with the trolley, as if pushing it down an icy track. On Twitter, #sochitrolley was trending. The Americans may have had the swankiest studio, the Russians may have won the most golds, but, in Britain, our audience made sure that a shopping trolley was the star of the show.

I was walking alone in Sochi, but even more beneficial to mental health is walking in groups.

Clinical psychologist Guy Holmes believes that lack of social interaction is dangerous to our health. He has done a lot of research into dealing with depression, alternatives to medication and the effects of trauma.

He has set up a walking group for people with mental-health problems called Walk and Talk. It is based in Shrewsbury, and I went there to meet Guy and the members of the group.

'If you get very isolated,' he told me, 'perhaps because you are a bit paranoid, or you're scared, or bad things have happened to you, or you've lost touch with people, just getting out of the house and being with people is incredibly powerful. The evidence shows that having no friends has a worse impact on your health than smoking. You are going to die a lot younger if you've got no friends – that's the grim reality.'

Guy is gentle but very direct. He has worked with victims of sexual abuse, survivors of extreme trauma, suicidal people and those who hear voices. He is an impressive man but, for the purposes of our walk, he was just another member of the group hoping it wouldn't rain, because he hadn't brought an umbrella.

Guy's Walk and Talk group had developed from a walking group I had met back in 2005, based at the Radbrook Day Centre.

Karen Gregor, who was producing this episode of *Ramblings*, has always been interested in the mental-health benefits of walking and wanted to explore the idea further in the series. She came across the research of Penny Priest, who was studying for a doctorate in clinical psychology and had joined the walking group to observe and report on the progress made by the people in it. Penny joined us on the original walk in 2005 and again in Shrewsbury nine years later.

'I came up with this model called the Healing Balm effect,' Penny said. 'It captured the reasons why people were walking and what they found to be the benefits. People can come together and be part of something, have company and feel safe. My research has helped legitimize the need for a walking group, and it's great to see it working.'

Watching the group gather in the Frankwell car park by the guildhall, it was as if oxygen was coming back into their bloodstream and, with it, colour to their cheeks. The proof of the power of friendship was there before my eyes as they talked and laughed together.

We crossed the River Severn and turned right into a park with wide pathways. I started to chat to a retired policeman who had spent over twenty years in the control room in a busy city but suffered badly when he stopped working and moved to the country. Then his marriage broke down and he fell into depression. He said that walking with the group was the highlight of his week.

'Four years ago I split up from my wife,' he explained. 'I live in a very isolated spot and I have no contact with anyone really. I got very depressed. First of all I was prescribed medication, and then my GP suggested I join this Walk and Talk group.'

He doesn't come on the walks for the views or the fresh air (he gets plenty of that living in the middle of the countryside with his nearest neighbour over a mile away) but for the human contact.

'Through coming to this, I've been able to come off the medication and, hopefully, I'm as right as rain. I was a policeman for twenty-five years in Manchester. When I first started there was an armed robbery once a week, but when I came out of the control room there was an armed robbery three or four times a week, and murders. It was horrendous.

'I had counselling when I left, but the counsellor hadn't been in the police force so they didn't understand. I've always been aware of mental issues because of being in the police and having to deal with people who have them, but it's not until it affects you personally that you can appreciate how bad and how low you can get. I was suicidal. I was that bad.'

He shook his head as if he didn't recognize the person he had been, then smiled.

'If I know I'm coming here on a Thursday, that keeps me going for the whole week. I just look forward to meeting people and having a chat with them.'

It seems such a small, insignificant thing, a walking group that meets once a week, but it is life-changing. People need to feel safe, they need to feel loved and they need a reason to meet up. We are not all gregarious, confident beings who will stride up to strangers and strike up a conversation. We need help.

We had climbed up a path towards Shrewsbury School and stood with our backs to the red-brick walls, looking down at the town. From up here, we could see the way the river bent right round in a U-shape, its ends nearly meeting at the top, almost creating an island in the middle. In the distance we could see in one direction the Wrekin and, in the other, the jagged quartz tor of the Stiperstones. Between them was the humpback whale of the Long Mynd and the ancient volcano of Caer Caradoc, with a hill fort on its summit. We were opposite a park called the Quarry, which has a beautiful manicured garden in its centre called the Dingle, designed by Percy Thrower.

One of the walkers, Gio, pointed out the landmarks to me, adding detail where I lacked knowledge. He first joined the group in 1995. He had suffered a breakdown when he was in his teens, studying for a degree. The pressure had frozen his brain and he started hearing voices. He has never fully recovered and is heavily medicated, a condition that he finds frustrating, because his brain feels as if it is constantly wrapped in a blanket, deadened to the world. He tried running and cycling, but the walking group worked differently.

'When I went for that first walk, I felt like I was being looked after and cared for,' he said. 'It feels safe in a way that a local ramblers' group wouldn't feel. Having had mental-health problems, we feel a bit vulnerable. We're a bit raw and more sensitive. The walking group provides a nice little atmosphere in which to have a safe walk and be part of a close-knit family group.

'It's a very meditative thing, more so than running. Walking tends to feel more like meditation.'

Penny's research has found this to be true because of the rhythm of walking. It seems that it's valuable for people to find a steady pace and stick to it, she said. 'We all experience various degrees of distress, and it can be useful for any person at any time, depending on what they're going through. Rhythm is very soothing. Think back to being a baby and being rocked.'

It had been threatening rain and, as the drops started falling, I was talking to Gio again. For him, the weather is irrelevant. Sometimes a grey, damp day can be a useful reflection of the mood inside. I have always tended to assume that people feel happier on a bright day, but in fact most of us identify strongly with our environment: it's comforting to be in a landscape that mirrors your mental state, rather than being in one that seems the opposite of how you feel.

'It doesn't matter what the weather is doing or where we are,' he said. 'It's always magical. When I get back to the van at the end, I feel relieved that the walk is over because of the tiring effect – that's the medication that makes me more tired – but there are times when I feel a flow of endorphins and I'm energized, which is rare when you're on medication.'

We had covered maybe four miles of a circular walk, crossing the river two or three times and climbing high enough to get a good view of Shrewsbury and across to those 'blue remembered hills', as described by the poet A. E. Housman. The aim of the group is not to climb mountains or cover miles, but it knows what its purpose is more clearly than most walking groups. Crucial to the experience is to go to a pub or a café after the walk, share a table, chat and recover. By that point, conversation is easy and problems are shared. There is nothing adversarial about it and the pressure is negligible. It sounds to me as if Guy would choose walking therapy over any other.

'I run psychotherapy groups,' he said, 'and they're absolutely terrifying places for people to sit in. This is much more relaxing. People can talk about their difficulties if they want to, but they don't have to. They can talk about other things if they want.

'Talking about your difficulties is of some help to some people some of the time, but people are much more than their problems. This group is open to all, so we have people who have no connection with mental-health services at all, but they get the same benefits.'

Walk and Talk has become self-sustaining, with members taking on the responsibility of organizing, planning routes and booking the pub. It can't be ruined by bureaucracy and, apart from Guy's time, it costs the state nothing. The research backs up the general feeling that walking is good for us and a group like Walk and Talk can quickly become a lifeline for its members.

Drug companies are never going to advocate walking as a medicine – there's no money in it for them – but there is emerging evidence that walking can help slow down the development of Alzheimer's and early-onset dementia.

I met a group near Swindon called Forget Me Not who firmly believe that to be the case. We were crowded into the living room of a house in a cul-de-sac. I wouldn't be able to find it again if I tried, because Swindon manages to hide houses in a way that only Basing-stoke or Milton Keynes can rival. The buzz of chatter in the room was fuelled by cups of tea and biscuits. We were discussing where we might walk that day, and the decision was not to be rushed.

Forget Me Not is run by Lynda Hughes, an occupational therap-ist who focuses on fitness, stimulation and independence. Members of the group have the responsibility of choosing where they will walk, providing the maps and helping make lunch. Lynda makes sure there is no pressure of time so, even after an hour of discus-sion, debate and looking at maps, she never once said, 'Have we decided yet?' or 'Let's get going, shall we?'

After an hour or so we piled into a minibus and headed off to our starting point. They had decided on a route near Wanborough, to the east of Swindon on the north side of the M4. Everyone had knapsacks stuffed with food and drink, maps and waterproof clothes. The windows steamed up as soon as we closed the doors and I started drawing love hearts in the mist. I can't help it. It's something about being in a minibus.

When we arrived at our start point, we piled out like children on a school trip. It felt exciting and new. People around me were smil-ing and laughing. They looked relaxed but eager to venture forth. Lynda believes that more and more of us will develop dementia, and that we need to learn to live with it.

'If people can feel more relaxed about it, can feel as if it's not the end of the world, then that goes a long way,' she explained. 'The early diagnosis is important because you want to understand what you've got; otherwise, you live in fear of it. There are thousands of people living entirely normal lives with just a few changes for years, and years, and years with Alzheimer's or early-onset dementia. The media only shows you the end stages, which are scary, but your life can be quite manageable with it.'

The Forget Me Not group is made up of about ten people, all

of whom have a diagnosis of early-onset memory problems. They were all under sixty-five, and no one person was in charge so they were all encouraged to take responsibility. They walk once a week, whatever the weather – in fact, the more inclement it is, the more of an adventure they have and the more everyone remembers it.

We headed off down a track towards a farm about a mile away. Lynda didn't lead the walk, nor did any of the other carers. I could see a man I knew was called Jamie up near the front, along with another, called Ian, who was looking at his map.

I had read plenty about Alzheimer's but had never had the chance to talk to anyone at length about living with it. For some it's a case of forgetting names or how to get home; for others it can affect coordination. One lady was less mobile than the rest. When it came to stiles, she couldn't always feel where her feet were or signal to her legs what to do next. Others gathered round to help, offering a hand or a gentle push from behind.

'One of the effects of any illness is that you're looked after and you lose the ability of being useful to other people,' Lynda said. 'All of us need to be useful to other people to feel good about our own existence. In this group they all help each other out, and it's just beautiful to see.'

They walk for five or six hours and nearly always get lost. But finding their way again is part of the challenge, so Lynda doesn't interfere. Being out walking is good for the members of the group but also gives their wife or husband a break from constant caring. Ian told me, 'Everyone is very relaxed and I like it that they don't do things for us that we can do for ourselves.' In the outside world, he explained, every mistake you make affects your confidence because of the reaction of other people. When you can't park the car properly, it can make you feel that you're messing everything up. 'Here, you feel a sense of normality,' he said.

We had been walking for a couple of hours before we stopped for lunch. Everyone was starving and fell upon the heaps of food, sharing sandwiches, crisps, fruit and cheese as we sat on the side of a hill looking at the Vale of the White Horse. I could hear the faint hum of the motorway in the distance, and I had no idea where we were or where we were headed.

After lunch, we followed the map as best we could but ended up in the middle of a field with no obvious exit. One of the faster members of the group said he would walk to the far corner to see if there was a stile and a footpath sign.

We watched him go and come back again, some fifteen minutes later.

'Was there a stile?' I asked.

'A stile?' he said. 'I have no idea.'

The others laughed and then he said, 'Did I go over there to see if there was a stile? Oh dear, that was a bad idea. I really can't remember whether there was or not.'

He didn't panic about not remembering, he just laughed because the others were laughing. It must be frustrating as hell not to be able to remember the most basic of things, but if you let that frustration take over you are living in a double hell. Lynda makes sure that everyone feels that, whatever happens, it's just fine.

Soon we had lost another walker, together with her 25-year-old carer. But then we could hear hysterical laughter.

'I fell in a bush!' said Sandy, emerging from the hedgerow. 'It was brilliant.'

It didn't matter that we were lost, because the group felt at home – and by 'home', I don't mean a house or a village, but a place where everyone can feel safe, loved and, most of all, relevant.

10

Long Way Round

'You look tired. Are you tired?'

Lucy can sound just like my mother.

'No, I'm not tired.' I said. 'I'm just not wearing any make-up.'

One of the joys of radio is that you don't have to wander about with layers of cake on your face. You don't have to dress up, you don't have to put on a costume or pretend to be someone louder, brighter and more colourful. Radio listeners don't want an act or what you think is an improved version of yourself. They like genuine people, warts 'n' all. They want you to share the real you, and on radio you can do that, in a way that television doesn't allow.

I worked recently with a well-known and talented broadcaster who told me, 'There is no amount of money they could offer me for a daily TV show that would make up for the complete loss of my life. I would much rather do radio – you get all the fun and none of the hassle.'

I love being able to do both but, if forced to choose, radio would win every time.

Anyway, Lucy clearly thought I looked dreadful. Annoyingly, I'd forgotten that a lovely man called Michael Harrison, who often recorded with us, was bringing a camera to film a 'behind the scenes' piece for the Radio 4 website. Lucy wasn't going to be the only one judging my appearance.

'Here,' she said, handing me her bag. 'I've got some powder and some lipstick. Do what you can.'

Lucy and I had come up with a rather different notion in 2009 for series thirteen of *Ramblings*. For the first time in ten years, we would walk a long-distance path. She had given me the choice of the Coast to Coast (unoriginal), the South-west Coast Path (very long), the West Highland Way (cold), the Pennine Way (exposed) or St Oswald's Way in Northumberland.

'Northumberland, please,' I quickly said.

'I knew you'd say that,' she replied. 'So I've started booking the guests and looking at places we can stay.'

In this instance, I didn't mind being predictable. Growing up, I had barely been to Northumberland, as it only had one racecourse, at Hexham. But the one time I had walked along the coast I adored it. There is so much space in Northumberland and, as it's not as popular a tourist destination as Cornwall or the Lake District, it never seems crowded. The historian G. M. Trevelyan called North-umberland 'the land of the far horizons', and I fancied a bit of that limitless space.

Trevelyan also believed that the French Revolution would never have happened if the French had played cricket. It sounds ridicu-lous, but his argument was that cricket in villages around England mixed the aristocracy and the rural workers, while in France the noblesse kept a distance from the 'peasants'. When the people rose up, these 'peasants' had no compunction about killing arrogant, aloof nobles they neither knew nor cared about.

Trevelyan was the first president of the Youth Hostels Association and worked throughout his life on behalf of the National
Trust to preserve houses and landscapes. He proudly avoided medical attention, saying, 'I have two doctors: my left leg and my right':
he was a firm believer in the restorative powers of walking. Trevelyan died at the age of eighty-six in 1962, just missing out on the
start of a new era for walkers.

The first long-distance path was opened in the UK in 1965, thirty
years after the journalist Tom Stephenson had first mooted the idea
in a *Daily Herald* article entitled 'Wanted: A Long Green Trail'. Pro-
tracted wrangling with farmers and landowners over access delayed
matters for decades until, finally, agreement was reached for a path
that stretches 268 miles from Edale in Derbyshire along the spine of
England to Kirk Yetholm in the Scottish Borders. The Pennine Way
is one of fifteen National Trails in England and Wales, with more in
Scotland (there known as the Great Trails) and one in Northern Ireland (the Ulster Way).

Things have come a long way since the mass trespass on Kinder
Scout in 1932, where walkers protested about lack of access to areas
of open country, and it's always worth remembering the struggle to
gain access to our green and pleasant land – and not to abuse that
right. It's up to us not to desecrate the land by dropping litter, behaving irresponsibly, leaving gates open or allowing dogs to chase
livestock. We have more varied and beautiful footpaths than any
country in the world and, just as much as it's the responsibility of
farmers, landowners and the National Trail Association, it's up to
those of us who walk them to protect them for future use.

I was excited about the challenge of the long-distance walk. This
would be a journey of slow and luxurious discovery – physically
demanding, but spiritually rewarding. There are few ways in which
we can feel truly connected with the ancient world, but this is one
of them. We walk in exactly the same way as our forefathers did
and, although our footwear may have improved, our stride length
and rhythm of walking is exactly the same.

A long-distance path can be as hard or as easy as you want to make it. You can do twenty-five miles a day or ten, camp out or stay in comfort. I know that some people feel that it's not a real experience unless you're sleeping under the stars, but I have never been a fan of camping. I'm too keen on sleeping on a mattress, having running water and a flushing loo. Lucy felt the same and had already booked the hotels.

So, we chose St Oswald's Way for our long-distance-path debut, or perhaps it chose us. It is England's newest long-distance route and runs for ninety-seven miles in total from Holy Island along the Northumberland coast, turning inland at Warkworth and finishing at Heavenfield, near Hexham. It starts with the best coastal walking you can find – cliffs, castles, fishing villages and beaches – and combines it with farmland, moorland, hill walking and, finally, a stretch of Hadrian's Wall. Lucy and I had six days to walk different sections of the route, with the option of shortening or extending our walks according to time and weather.

The start and end point are both hugely significant to the memory of St Oswald, who brought the Irish monk and missionary Aidan from Iona. St Aidan (as he became) was the first Bishop of Lindisfarne and, without him, there would have been no Holy Island, because he was the one who picked it as a place to establish a monastery for himself and his Ionian monks, to follow the Celtic school of Christianity. Heavenfield, where the walk ends, is where Oswald won the battle that made him King of Northumbria in the year 634 (or thereabouts).

The Venerable Bede described St Aidan as a 'man beloved of God' because he brought Christianity to the North-east and did his best to protect it.

Oswald was eventually killed in battle – as they all tended to be – fighting the tribal kings of Mercia and Gwynedd. His body was dismembered, with his head and arms fixed to stakes in Shropshire, where they were fighting. The following year, his brother rescued what was left of Oswald and took his remains to his headquarters at Bamburgh. His head was given to the monks at Lindisfarne. They did give some funny Christmas presents in those days.

It seemed to make sense for us to start at Lindisfarne Priory, in the middle of Holy Island, because of its link with St Aidan and St Oswald. Holy Island is a tidal island with a permanent population of about 160 but an influx of approximately 65,000 visitors a year. Quite often drivers get the tide times wrong and are left stranded on the island or, worse, halfway across the causeway.

There are no big shopping chains on Holy Island, no Costa Coffee or McDonald's. That's not to say it isn't commercial, but it takes your money with style. It has independent shops, dog-friendly pubs and small cafés, a gift shop and galleries: everything the tourist might need or want. The huge bonus for its permanent residents is that it also has a cut-off point every day when the visitors have to leave before the tide comes in. The island can breathe a sigh of relief and go back to being itself.

Lucy and I had divided St Oswald's Way into six chunks, which we would walk with different people. We started with the man who came up with the idea of the path as a millennium project – the Revd Michael Mountney. He wanted to design a sort of pilgrimage to link the various parishes of the North-east. It turned into something rather bigger and more wonderful, and he seemed genuinely surprised by its success. He struck me as a man who was perhaps more used to fighting the good fight and coping bravely with disappointment than bathing in the glory of a hit.

Michael did not look like a vicar. I know they come in all shapes and sizes and there is not a shop that dispenses identikit 'Vicars', but there is usually a giveaway expression or tone. So much did Michael not look like a vicar that I walked past him twice and, even when I was introduced to him, I still wasn't sure. He was wearing shorts, a grey T-shirt and a bright yellow plastic mac. He had short-cropped greying hair and was carrying a red-and-yellow flag, waving it like a child.

'It's the flag of Northumberland,' he explained, sweeping it from side to side. The red and yellow alternate in offset vertical stripes, creating a row of red 'u's at the top and red 'n's at the bottom. It was apparently adapted from a purple-and-gold banner that hung over St

Oswald's coffin after he was killed. Michael, Lucy and I were joined by Jenny Walters, who is a long-distance-walking expert and who I was hoping would make sure we didn't suffer too much over the coming days.

Michael explained the genesis of St Oswald's Way as we removed our boots and socks and I zipped off the bottom of my trousers. I congratulated myself on wearing them, as it was one of the few times they were genuinely useful, rather than just looking like a pair of trousers with an ugly zip around the knee.

'There's a spiritual and a historical core to it,' he told me.

I should clarify that stripping off to the knee was not a holy ritual but a practical necessity: the first section would be three miles across the mudflats to the mainland. It was the perfect way to lose the madding crowd on the island, and also a symbolic start: we were casting off baggage, unloading ourselves of unnecessary extras, getting closer to the elements – and saving our boots from seawater rotting.

Michael Harrison watched us leave with the video camera and then, thankfully, returned to his car. I say this not because I don't like him but because as soon as you introduce a camera into the scenario you lose the intimacy of the walk. I don't want anyone to be distracted by what we look like, nor do I want to be judged for wearing a scruffy T-shirt and a pair of ill-fitting, zip-off trousers.

We followed the line of ten-foot-tall posts that show walkers the most direct route and mark the Pilgrim's Path. It was hard to imagine that in a few hours, when the tide came in, they would barely poke out above the water and that the whole road would be covered. I guess it's precisely because it's hard to imagine that so many people get stranded.

Halfway across, I turned to look back at Holy Island, the silhouette of Lindisfarne Castle rising out of the volcanic rocky outcrop on the south-east of the island, the buzz of the tourists now a distant murmur.

We squelched on through the mud, hopping over the wider rivulets of water and gazing into the distance at the beginnings of low hills, trees and the darker lumps on the horizon that are the Cheviot Hills. I was looking at the opening paragraph to the giant tome that is Northumberland, and it was seriously impressive. As we stood, we realized that the eerie sound in the air was not the wind, but seals howling. They make a noise like cows, and it carries over the water and the rocks, floating around us like ghosts.

As we reached the shore, I could see grassed-over sand dunes to the right with mad, wavy hair blowing in the breeze. Streams of cars were driving towards Holy Island, but we, on our feet, were alone. We were special. We smelt special too, the combination of seaweed, saltwater and mud not being a favourite for lovers of Jo Malone.

Walking three miles in mud is quite hard work, let me tell you, and, for all the symbolic hoo-ha, it was a relief to be on dry land. I washed my feet off and dried them on some grass as I hummed 'These Boots were Made for Walking' and considered the challenge ahead. If you are going to undertake a long-distance walk, the advice is to build up over a few weeks, walking six or seven miles a day and then further at weekends, to make sure that you can cope. Of course, I hadn't done any of this and neither had Lucy.

It was a major step forward that I was carrying a rucksack with food and a change of clothes. Lucy had the first-aid kit and the recording equipment. We figured we would get fit as we went along and, if the worst came to the worst, we could always take a bus or a taxi. Yes, I realize that would be cheating, but I mean if I broke a leg or something. Thinking of the taxi, I said, 'Have you got money?' I wondered why I hadn't asked this before we left the island, when we might still have been able to do something about it.

'Yes,' she said wearily. 'Of course I've got money.'

I have a bad habit of forgetting to take cash with me when I go walking. Alice says I think I'm the Queen and that I don't need money. I don't, by the way, I just forget. I usually have a credit card, but that's not much good when you're in the middle of nowhere and want to buy an ice cream. That's why Alice and Lucy always carry cash, which is good news for me.

We headed south, down the coast for a short stretch, looking out at the Farne Islands surging up out of the sea like surfacing submarines. Their big black volcanic rock, the Whin Sill, is a haven for puffins, guillemots, shags, kittiwakes, Arctic tern, eider ducks and grey seals.

We followed the signs with a black raven emblem, turning further inland, crossing the A1 and walking through the village of Fenwick. Michael wanted to take me a mile off the route so I could see St Cuthbert's Cave.

Michael was so proud of the walk and the fact that people had clearly been using it. He pointed out each signpost enthusiastically and was wonderfully excited about showing us the first section.

'What thrills me is that people are discovering St Oswald's Way and being introduced to Northumberland,' he said. 'They can learn about his history and know about the religious connection, or just walk it and enjoy the county.'

It started to rain as we got to St Cuthbert's Cave, and the drips echoed off its stone walls. It's a weirdly moving place: an over-hanging slab of sandstone rock, perched precariously, giving a wide-mouthed opening to a damp, cold, dark cave. There were the remains of a fire and signs that campers had stayed the night. Rather them than me.

St Cuthbert (of the cave) was renowned for his patience and sensitivity. He died in solitude on the Farne Islands in AD 687 and was buried at Lindisfarne, where he had been bishop. A cult of St Cuthbert grew up after he died and he had to be moved to protect him from the invading Vikings. When the monks raised his coffin, they didn't find a skeleton but a body that looked as if it was sleeping, still fully flexible, with hair, flesh and skin. This was seen as a sign of the bishop's great purity and holiness, and the monks vowed to take him to safety. So they began a trek across northern England, carrying his coffin, and this cave was said to be one of the places they spent the night.

Legend has it that St Cuthbert himself chose his final resting place when the monks couldn't lift his coffin at a bend in the river in

Durham. They pushed and pulled and tried to shift it, but it wasn't going anywhere. This was where it wanted to stay. St Cuthbert's shrine was therefore created at the place where Durham Cathedral now stands.

It became a popular pilgrimage point through the Middle Ages and, in 1104, more than four hundred years after his death, nine monks decided to have a look for themselves to see if the myth of his uncorrupt body was true. They took his coffin into the newly built cathedral to examine it. You can imagine the trepidation with which they opened the creaking lid and their amazement when they saw that there was Cuthbert, lying on his side as if he was asleep, complete still with hair, skin and flesh.

His body was examined again during the Dissolution of the Monasteries and, again, it was found to be whole and undecayed, which must have freaked out Henry VIII's men. They were busy smashing up everything, but didn't know what to do with the body so decided to leave it to the King, a delay that gave Benedictine monks a chance to hide his body. There is strong evidence to suggest that St Cuthbert was returned to Durham Cathedral, where he still lies, although a nineteenth-century examination found only bones and glorious robes in the coffin.

So the body either eventually disintegrated or it was a substitute and the real thing still lies in a top-secret hiding place known only to a handful of Benedictine monks. Whatever the truth, St Cuthbert is everywhere in Durham – his cross is on the flag of the county and the coat of arms of Durham University, while the modern sculpture chosen for Millennium Place in 2008 is of six hooded monks carrying his coffin as they try to find a safe place to take him.

Having taken our diversion to St Cuthbert's Cave, Lucy and I left Michael and headed off to Bamburgh, where we were staying in a bed and breakfast. Anyone who travels a lot for work will tell you that there is a huge difference between cheap hotels and equally cheap B&Bs. One will have plastic undersheets, plastic glasses (often bizarrely encased in a plastic bag), little plastic UHT milk containers, and small soaps (of course) covered in plastic. The other won't have any plastic. It will have lovely sheets and pillows, proper tea and real milk, a bathroom that doesn't smell and curtains that shut. If you're lucky you will have biscuits in your room, and I've even had a piece of home-made cake left for me because the owner was worried I'd be hungry.

B&Bs are sometimes fractionally more expensive than certain chains that build their hotels next to motorways and dual carriageways, but they are way better value, because you can actually sleep *and* you get breakfast.

They also tend to be in the place where you want to stay, not twenty miles away. I was doing a series a few years ago called *Britain by Bike*, which followed the routes detailed in a series of books by a cycling journalist called Harold Briercliffe. The idea was that I would cycle the routes on Harold's own bicycle, a 1957 Dawes Galaxy. Brilliant idea. Except that bike had a crossbar so high that I couldn't climb into the saddle and only three gears, with a gear shift so stiff it was impossible to switch between them. I learned to hate that ruddy bike.

We started our recording on the edge of the Cotswolds but, for some reason, our production coordinator decided to book us all into a Travelodge on the ring road in Oxford. I know there are hundreds of wonderful B&Bs throughout the area, but no, far better to drive in crawling rush hour to a car park on the ring road to stay in what amounts to a collection of cardboard boxes stacked on top of each other. When I got to my room I removed the plastic undersheet (you have to do this straightaway, because when you are dripping with sweat at 2 a.m. you will be too tired to work it out) and tried to draw the curtains. They were broken.

On the faux-wooden sideboard, there was a packet of Pringles, a Tracker bar and a can of Diet Coke. I was taken aback, as I didn't think they did that sort of thing.

'They don't,' Amber the production assistant said when we met in the pub for a drink. 'I put them there to try and liven the place up a bit.'

She was gold dust, was Amber. She came from Devon and spoke

with the West Country burr that is my favourite accent, mainly because it's one I can really do. Every conversation had to be sprinkled liberally with 'All right, my lover?', which made us laugh. It's pathetic, I know, but when you're on the road trying to ride a 1950s bike with gears you can't change and a crossbar so high you get groin strain every time you climb on it, you need silly things to laugh about.

Our crew for *Britain by Bike* was me, Amber and Alison, who was a self-shooting director, which means she did all the filming and all the directing. She basically ran the show while Amber and I said, 'All right, my lover?' to each other. Exploring the countryside by bike, even a bike that I hated, is much faster than walking it. You can still stop and enjoy the view and you can throw the bike down (always a temptation) and walk off track to see, for example, Offa's Dyke or Broadway Tower.

We worked from sunrise until it was dark every day because we were packing a lot into a very short space of time, and we got along beautifully. Our only problem was that we were being organized from afar, so hotel bookings were never great and transport arrangements always caused confusion. The worst example was when we were on the Isle of Wight and Alison wanted to film me on the ferry from Yarmouth to Lymington because it was on that journey that Tennyson wrote 'Crossing the Bar'.

Amber phoned the production coordinator, who was in an office in Glasgow, and asked her to book the tickets.

Three hours later we had a text message: 'Can't see any ferries from Yarmouth to mainland. Can only find superfast ferry from Yarmouth to the Netherlands. Will that do?'

I would have quite enjoyed a trip to Amsterdam, but as we were in Yarmouth on the Isle of Wight, not Great Yarmouth, Norfolk, and I quite wanted to get home, it wasn't the most helpful suggestion.

Luckily, Lucy had actually looked at a map to work out where we should stay for St Oswald's Way. Our first stop was at the B&B in Bamburgh, within sight of the castle, which had been King Oswald's royal headquarters when he was King of Northumbria.

The castle is built on nine acres of the same rock type as the Farne Islands, Whin Sill, which means it is in no danger of slipping into the sea, but it is not immune to attack and holds the distinction of being the first castle to be destroyed by gunfire during the Wars of the Roses. It stood as a ruin and was used as a hospital and a coastguard station until Lord Armstrong, engineer, inventor and arms manufacturer, bought it in 1894.

Armstrong spent a million pounds (more than £60 million in today's money) renovating the castle and ensuring that it had the benefits of his latest inventions, like central heating and air conditioning. He died a week before the work was complete, but the conversion of the castle into a home has lasted: the Armstrong family still live at Bamburgh Castle. It's open all year round and I would thoroughly recommend a visit. You can even get married in the King's Hall, should the desire grasp you.

I would love to have wandered round the castle for hours, but I was shattered. We headed to our B&B, left our mud-caked boots by the front door and repaired to our rooms. All I wanted was a hot bath and to peel off my damp clothes, in whichever order happened most easily.

We had supper in a local pub, thrilled that we could order pie and mash without fear of calories. There is nothing better than a really good meal when you know you deserve it. The only problem was finding the energy to raise the fork.

I was in bed by ten o'clock and fast asleep by one minute past. I woke up the next morning in exactly the same position. I had a few seconds of confusion as I worked out where I was and which sport I was covering. But then it came to me: I was walking. My only concern would be blister plasters and snacks. There is a huge joy in paring back life to the bare essentials.

It felt as if we'd only just had supper, but you must take food when it's available, so Lucy and I tucked into a full English breakfast. My shoulders were a bit sore, but my legs felt good. Lucy insisted on walking in jeans, which I thought would chafe, but I wasn't going to argue. We had five more days of walking together so it seemed better to let her get on with it. I would say 'I told you so' on day six.

The second section of St Oswald's Way is fourteen miles from Bamburgh Castle to Craster, all along the coast, but we tracked back a bit to do a section we had missed the day before. We started inland at Spindlestone Mill and walked through fields and woodland in the company of Iain Robson, who is in charge of maintaining the Northumberland Coast Path, and Tom Cadwallender, who was the Natural and Cultural Heritage Officer for the Northumberland Coast Area of Outstanding Natural Beauty. Butterflies danced around us as the two men explained the balancing act for those who work in the tourism trade of maintaining the very thing that people come for – the solitude and the space – while promoting the area so that the local economy can benefit.

After a couple of miles we reached the coast at Budle Bay and could see back to Holy Island.

'Oh,' I said. 'It doesn't seem very far away.'

'Don't worry.' Iain sensed my despair. 'It looks closer than it is and you can't walk directly there because the sea is in the way.'

Tom and Iain were both in shorts and I'd thrillingly zipped off my trousers again to let the sun see my legs. I lived in hope that, by the time we finished, they would be vaguely bronzed. I was to be disappointed.

We had to cut along the edge of a golf course (there are eight in total on St Oswald's Way) and, as an enthusiastic but erratic golfer, I felt as if I was a gamekeeper turned poacher. Walkers don't like golfers and golfers certainly don't like walkers, but Iain insisted we should all exist happily together as long as we respected each other's rights. I put my finger to my lips to tell him to shush as a man in a pale-pink-and-yellow diamond jumper was about to tee off twenty feet away from us.

'Good drive,' I said helpfully as he sliced the ball off the tee. He glared at us.

Bamburgh Castle was looking magnificent in the early-morning sunshine and, as the tide was out, we cut down to the beach to walk on the compacted sand.

'Look at that.' Iain pointed to Harkess Rocks, jutting out into the sea.

They are known locally as Stag Rocks because of the bright-white stag painted on to the rock side. Apparently, it was put there in honour of an albino stag who was chased by hounds to the point of the cliff and, rather than be caught, jumped into the North Sea. Either that or it was painted by Italian prisoners of war during the Second World War. You would think someone would know. It's quite a thing to have appeared overnight, but it remains a mystery.

As well as the castle, Bamburgh is the home of the Royal National Lifeboat Institution Grace Darling Museum. Grace Darling was the first woman to be awarded the RNLI Silver Medal for Gallantry, for her part in the rescue of survivors from the SS *Forfarshire*, a luxury paddle steamer that was wrecked off the rocks near the Farne Islands in September 1838.

The boilers of the steamer had been giving trouble and as the captain tried to navigate the sixty-two on board to safety, he got caught in a terrible storm. He made the mistake of sailing towards Longstone Lighthouse, where Grace's father, William, was the lighthouse keeper, and crashed into the rocks from which it was meant to warn him away. Some crew members escaped on the only lifeboat but, when the ship split in two, those left behind had little chance of survival. A small group of nine swam to the nearby Big Harcar rocks.

Early in the morning, Grace spotted movement through her telescope and persuaded her father to take out the rowing boat to attempt a rescue. She had to keep the boat steady in the stormy waters while her father climbed on to the rocks to help people to safety. The rescue of the nine survivors was a success.

That bit of the story is very well known. What is less discussed is what happened to Grace Darling afterwards.

The press loved the unlikely story of survival against the odds and the young woman at the centre of it all. The letters pages of *The Times* were full of admirers, with one correspondent writing, 'Is there in the whole field of history, or of fiction even, one instance of female heroism to compare for one moment with this?'

Grace Darling became a celebrity. People sent her letters and presents, and even the young Queen Victoria sent her fifty pounds, which was a fortune to a girl who lived in a lighthouse. People hired boats at Seahouses to come out to Longstone to try to catch a glimpse of the famous sea heroine. It all, frankly, got a bit weird.

Artists arrived to paint her portrait, there were mugs, jugs and chinaware with her image on them and her fame spread around the world. A circus owner tried to take advantage of her popularity by asking her to appear at his show in Edinburgh, but the prospect of her being used to pull in the punters appalled some of her fans, who wrote to her urging her not to lower herself by appearing at Batty's Circus. Grace got upset and decided to give the circus a miss. She was offered a part in a stage play at the Adelphi Theatre in London called *The Wreck at Sea*, in which she would play herself. She turned that down, as well as most public appearances and the many proposals of marriage from men she had never met.

Not long after the rescue, Grace and her father were presented with medals by the Duke and Duchess of Northumberland. The Duke offered to become Grace's guardian to help her handle the attention and the funds that were coming her way, but even he couldn't contain or control the interest. Poems were written about her, novels based on her, ballads sung for her and endless letters written to her.

All Grace wanted to do was live quietly at Longstone Lighthouse, but that would be like David Beckham deciding he wanted to play for a village football team. William Darling was conscious of his daughter's reluctance. He wrote in a letter turning down yet another request for an appearance, 'You can hardly form an idea how

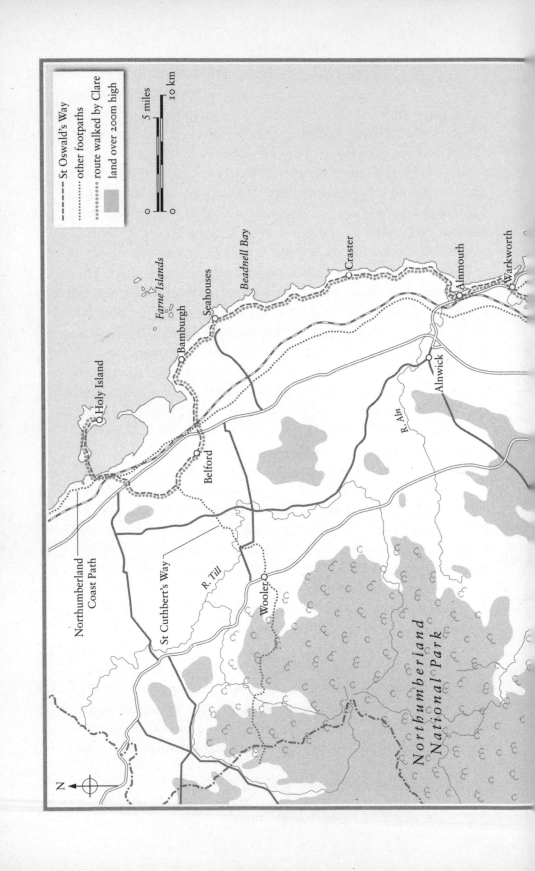

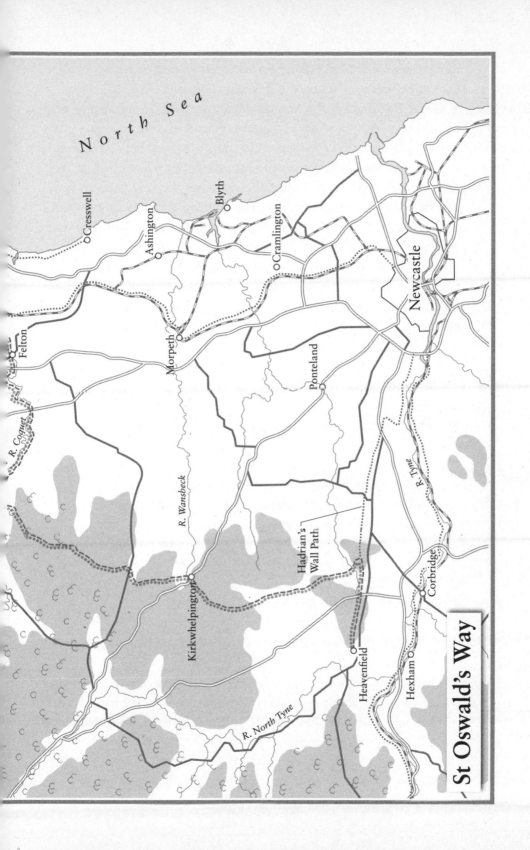

St Oswald's Way

disagreeable it is to my daughter to show herself in public . . . You cannot believe how much she has been annoyed by it all.'

Grace Darling was the first media icon of the Victorian age, and hated it. In 1842, four years after the rescue, she picked up a virus and couldn't get rid of a cough. Her family moved her to the mainland so that she could get proper attention, but it was too late. She was wracked with guilt about the requests she had turned down and began to have visions of people staring at her. She was weak and fading fast. The Duchess of Northumberland asked her own doctor to examine Grace. He diagnosed tuberculosis.

Grace died in her father's arms on 20 October 1842. She was twenty-six years old. Thousands came to her funeral at St Aidan's Church in Bamburgh, and the country mourned. A black iron fence surrounds a memorial to her, which looks like a Gothic four-poster bed with her stone body lying beneath the canopy, an oar by her side.

She is still famous today, and my nephew Jonno has just been learning about her at school. As recently as 1974, a song by The Strawbs was called 'Grace Darling'. The first verse goes like this:

> You have been my lighthouse in every storm
> You have given shelter, you have kept me safe and warm
> And in my darkest nights you have shone your brightest lights
> You are my saving grace, darling, I love you.

I find her story desperately sad. We think of uncontrollable, unwelcome fame as a purely modern plague, but the story of Grace Darling proves otherwise.

We walked on to Seahouses, crossing a massive stone-step stile and approaching the town not from its prettiest side. Seahouses is a fish 'n' chip paradise, and the seagulls love it. The town grew from the early railway tourists coming out of Newcastle, and it's bustling.

My shoulders were hurting from the rucksack and I was starting to whinge.

'Do belt up,' said Lucy. 'We're staying somewhere really nice tonight.'

We pushed on through Seahouses to Beadnell Bay, where I kicked off my boots and socks and thought I'd do what Dad used to do when racehorses had sore shins – bathe them in cold water.

My, oh my, the North Sea is *cold*. It was a gorgeous late-summer's day, warm evening sunshine persuading people to go windsurfing and jet-skiing. Children were splashing, their screams dancing down the bay. A woman and a Parson Russell terrier were playing tug of war with a rope of kelp, him snarling as he tried to win the prize. A man was checking his lobster pots and, on the horizon, I could see a tanker out at sea. I stood trying to distract myself with all of these sights as my legs quietly froze in the water.

'What's good for the horses is good for me,' I thought.

When I couldn't feel my lower legs any more, I walked back up the beach.

Thankfully, Lucy hadn't been lying about the quality of our accommodation. St Cuthbert's House is a renovated Presbyterian church and went instantly to the top of my 'best ever B&Bs' list. In fact, I would describe it as a luxury small hotel with a family feel, but that might not fit on the signs.

Paradise came in the form of fresh linen sheets and a three-course home-cooked dinner in the galleried dining room.

Our next day's section was meant to be from Craster to Warkworth, but when we woke the wind and rain were lashing the windows of St Cuthbert's House. It was the tail end of Hurricane Bill, which had wreaked havoc along the east coast of Canada and North America before hitting Ireland and the UK with heavy rainfall and strong winds.

'What do you want to do?' I asked Lucy over our steaming porridge.

I was quite happy to hang about all morning drinking coffee and reading the papers, but we had to go out at some stage. We were due to meet an artist and a photographer in Boulmer (pronounced Boomer) to discuss the visual glory of Northumberland.

'I'll call them and discuss our options,' said Lucy.

One of the reasons that Lucy and I get on so well is that we are both up for having unusual adventures but we are also quite pragmatic in our outlook. Years ago, when we'd done about ten series of *Ramblings* together, I said that we should choose walks that we wanted to do and live the experience for ourselves.

That way, the programmes would be authentic, better to listen to and our lives would be enhanced. With only a few mistakes – the opera singer who was far too aware of being on the radio ('Gate closing,' she said, as the gate closed), the tour guide who spoke in that tour-guide voice, the ramblers who wouldn't stop to look at the view, the trainee producer they gave me who I was supposed to help educate (terrible idea) – we've done pretty well at sticking to our ethos. If we are discovering new things and are genuinely excited by them, the listener will be, too.

In this instance, the new experience I was keen to have was an easy morning. Day three of a long-distance walk, it starts to hurt. You are over the feeling of invincibility and the novelty has worn off.

'Right,' said Lucy, who had made her phone call. 'We're going to meet them in Boulmer and walk for as long as we can without this getting soaked.'

She pointed to the recording device hanging round her neck. Lucy had refashioned a see-through washbag into a plastic cover for the recording kit and hoped that would keep it watertight. She needed to be able to see the screen and the red light that told her we were recording, so she couldn't hide it under her coat. I was happy to use the safety of the recording kit as an excuse to cut our walk down to the bare minimum, but my one regret in skipping south to Boulmer was that we would miss Dunstanburgh Castle.

I had walked there before, and I recommend the route from Craster up to the castle and back again, though it's often quite busy. There are some holiday cottages on the clifftops that I fancy – even if it was stormy, you could sit and watch the North Sea whipping up a lather. I do love a good storm.

Dunstanburgh Castle was built by the 2nd Earl of Lancaster, a grandson of Henry III, but he had his head chopped off by Edward II in 1322 for leading a rebellion a year earlier, before he could enjoy the luxury of his fortified retreat. It was designed on a massive scale, far bigger than Bamburgh Castle, and even the ruins stretch across eleven acres. It is isolated and exposed to the North Sea. J. M. W. Turner visited in 1797 and painted the coastline being ravaged by waves, the castle ruins forming a haunting backdrop.

Turner would have loved this kind of a day on the Northumberland coast; the artist I was meeting, Sue Fenlon, was similarly moved.

'I find it's a very emotional coastline,' she said. 'Growling grey skies, muddy, olivey green seaweed and always throwing up different shapes with the stones and line of seaweed coming up towards sand dunes. There's so much atmosphere with the sounds of the birds and the seals.'

We couldn't hear that much because it was raining so hard, but I got her drift.

Boulmer is a tiny fishing village which was the smuggling capital of the north. Smugglers and pirates from across Northumberland and Scotland would meet in the Fishing Boat Inn to trade their stash of stolen goods. The most famous was William Faa II, King of the Gypsy Kingdom. He owned an inn in Kirk Yetholm (now a tourist attraction at the end of the Pennine Way) from where he would smuggle whisky over the border into England and take tobacco and Dutch gin or brandy back with him.

Apart from the Fishing Boat Inn (which is still there), Boulmer is a collection of low stone sea-facing cottages with no shops or post office. Behind the cottages are walled fields where sheep were huddling against each other and into the walls to keep dry.

As the tide was out, we walked down to the beach, where ours were the only footprints in the sand. The weather was filthy but, once we got into our stride, it became a challenge that was strangely invigorating.

I was sporting a 'showerproof' jacket, which is about as useful as a chocolate teapot. I don't quite understand the concept of 'shower-proof'. Most clothes are technically showerproof, as your skin won't get wet for a few minutes if it's only a passing shower, but what's the point of advertising the fact that an item of clothing keeps out any water at all if it patently doesn't? It would be better if they labelled it 'not waterproof'.

Within minutes I was wet through.

The only group seeming to be really enjoying the weather were the black and white oystercatchers, who were running along with their long orange bills open, squealing with delight. They looked like children let out of school early, not sure what to do with themselves but very, very excited about it.

When we got ourselves back on the main footpath, we saw a man coming the other way, bent double against the wind to carry the weight of the enormous rucksack on his back.

'Glad to know there're more crazy people out in this weather, not just me,' he said, before explaining that he was walking St Oswald's Way from south to north and had been wild camping. I wondered how much fun that had been last night, with Hurricane Bill for company.

'Oh, it was fine,' he said. 'I've been up in Scotland for three months' walking.'

I'm not sure if that was meant to be an explanation as to why it was fine last night or just a change in direction, but he was clearly a committed hiker. He didn't really care what the weather was doing, as long as he was in it.

It was all a blur until we got to Alnmouth. I peeled off my clothes, which were stuck to my skin. I tried not to dwell on how lovely it would have been to have stayed snuggled up on the sofa at St Cuthbert's House with the papers and a pot of real coffee.

Weather and energy allowing, followers of St Oswald's Way would walk on down the coast to Warkworth, site of another cracking castle, this one from the twelfth century, and more good B&Bs.

I walked round Warkworth (try repeating that quickly) a year or so ago with an amazing all-female choir called Werca's Folk. The name comes from the woman after whom Warkworth was named. Werca was described as a 'wild and witchy woman' by some and as 'saintly' by others. Sandra Kerr, who leads the choir, likes to think the choir has that combination of power and goodness with a naughty edge.

She doesn't hold auditions because, to her mind, commitment to the cause is more important than a natural ability to sing. She knows she can teach someone to sing better, but she says she can't teach dedication. Werca's Folk perform without music, so they all have to learn the words and harmonies to every song, and they can call on any one of eighty songs from memory.

Where I believe in the ability of walking to solve the problems of the world, Sandra is a passionate advocate of the power of music.

'We enjoy doing it, it makes us feel good, we feel better when we've done it, and so it goes on. We all know singing is good for us. It releases the same feel-good endorphins as sex and chocolate,' she told me, amid much laughter from her choir, 'but it's much cheaper and less messy.'

There are twenty women in the choir, most of whom have been members for eighteen years, singing and walking together. We set off from Warkworth Castle, past the Church of St Lawrence, where they all dived inside to make the most of the acoustics with a quick tune, then down to the riverbank and back in a big circle to Warkworth. They told me how much they valued their Thursday nights at choir practice as their own time to do something that required their entire concentration and wasn't about the demands of family or work.

They stopped opposite the Hermitage on the River Coquet to sing a haunting harmony called 'Blood and Gold'. Sandra threw herself into energetic conducting. I watched their faces fill with joy and wondered what it would be like to be able to create a sound so beautiful. Sandra asked me to become a patron of Werca's Folk and I accepted because I just love their spirit.

I am not a natural singer – as Alice frequently reminds me. I can follow a tune if she is singing it (she has a great voice and was in *Evita*), but I can't create one of my own, nor can I hold a note. So, all in all, I really can't sing, even though Sandra tried to persuade me otherwise. Luckily, the microphone was not switched on at the time.

The coastal stretch of St Oswald's Way ends at Warkworth, where the route turns inland, along the River Coquet towards Rothbury. We joined a group for section four who were being guided by a former shepherd who had turned his attention to herding people rather than sheep.

Jon Monks set up Shepherds Walks and takes people all over Northumberland, introducing them to the landscape (and the sheep). He's a great guide because he gives everyone in the group the confidence that he knows where he's going and that they are capable of walking as far as he can. He leads the walk but makes sure that he talks to all, cajoling those who need encouragement and steadying those who race ahead. He knows the land intimately, and plenty of the history of Northumberland as well. Jon is a fan of its newest long-distance path.

'It's more of a thinking person's trail,' he said. 'It's not got to the stage of attracting walkers who just want to tick off a long-distance path.'

Part of the path follows the route of the Devil's Causeway, a Roman road which goes from Port Gate to Berwick-upon-Tweed. It was the marching route to Scotland, and we tramped along in the footsteps of soldiers long gone.

The North Sea Trail goes up the North Yorkshire coast from Filey, past Scarborough and Whitby, all the way to Saltburn. It links parts of Scotland with Denmark, the Netherlands, Norway, Sweden and Germany and is a rather clever idea to promote tourism in North Sea coastal areas.

We switched off the microphone for an hour because we were walking much further than we needed for the programme (to take back too much material just makes it a pain for Lucy, who has to listen to it all and chop out the boring bits – of which she says there are many). The benefit of switching off was that I could talk to Alice, who had joined us for the second half of St Oswald's Way.

She had never been to Northumberland before and I had done a big sell on the county. Sadly, she had been busy working so had missed all the coastal walking. I tried not to keep saying that we'd already done the best bits and stayed in the world's finest B&B, but it was difficult.

On the plus side, the route inland was very pretty. The sound of the River Coquet accompanied our every step as we walked through woodland and across fields. We crossed over a wide, solid stone bridge and stopped in the middle of a field for lunch. The grass was soft underneath and Jon had picked a spot with a view. The group chatted away and I could sense everyone relaxing a bit as they got to know each other better and compared sandwiches.

I started talking to a retired doctor about the benefits of walking. She had seen good results with her patients, but she also knew the benefits from her own personal experience. She had suffered from depression and was in no doubt that walking had helped get her through it.

'The trouble is,' she said, 'you can't tell someone who is depressed to get out and exercise more, because they just don't feel like it. I had friends who came with me and we started very gently. Eventually, I had the confidence to go out on my own, and it definitely helped.'

We packed our lunch remains away and headed off again via Pauperhaugh and Thistleyhaugh towards Rothbury. 'Haugh' (pronounced 'hoff') means a flat area next to the river; there used to be a workhouse at Pauperhaugh, so the place was named after poor people living adjacent to the river. I know this because Jon told me. Thistleyhaugh is a thistly area near the river, and Cow Haugh car park is where they used to graze the cows – near the river, of course.

We arrived in Rothbury by mid-afternoon and checked into a rather austere country house that had been converted into a hotel. Our room was a little bit damp and the bathroom had soap in a plastic cover. I started to tell Alice how lovely St Cuthbert's House was but stopped when she gave me a funny look.

We took the hire car to have a little drive around Rothbury and to see Cragside, where Lord Armstrong (of Bamburgh Castle fame) built the first house in the world to use hydroelectric power for its lighting. It was past closing time but I was at the wheel and feeling brave.

'It says "Deliveries Only"! You can't go up there,' chorused Lucy and Alice.

'Oh, come on.' I laughed. 'Let's live a little dangerously. We won't cause any harm and I just want to have a look at the house.'

You can't see anything of the house or the estate from the road, mainly because Lord Armstrong planted 7 million trees. Yes, 7 *million*.

I wish I could tell you more about what Cragside was like but I was too busy looking out for security guards. I think it was Elizabethan in style, but when we got to the top of the drive I panicked because there wasn't anywhere to turn around. So I bumped too quickly over a ramp and drove through the arch. We found ourselves right in front of the house and I kept driving, trying to look as if I knew exactly what I was doing and where I was going.

'Keep moving!' Lucy shouted.

Apparently, the gardens are worth a long visit and the house is fascinating. I put my foot down, my heart racing, and sped out of there as quickly as I could.

We took the car back to the hotel and went for a wander around Rothbury, which has an old-fashioned feel. Most of the shops are independents and it's full of people who actually live and work there, rather than holiday cottages that are empty fifty weeks of the year. The locals are in constant dispute as to whether it's a town or a village, but either way it's very charming and deserves much better than the fame it achieved a year later than I was there as the hiding place of a murderer on the run.

The next morning we set off from Rothbury with Russell Tait, the senior ranger for the Northumberland National Park. Let me paint you a picture of Russell, because it's easy enough. He looks like George Clooney and he ticks off 24-mile walks for fun. He is happily married and lives in Rothbury. He and his wife drive out to the coast sometimes to watch the sunset because, he says, 'It's a lovely way to end the day.' So, he's handsome, athletic, faithful and romantic.

I know, I know. Completely wasted on me and Alice.

Or not, as it happens, because we thoroughly enjoyed his company and left Lucy to drool over his manly perfection. Russell told me that there used to be a racecourse in Rothbury and was thrilled to find someone who was actually interested in that fact. It staged one meeting a year, in April, but was closed in 1965, not long after the railway line had shut down for good.

My God was Russell a walker. I mean a real walker. Not mucking about like us. He didn't stop and pretend to look at the view while getting his breath back, or make out that a shoelace was undone so that he could rest for a minute, or give himself a secret reward of a chocolate eclair every mile. He just strode on, relentlessly. It was quite steep, that climb out of Rothbury to Simonside.

I'd thought I was quite fit until that point, or at least that St Oswald's Way had made me fitter. Turns out you can't get fit in just four days, and I was puffing so much I couldn't talk, which would be fine if I hadn't been trying to make a radio programme. Lucy and Alice had gone red in the face and I found that strangely comforting: at least we would all die together.

We headed up a stone path on the side of the hill built to protect walkers from sinking into the peat and to protect the hill from the erosion caused by footfall and the channels of water that rush down the path, washing vegetation away as they go. It was made from reclaimed stone from the Lancashire cotton mills.

When we had finally hauled our way to the top, Russell stopped to show us the view of the Cheviot, the highest hill in Northumberland. From where I was looking – with my hands on my knees, gasping for air – it looked like a huge dark whale. I needed something to lean against, but there was nothing around. Bloody moorland.

It's so selfish to be that bare. I drank some water and ate a flapjack. That would work, I was sure.

I tried to enjoy the views across to the coast, the North Sea quiet and seemingly calm in the distance.

'How far are we actually walking?' asked Alice, looking alarmed. I never know when answering questions like that whether one should be accurate or just lie so that the person feels better. I went for the latter option.

'Oh, I'm sure it's not much further,' I said. I had no idea. Based on our sections so far, it couldn't be more than fourteen miles. We must be halfway. 'At least we've done all the climbing now.'

I said that last bit for my own benefit and was relieved to see Russell nod and smile. If he was lying to me to make me feel better, I would kill him.

As we climbed the Simonside Hills, Russell told us to keep an eye out for a Duergar, although I was unlikely to see one during daylight hours. Duergars are the Simonside dwarves. They are hairy, ugly, tough little creatures who wear sheepskin coats and hats made of moss. I had heard tales that they took walkers and would roast them on a peat fire. Russell said not to worry as they were usually vegetarian, living on cloudberries, mushrooms, nuts and fruits of the forest . . . but they might lead you astray, perhaps into a bog.

If Russell was telling me this to make me hurry up, it worked. I didn't want still to be on the hillside when dusk fell. He explained that there used to be outlaws in the hills, which is probably where the legend of the Duergars came from. A few people had gone missing but, he assured me, not for many years.

'Duergar spotting' could be a major tourist attraction, and even a new sport. If the Loch Ness Monster could spawn a whole industry, I didn't see why Duergars couldn't do the same.

The heather made it very hard walking until we came into the forest and could walk on a Forestry Commission path. We thought it would make it easier but in fact it became very tiring on the feet. I was feeling guilty that I'd inflicted such a long and difficult walk on Alice. It might put her off for life.

'It's not normally like this,' said Lucy, her face flushed with effort.

Russell grades his walk differently to most guides, who will tell you it is challenging, medium or easy. His walks are ranked according to food.

'I would call this a two-sandwich-and-fruitcake walk,' he said.

I would have called it a three-course-dinner-and-coffee walk.

When the torture finally ended, we bade the George Clooney lookalike goodbye. He was probably going off for an evening stroll of twenty miles or so. We were just hoping our hotel didn't have stairs. As luck would have it, it didn't. It was one of those faded, jaded places where bus parties go before heading off to look at Hadrian's Wall or Alnwick Castle. Our room was down a long corridor and smelt of smoke and damp.

I had stupidly suggested to Lucy that we mix up our accommodation to get a variety of B&Bs and hotels. I don't know why I thought that was a good idea. We decided not to eat at the hotel, which was still in the age of a glass of orange juice being a starter, and went out to a wonderful pub called the Red Lion in Newbrough. Alice and I both ordered the twice-baked cheese soufflé and made little squeaks of joy as we spooned it up. I wanted to pick up the bowl and lick it out but I thought better of it. The other diners might not have appreciated how much we needed that food.

The next day was our final section on St Oswald's Way. We had covered coastline, farmland, heather-covered moorland; we had seen castles, wandered through villages; now we would finish with a bit of ancient history on Hadrian's Wall.

In celebration of St Oswald's Way, we were joined by Gary Campbell, who organized the project partners and funds needed to make it happen, and Martin Paminter, who mapped the route and wrote the guidebook. They agreed that the key to a good long-distance path is a variety of scenery, as well as good signage and clear paths.

'We tried to have a village or a town at the end of each section so there were places to stay, and there are often pubs on the way,' Martin said. Wise chap.

If you're wondering how much money it takes to organize and

launch a long-distance path, I can tell you, because Gary told me. It cost £88,000 to complete the path, and they've worked out that walkers spend on average £80 a day in the local area, taking about seven days to finish the whole walk. Simple maths (which I can't do without a calculator) suggests that walkers are contributing at least £170,000 a year to the local economy. Happy days.

The one thing Gary and Martin can't control is the weather, and for our final day it was chucking it down. Proper, relentless, wet rain. I had my 'showerproof' jacket on and had resigned myself to getting soaked. Alice had decent waterproofs but was looking a little miserable and Lucy just wanted to get the recording done and go home. I won't lie to you – Hadrian's Wall in the rain is grim.

It's not even a wall in most parts. It's a ditch and a few rocks. The actual wall is underneath the military road, its stones having been used to make the foundations in the eighteenth century.

'In my opinion,' Martin said, 'this is the most serious piece of archaeological vandalism our country has ever seen. All that's left is the Vallum [the enormous ditch and mounds that form an essential part of the defence] and all those walls over there.'

He pointed to the small, pretty walls dividing the fields. They were lovely, but they weren't exactly a representation of one of the greatest ever feats of manual engineering. (There are, of course, much better sections of Hadrian's Wall to enjoy; it stretches for eighty miles from the Solway Coast in Cumbria to Newcastle. I'd recommend the 10-mile stretch from the Roman Army Museum run by the Vindolanda Trust past Windshields, Highshield and Hotbank Crags to Housesteads Fort.)

So we were trudging along in the rain feeling sorry for ourselves when we saw the walkers' equivalent of an oasis in the desert. A white van serving coffee! It had 'RAMBLER'S REST' written on the side of it. I started running towards it, worried it might vanish in the rain like a soggy mirage.

'Morning!' said a cheery man in the van.

I was so pleased to see him I started jabbering about coffee and hot chocolate and flapjacks and brownies. I would happily stay here under his awning all day. In a rather pathetic attempt to make our stop seem like a useful part of the programme, I asked him what sort of business he did.

'Oh, I get a steady trade from walkers and cyclists,' he said. 'Today I haven't seen any walkers apart from yourselves but, when the weather's better, we do well.'

In a way, you get a strange sense of pride from walking in really terrible weather. In another way, you just get wet.

Everything around us had a fuzzy quality and, although we could see about five miles into the distance, I couldn't make out any features. Gary told me that we could see south to the Tyne Valley and, if I turned round (I didn't much fancy this because of the rain), I could see the Hexhamshire Moors and the North Pennines.

'Lovely,' I said, pulling my cap further down over my face.

After what seemed like hours we arrived at Heavenfield. This was where Oswald won the battle that made him king. I am not very good at imagining battles, apart from in Wiltshire, where I have clear visions of cavalries coming over opposing hills. This looked like a field to me. A very nice field with a tiny church right in the middle of it. Now that's not something you see every day, especially a church with a bright-red door.

It's the Church of St Oswald. We sat on one of the seven pews and contemplated the end. Not the end of life, the end of the walk. Lucy and I had done it all and, even though we were soggy, exhausted and cold, we felt a surge of achievement and delight. Martin and Gary can be justly proud of what they and the Revd Michael Mountney have created. St Oswald's Way is a varied and exhilarating delight, even in the rain.

Although Lucy and I struggled in parts, we have caught the long-distance-walking bug.

Since then we have done the South Downs Way, which stretches a hundred miles from Eastbourne to Winchester, starting on the coast and then along the high chalk downlands of the South Downs. It was glorious, apart from the section we did with a group of Gurkhas, who do sixty miles of the path as an endurance challenge with heavy packs on their backs. The 'Trailwalker' takes most teams about twenty-seven hours to complete. The record time was set by a team of Gurkhas and stands at nine hours and fifty minutes. I know. It's ridiculous. But even more ridiculous was the sight of me trying to keep up as a charming and fit Gurkha jogged along to show me the pace they set.

England alone has nearly 120,000 miles of rights of way, and we owe a debt of gratitude for their preservation to the Ramblers Association and the Open Spaces Society, who campaigned for years to secure the CROW (Countryside and Rights of Way) Act of 2000. There is so much to explore. Every right of way is there for a reason, a footpath that has existed for centuries as a drovers' path or a way to church or school, a pilgrimage or a trade route. When we walk those paths we tread in the footsteps of our ancestors. We become living history.

There are long-distance paths abroad that I would love to travel, like the Santiago de Compostela in Northern Spain or the Inca Trail in Peru, the GR20 in Corsica, the Lycian Way in Turkey, the Cinque Terre in Italy or the Haute Route from France to Switzerland.

More than any of those, however, I want to do the Dales Way, from Harrogate (which seems a fine place to start) to Bowness in the Lake District. Colin Speakman has written a superb guide to the Dales Way, including a planner showing B&Bs, pubs, shops and cafés. He knows what is needed. He also explains rather beautifully the difference between the daily walk and the epic nature of the long-distance walk:

> Short circular strolls back to the security of the car, whilst welcome, never really shake off that psychological umbilical cord, that invisible chain which draws you back to that little bit of urban living. True freedom is to stride out, for days on end, with a real sense of purpose, which Germans call *Zielwanderung*, or destination walking.

There is perhaps no finer way of understanding the scale and complexity of a landscape and personal satisfaction in achieving that goal than to walk to somewhere special, the twenty-first-century equivalent of a pilgrimage.

I will do the Dales Way with Lucy, Alice and Archie and our friend Sally, who lives near the start. We may do it for *Ramblings*, we may do it purely for pleasure or, most likely, we will combine both. Sally says she will have us to stay as long as Archie behaves himself and doesn't try to get on the sofa or the bed.

We'll see how that goes.

11

Puppy Love

'Your biological clock will be ticking,' predicted Matthew. 'Trust me, you'll be desperate for a baby and you'll be pregnant before your thirty-fifth birthday.'

Matthew Norman is a journalist. I like him. His writing had always amused me and during our years working on the *London Evening Standard* we had found each other a safe port in the storm of the Christmas party. His certainty on this issue baffled me. I had never wanted babies. Never.

'You don't understand,' I said. 'I just want a puppy.'

He laughed. The laugh of a man who is sure he knows.

'A puppy? Don't be ridiculous. I bet you'll be pregnant within the next five years.'

I fell back on an old tactic I had learned when boys at parties didn't think I understood football.

'Fine,' I said. 'We'll have a bet. I'll give you 6:4 on me being pregnant within the next five years.'

He thought it a generous offer – he considered it an odds-on shot. To be honest, I knew it wasn't. I could have offered him 100:1, but I thought I'd better make it sound vaguely likely. There was also the worry in the back of my mind that the ticking of this mythical biological clock might get me in the end.

Matthew didn't hesitate.

'I'll have a thousand pounds at 6:4. Done.' He shook my hand. I was shocked at the amount he was prepared to stake but didn't want to show it. I may have grown up in the racing world, surrounded by gamblers, but I don't bet much myself and certainly not in large amounts.

Eight years later we met up for dinner. His wife was far from impressed at his attempted reading of the female mind and I felt vaguely guilty that Matthew hadn't known at that stage that I was never going to get pregnant by accident – as I wasn't sharing my life, or my bed, with a man.

I took some of the stake – a bet's a bet – but not the whole amount.

As for getting a *puppy* before my thirty-fifth birthday, well, this was a serious business. Not something to be rushed into. My mother, who had been putting me off for years, couldn't really understand the desire to have a dog in London.

'Well, you'll have to get a *London* dog, I suppose,' she said, with her usual slightly contemptuous pronunciation of 'London'.

I had no idea until my mother told me, but apparently a convertible is 'a *London* car' and any pair of suede boots are 'fine, I suppose, for *London*, but totally impractical for the country'. Ditto white jeans, which I was never allowed as a child.

I'm not sure my mother has ever entirely forgiven me for living and working in London. It's a phase that she hopes will pass. One day, she has no doubt, I will see sense and come back home. Then I can have a real dog.

Alice and I had been together for two years. I was fairly certain this was the person with whom I wanted to grow old, but there was one killer question yet to be asked. I was nervous. This was a big step. So I waited for a rare shared day off and popped the big question.

This was the real deal, a statement of commitment that I had never before asked of anyone.

'Would you like . . .' Long pause, while I built up confidence and looked earnest. '. . . to get a dog?' I blurted out.

Where I am a slightly idealistic, romantic dreamer, Alice is a practical soul. She knew that during the long weeks of summer sport or during an Olympics or Commonwealth Games, she would be left in charge of 'the dog'.

There was also the problem of allergies. Alice is asthmatic and allergic to horse hair, cat hair and dog hair.

There was silence. I wondered what I would do if she said no. I blew air out of the side of my mouth, waiting for the answer. Finally, it came.

'I think that's a lovely idea.'

Three months later, we were on our way to Gloucestershire to see a litter of Tibetan terrier puppies. The breed was hypoallergenic, non-shedding, medium-sized, good travellers, protective of their owners, intelligent and biddable, and Alice had decided that this was the dog we should have. I didn't mind which breed we chose – I hadn't really got that far in my head – I was just beside myself with excitement that we were actually getting a puppy.

We had contacted reputable Kennel Club registered breeders and were told that a litter had just been born in which there may be one puppy available. Knowing how my mother was with potential owners of her boxer puppies, I realized that this visit was as much about us proving ourselves responsible owners as it was about us choosing a puppy. Good breeders will always vet their buyers as thoroughly as they would their dogs.

We met the mother first, who was a sweet, kind bitch with short-cropped hair. Tibetan terriers can grow hair down to the ground – show dogs all have long, flowing hair – but for functional, pet-owning reasons, a regular haircut is necessary. After plenty of questions about our working hours, our house, the size of our garden, the proximity to a park and our relationship, we were finally allowed to see the litter of puppies.

Oh. My. Word. No bigger than the palm of my hand, these little balls of fluff were play-fighting in their large pen. I climbed in and sat in the corner. Within seconds, they were all over me, chewing my hair, batting me with their paws and sliding down the sides of my legs like children at a theme park.

'The bitches are all taken,' explained Ken, the breeder, 'and two of the boys have gone, so there's just one left. It's the white one over there.'

Ken pointed to the smallest of the litter. He was a little nervous and quieter than his brothers and sisters. As if he knew he was being talked about, he chose that moment to climb along my legs, up my chest and towards my face. I put my arm under him to support him and he started to suck on my chin.

'Well, he knows how to make a girl feel special,' I said.

'He's just gone for the bit that sticks out the most.' Alice laughed. She winked at me. We were sold.

Percy, for that would be his name, was ours.

Alice went back to collect Percy when he was eight weeks old. I couldn't wait to get home to see him and, as I came through the front door, I could hear noises from the kitchen. I got down on all fours and called him. He came running along the hallway and skidded to a halt in front of me, jumping up to lick my face. I picked him up; he was all soft and cuddly.

'Group hug,' I said to Alice. 'Now we're a family.'

Percy was never the bravest little soldier. He got himself up the stairs and then couldn't work out how to get down again, so he stood peering from the top step as I waited halfway.

'Come on, you can do it,' I said encouragingly. 'Just one step at a time.' He slid down the first one, stopped and then took the next at greater speed. He lost his balance and tumbled into my arms. I set him back on his feet and made him take the remaining six stairs slowly. He picked it up and soon was haring up and down the stairs, just because he could.

His white hair wasn't the easiest to deal with and, not surprisingly, my mother was horrified. A white dog? Good Lord, how *London* can you get? He developed little brown marks under his eyes, and no matter which magic tear-stain-removal lotion Alice tried, they wouldn't go away. On the plus side, his white hair was as soft as silk and he was the cuddliest little chap.

Even Alice's mother, who is not a dog person, fell for him,

'Oh darling, he's divine,' she said on first meeting. 'But he looks like a teddy bear, honestly he does. Are you sure he's a dog?'

A few weeks later, she proved her point by giving us a teddy bear that looked just like him, and we played spot the difference. Other than the scarf on the teddy bear, there wasn't much to tell them apart.

We bought every bit of dog kit on the market – from puppy pads (newspaper wasn't good enough) to organic dog food, dental-brush chews to designer collar and dog bed. Percy wanted for nothing. Yes, he was spoilt. Yes, we let him on the sofa. Yes, we probably weren't strict enough, but we adored him. Absolutely adored him.

You make a deal when you get an animal, and I knew that better than anyone. We'd had dogs, horses and ponies all my childhood and I knew that the love came at a price. You had to learn the hard way that there is an equation of love to pain and, the more you love, the more it will hurt when you lose what you love.

We had one Christmas with Percy. He was an angel. He was even more excited by Christmas stockings than me, and that takes some doing. He had presents of his own from everyone – including my mother, much against her better judgement. My father, who thought him the most ridiculous dog, was impressed when he saw him bounding through the fields at home, his legs black with mud and his coat heavy with rain.

'He's a tough little thing, isn't he? Shame he's white but, hey ho, I suppose you girls will keep him clean,' he said.

Poor Percy spent most of his life in the bath, one way or another.

When Alice had late shifts I had him for company, and when I was away covering sport, she had him. He gave purpose to our days. Every morning we'd be out in the sun or the rain walking to the park. We trained him to sit and stay, to come when called and to give us his paw in a handshake on cue.

We discovered local parks we had no idea existed and stumbled upon a whole new social world of dog owners. It may be considered weird to start a conversation with a complete stranger in the park, but it's not at all strange if your dogs bound up to each other and sniff each other's bums. Maybe life would be easier if we were more brazen, but it certainly helps that our dogs can do the introductions for us, getting the awkward bit out of the way.

Suddenly you have a network of friends, all of whose dogs you can name and age before you've quite worked out whether their owner said her name was Jocelyn or Jemima. Our London friends are all fellow dog walkers and, because we see each other nearly every day, we know more than we probably should about each other's lives.

Derek and Chris own a fencing company and a timber merchant's but, more importantly, they have a whippet called Sid who shakes when he hears loud noises. Bonfire Night, Diwali and New Year's Eve are all a nightmare for poor Sid, who lies trembling in a corner. We always know when Derek is tipsy because he starts hugging everyone and telling us all how much he loves us.

'We're family, aren't we?' he says, again and again.

The most glamorous member of our group is Dariel. Until fairly recently, her age was a mystery, and I will not reveal it here. She has a Tibetan terrier called Sunny who is very calm and sensible – until the postman puts his hand through the door, at which point he goes nuts.

Dariel glides through the park in designer clothes, rarely looking ruffled. However, she has a worrying ability to break bones. On holiday in Corfu with the gang (dogs left at home, apart from Sid, who likes the sun and the swimming pool), she broke her ankle coming out of the local shop. It was ten o'clock in the morning so, as she told her husband, Harry, on the phone, she was not drunk. Maggie, who runs a sheltered housing unit, was also there, and her nursing skills came to the fore and she took Dariel to the local hospital, with her passport as proof of identity. This meant that Maggie found out her date of birth, but despite generous amounts of alcohol, offers of bribes and brute force, she would not be broken. Dariel hobbled around on crutches for the rest of the holiday, still managing to look admirably glamorous.

We get together for evening meals at dog-friendly pubs and we laugh a lot. We have a New Year's Eve tradition of swapping our worst Christmas presents in a weird distortion of Secret Santa. Alice has a pair of revolting frog slippers that Maggie had been given, Derek is the proud owner of a laughing gnome and Jocelyn now has a pair of XXL boxer shorts that light up to read 'Happy Christmas'. We got together despite our different jobs, different backgrounds, different family situations and different ages. We became friends through our dogs.

For each one of us, our dog is an essential member of the family and a part of our relationship. We also know that we will outlive our dogs and will have to comfort each other when we lose them. What we hope is that we'll get a good length of time with them before the inevitable happens. With Percy, Alice and I did not have that luxury.

It was Easter Monday and, perhaps for the first time ever, we both had a bank-holiday Monday off. We took Percy to Gunnersbury Park, threw a tennis ball, practised his recall, and laughed at him venturing near strange dogs then bolting back to us.

Safely home, I remembered I'd left something in the car, so I popped out to get it and, as I came in, Percy slipped past me on to the garden path. The gate on to the pavement, normally closed, was ajar.

'Percy, come!' I called. 'Percy – good boy – come!'

He turned and looked at me and, for the only time in his life, wilfully ignored a command. We lived in a quiet, residential street. It wasn't a cut-through road. Cars didn't come down there fast. Not usually.

The following week, Alice stood on that road for an hour and only one car came past, slowly.

So why, at that moment, on that day, at the exact moment that Percy decided to step into the road, did there have to be a car? Why? And why did it have to be going so fast?

It happened in an instant. I heard the car, I was calling Percy, I was running into the road. I heard the thud. Percy squealed as he was thrown into the air. The driver stopped. I was by Percy's side. I could hear a voice saying, 'Percy's been hit, he's been hit by a car.' It was my voice.

Alice came out of the house to find me cradling his head in my lap. He had let out a big gasp of breath and weed himself in the street. I know now that was the moment he died.

The driver was apologizing, saying he had been in a hurry because he was going to see his sister in hospital. I can't remember what either of us said, but I remember being incredibly polite. Again a voice that sounded like mine said, 'Don't worry, it's not your fault. It's my fault. I shouldn't have let him out. I'm so sorry, I'm so sorry.' This last bit was said into Percy's ear, my face buried in his. Alice told the driver to go away, firmly but politely, and we carried Percy into the house.

I did what I always do in moments of complete panic. I called my mother. She said to wrap him in a blanket, keep him warm and, if he was still breathing, to get him to a vet as soon as possible.

I only remember fragments of the next hour. The confusion about where to find the only vet open on a bank holiday. Me trying to give Percy mouth-to-mouth in the car. My father ringing to say he was at Kempton racecourse and Simon the vet could come to the house if we needed him. Carrying Percy into the vet's surgery when we eventually found one. Kicking the boxes in the corner of the room and screaming when she said, 'I'm so sorry. He's gone.'

Even now, when I drive past that 24-hour vet's surgery, I feel the sharp needle of pain.

My mother rang again. I told her he was dead. We wanted to bring him down to the country to bury him there, and she said she'd meet us. We drove in silence, Percy wrapped in a blanket in a box on the back seat. When we arrived, my mother was waiting. She had organized for a hole to be dug in the dry riverbed so that we could bury him.

My mother is not one for public displays of affection or wildly emotional scenes, but that was the most considerate thing anyone could have done.

'I think you should both come for a walk,' she said. 'You can't stay here all day crying, and it will do you good.'

Now that I know about the bereavement walking group in Shropshire, I know this was the best thing she could have suggested.

So we went for a walk with Mum and her boxers, Molly and Ruby. We didn't say much. There wasn't much to say. We couldn't stay and we didn't want to go home. We were without a safe place, and all we had was us. We held each other and cried. Big, gulping sobs of grief.

When we eventually drove back to London, there was a small indentation on the sofa where Percy had last lain. His toys were all over the floor and his lead was hanging over the banister. The house was empty. And quiet. In the morning I thought it might all have been a horrible nightmare, but when I came down to the kitchen all I saw was the gaping hole in our lives where he used to be.

Alice went to the park the next day by herself. She sat on a bench and cried. A well-dressed woman with a black-and-white Tibetan terrier sat next to her and asked her what had happened. Alice told her everything, and soon Dariel was holding her in her arms as she sobbed. That is how Dariel became our friend, along with Derek and Chris, David and Jocelyn, Maggie and Richard, Toby and Martin. They all understood.

My father is a good letter writer. He wrote to me a few times at school, once at university and a couple of times since. The letter he wrote after Percy died was a masterpiece. It was to both of us. He told us how much he had enjoyed seeing us with Percy and how happy we looked, how good we were as dog owners and how much we cared. He told us that he had once run over his mother's dog and how awful it had been. He also pointed out, gently, that the good thing about loving a dog is that you can get another dog who you will love equally, if not more. You cannot replace a person when they die, but you can replace, if not the dog, at least the dog-shaped space.

We did fill the dog-shaped hole in our lives, and we now have Archie.

Archie is nine years old and still looks like a puppy. He is far from perfect, but he's ours. We walk him together as often as we can, we laugh at him running through the park or despair at him rolling in something smelly. Our time with him is 'family time' but without the pressure of worrying what his school report says or what subjects he should do for GCSE. He is quite naughty and has just recently started stealing food off the kitchen counter; one evening we got back home to find he'd eaten half a loaf of soda bread that had been sitting by the toaster. (His stomach gurgled, and let's just say he was still suffering the effects the following morning.)

Our daily walks with Archie mean that Alice and I get precious time together. We remember things half an hour into a walk that we've forgotten to tell each other, and we can discuss decisions about work or life without the distraction of phones or email. We fall into a rhythm and we explore our local parks or the countryside together.

Walking. It can be a medicine for grief, a key to love, a therapy for illness. It can lift your spirits from the depths.

Litchfield–Cannon Heath Down

I hadn't noticed it before, but Mum, Alice and I look as if we are dressed for a team competition. We are all wearing the same shade of powder blue. Mum is in a jacket I gave her, Alice is in one of my sleeveless jackets and I am wearing a fleece top of my own.

I could open a shop selling jackets or jumpers in exactly that shade of blue. Any time we go shopping, I find something and say, 'Isn't this nice?'

'Yes. And it's exactly the same colour as 50 per cent of your wardrobe,' Alice mutters.

Of course I buy it anyway, and every six months or so I go through my clothes to share them around, to give everyone a little bit of blue in their life.

One of the benefits of walking so much is that I have lost a lot

Wayfarer's Walk

of weight. This is all down to my mother. In the summer of 2013 I had got rather tubby. I knew it, Alice knew it and the TV camera most certainly knew it. I caught sight of myself on a monitor at the Newmarket July meeting and I was appalled. I looked as if I'd been blown up with a bicycle pump. The same week, my mother phoned Alice.

'I think Clare and I both need to lose weight,' she said. 'I'll take her on in a competition.'

'That's my mother telling *me* I need to lose weight,' I said to Alice grumpily.

'No,' she said. 'I genuinely don't think it is. She wants to lose a few pounds and she knows you'll egg her on, and vice versa.'

I emailed my mother and said I was willing to take on the challenge. We would give ourselves three months and have a bet: £100 per pound shed to whoever lost more. If we put on any weight between the end date and Christmas, the money was to be paid back. We all need an incentive and the double whammy of winning a competition and money from my mother was the perfect calorie-controlled carrot for me.

There have been a couple of times since I had my thyroid removed in 2006 that I have tried to lose weight, but I didn't keep at it for very long. My doctor had told me that thyroxine would boost my metabolism into action and that I would be able to eat pretty much what I wanted. I took him at his word and stuffed my face.

I remembered a conversation I'd had with the world-champion open-water swimmer Keri-Anne Payne in the autumn of 2012.

'I meant to lose half a stone before the Olympics,' I told her. 'But looking back on it now, I'm not sure it would have made any difference.'

'Oh, it would have done,' she replied.

'Thanks a lot!' I laughed, thinking she was being a little more honest than I desired.

Then she explained: 'You'd have been obsessed with what you were eating, or not eating. Your concentration would've been affected, your energy levels would have dropped and you'd have suffered because you wouldn't have got through those long days or remembered all the things you had to remember. It would definitely have made a difference – in a bad way.'

It was the first time anyone had talked to me about a diet as a negative thing. I had spent my life associating eating with greed rather than necessity. Now I realized that you have to pick your time to lose weight, and the summer of 2012 was not a good time for me to be mucking about with my calorie intake. The summer of 2013 was a different matter, and I'd got to a stage where I knew I had to do something about it. Instead of lying in bed dreaming of taking exercise, I would actually do it.

The worst part was standing on the scales. I hadn't weighed myself since my racing days and I didn't want to look. It was bad, but on the plus side, I was starting at a much higher point than my mother: in terms of our challenge I could probably lose more.

On 14 July Alice and I went on a few days' break to Devon and Cornwall. I downloaded an app called 'My Fitness Pal' and entered everything I ate and drank into the phone. It gave me

Wayfarer's Walk

1,200 calories a day but I could earn back calories if I exercised. Alice agreed to do it with me, which was sweet of her, as she weighs less than eight stone and has never needed to diet in her life. Poor Archie didn't know what had hit him as we started pounding up the slopes of Dartmoor, sweating buckets, then doing sit-ups on top of the tor.

Every day, I stuck to my calorie intake. If I had calories to spare, I could have a treat, like a mini packet of Maltesers (99 calories) or a Guylian sea shell (54 calories). We bought low-fat butter, low-fat mayonnaise and low-calorie ready-made meals. Plus, we walked. After a week, I felt my trousers becoming looser, and then the pounds started falling off. After three months, I had lost thirty pounds. Mum had lost ten, which isn't bad, but was still twenty pounds less than me. You do the math, as the Americans say.

Between October and Christmas I even lost a few more pounds. By the night of *BBC Sports Personality of the Year* I had lost two and a half stone, and it showed. Double Olympic gold medallist Becky Adlington was in raptures.

'I just can't believe it,' she said. 'I just can't believe it. You look *amazing*! I kept saying to Harry [her boyfriend], "Look at Clare, just look at Clare!" In the end I think he was getting a bit worried about me but, honestly, I just can't believe it.'

Swimmers are very aware of their bodies and they are used to the calorie intake/outtake exchange, but it was all new to me. I was a bit surprised that everyone noticed, although it was lovely to be able to wear an outfit that I felt really comfortable in and that I knew made me look streamlined. It's hard enough presenting a big TV programme without constantly worrying whether your bum, tum and arms 'look big in this' and knowing that the answer is undoubtedly 'yes'.

There is an obsession in this country with how people look, and women are particularly targeted. What I say on any programme never gets as much comment or attention as how I look. I have learned to live with that. Ted Walsh, who works on *Channel 4 Racing* at Cheltenham, said to me, 'Jeez, I wouldn't want to be a woman for anything! All they're saying over there is "I liked what Clare wore yesterday better" or "That colour looks nice." My God, it's like you're just a clothes horse.'

I don't much enjoy having my photo taken, knowing that it will inevitably lead to discussions about my figure and what I'm wearing. I'm happiest in a pair of jeans and a jumper, and no make-up. I never blow-dry my hair and I rarely brush it. Only recently did I have a few highlights put in it for the first time, to brighten it up over the winter months.

Having said all that, I have more energy now, and it's easier to dress for an occasion because I am not trying to hide my tummy with a scarf. It's a sense of shame we carry, but it's also confirmed by a society that does not value the fuller-figured woman.

I am walking in front of my mother on the smooth, chalky downland turf when she says, 'You aren't going to lose any more weight, are you?'

'No,' I reply cheerily. 'I'm not even counting calories now. Just walking every day and doing my ten thousand steps.'

Wayfarer's Walk

'Good,' she says. 'Because I think you're just perfect as you are.'

I swing round and smile at her. The joke has always been that my brother can do no wrong and is Peter Perfect.

'I've been waiting my whole life to hear you say that, Mum,' I laugh.

We go through a gate on to a deeply rutted muddy track. The sign reads 'BYWAY' and, looking at the ruts, it seems that every vehicle that could use it has done.

'You'd need a tractor to get down this,' I say. Then we hear the roar of a motorbike and see a helmeted man coming towards us. 'Or a bike.'

The track leads to the new A34, built to bypass Newbury's gridlocked roundabouts in the mid-nineties. There was a big protest about the woods that would be destroyed – the 'Third Battle of Newbury' (after the two during the Civil War). Eco-warriors dangled from trees and dug underground tunnels, where they hid to prevent heavy machinery moving. The last protestor to be removed from the tunnels came from the New-bury area; his name was Daniel Hooper but he was better known as Swampy.

It caused quite a stir and put Newbury in the headlines daily. The broadcaster and botanist David Bellamy addressed a meet-ing of protestors and, in February 1996, five thousand people marched. Their cries fell on ears which did not want to hear and the bypass was completed by the end of 1998. Walking towards it, you see the lorries rattling along before you hear them. Weirdly, the noise doesn't hit you until you are nearly underneath it.

On our right is a stone memorial marking a piece of aviation history:

Geoffrey de Havilland, assisted by Frank Hearle, carried out his first flight in his home-made aeroplane here at Seven Barrows on 10 September 1910.

It may sound as if a Boy Scout was experimenting with a toy, but the 5th Earl of Carnarvon (the same one who funded the discovery of Tutankhamun's tomb) had encouraged de Havilland and his team to base themselves at Highclere, and he witnessed that first biplane flight. He was said to be 'elated at the success which attended the efforts of the flying men'.

You can just imagine the thrill and the danger of those early flights, defying gravity and nature with science. De Havilland moved from Highclere to work for the Royal Aircraft Factory in Farnborough, Airco in Hendon and, finally, set up the de Havilland Aircraft Company. He designed aircraft used in both World Wars, including the Gypsy Moth and the Mosquito. He was knighted in 1944 and continued flying until he was seventy. What a life.

The ability to take flight for a few yards would serve us well now we are at the A34. The dual carriageway cuts right across the Wayfarer's Walk and the route across is not straightforward,

Wayfarer's Walk

unless you want to take on the traffic. We follow the way marked by a board and turn right, heading uphill on a slippery, filthy track.

Mum suggests we walk further into the field, where it is drier, but I can see a fence up ahead where we need to turn left into the underpass, and I think we'll get stuck the wrong side of it if we don't keep to the path. Five muddy minutes later, with Boris pulling Mum one way and another, we realize I am wrong. We could have avoided the ankle-deep mud altogether.

My mother restrains herself from saying 'I told you so', because we now have a bigger problem to overcome. Flooding.

'Shall I send Boris through to see how deep it is?' my mother suggests.

Boris is enthusiastic about most things but, after putting a toe gingerly in the murky water, he turns his wrinkled face towards us and I could swear he shakes his head. The water is too deep. We will have to find another way. I consult my phone and decide that if we carry on towards Litchfield we can cross under the A34 and pick up a footpath that eventually links to the Wayfarer's Walk.

Dad has tried to call again. He wants to know what time he should meet us on the Downs to walk the last section. Mum tells him we have had to take a bit of a diversion and will call him when we are closer. He rings again five minutes later. Mum ignores him.

'He'll just want to know if I've seen his glasses, because he'll have lost them,' she says. 'Or it'll be his diary, or his all-colour biro.'

It was the soundtrack of my childhood.

'*Emma! Ems*, where are you?' Dad would shout. 'I can't find my . . . [fill in the gap]. Where is it?'

I would've shouted back 'How the hell do I know?' and made him find it himself, but my mother is more tolerant. Forty-five years on, and she's still helping him find the things he has lost.

We pound up the hill towards Litchfield. Our limbs are feeling the effort by now – being forced into a diversion when you are walking is mentally as well as physically demanding. A mile or two out of your way seems like a marathon. Especially if you won't listen to your mother.

Mum says we should cut back parallel to the A34 to link up with the walk where it meets the underpass, but I have a better idea. I think we can carry on up another steep hill and then cut left on a track opposite Down Farm and link up again near Ladle Hill and Sydmonton. This is a fine plan, until we get to the top of the hill and see a sign on the left that reads 'PRIVATE ROAD'. My mother is more respectful of private property than either my father or my brother, so we think it best to continue on the foot-path. We know we are less than seven miles from home and that we'll recognize our local area soon enough.

Archie has picked up heavy mud on the path to the flooded underpass and it is compacting in his toes. He's limping and keeps rolling on the path, as if to remove some kind of itch. I want to find a stream to wash his feet off but, without an OS map, I don't know where one would be. Luckily, I can see a trough up ahead that is a hangover from an old field boundary;

Wayfarer's Walk

it isn't used any more by sheep or cattle but is still there, gathering water. I lift Archie up and Alice washes his feet – mud, stones and bits of hedge come from between his toes. No wonder he has been so uncomfortable. He shakes himself thoroughly and trots off up the path. A dog transformed.

Archie is happy, Boris has settled down into a fairly controlled gait and the sun is shining. The only problem is our location, or lack of it.

One field looks much like another and we are coming at the Downs from a direction we've never come from before. My mother grew up in Kingsclere and has lived there all her adult life. That's over fifty years of riding, walking and driving in the area.

'Why didn't you bring a map?' she asks me.

'Because I knew I had you,' I reply, staring at the photos I've taken of a map on my phone. The trouble is, we aren't on the Wayfarer's Walk any more and we've gone off the side of the map. I have no idea where we are.

'Why don't we ring Ian?' says Alice. That's my dad.

'No!' Mum and I respond in unison.

We don't want to admit to him that we are lost and, anyway, we can't tell him where to come and get us because we are *lost*. We can't see the mast at Hannington, but I reckon if we turn left and head a bit further up to the brow of the next hill, we will get our bearings. There are no longer any footpath signs so we follow the wide verges of fields in the hope that we are more or less obeying the laws of the countryside.

Eventually we see signs we recognize for Cannon Heath Farm

(our home downs are Cannon Heath Down, so we have to be close). We spot the mast in the distance and I can see the ghastly white fencing that Dad has put along the Downs to stop people straying on to the gallops. It's not that he doesn't want them to enjoy the space and the views, it's to prevent them leaving the detritus of picnics in the middle of a stretch where a bunch of two-year-olds will gallop.

By now we are all quite tired and conversation is limited to where we are going and whether or not it's time to ring Dad. I can see a man in a tractor having his sandwiches and an apple, so I decide the best policy is just to ask how we can get to where we're going.

'Oh, hello,' he says when I appear at his cab door. 'Where are you going to then?'

I explain that we have walked the Wayfarer's Walk from Combe Gibbet, but we've had to divert for flooding and are a bit lost. He's wearing a jacket that reads 'SYDMONTON FARMS', part of the estate owned by Andrew Lloyd Webber.

'Oh, I know where you're meant to be,' says the man. 'My wife did it last year. Lovely walk. You're well off track, aren't you?'

I look sheepish.

'Never mind. Head for those three trees over there [he pointed half a mile in the distance] and you'll be back on your downs. I'll just ring the gamekeeper and tell him I've sent you that way.'

We couldn't be more grateful. He is basically giving us permission to cut a corner and, when the gamekeeper comes rattling along in his four-wheel drive with his baby on the seat beside

Wayfarer's Walk

him, it is only to say hello and check we are all right. The kindness of strangers is what gets you through when you make mistakes in life.

In the distance I can see Dad's blue Jimny. I look at my phone. Five missed calls. Mum looks at hers. Six missed calls. He's a bit impatient, my father. Suddenly the car starts moving in the wrong direction. He's heading home.

'Quick, call him!' Mum says, panic rising in her voice. She has come such a long way, but the thought of the final mile or two home is too much. We have gone so far off our route that all of us are running on empty. I call Dad and tell him to wait.

He is shaking his head as we approach the gate.

'What are you doing coming from that direction?' he asks, as Mac the lurcher sniffs around for something to kill, totally uninterested in us or Boris or Archie.

'Oh, it's a long story,' I say, not wanting to admit we'd got lost. 'We were forced into a diversion and it's taken us this way. Lovely farmer said we could cut across and, in fact, we've all decided that we'll do the last section from Ladle Hill to home another time, with the whole family. You can come, too, if you like. It's only about seven miles and it'll be lovely.'

As I am inventing my alternative plan, Archie takes a decision on behalf of us all and jumps into the car. He's had enough. Alice and I cram into the back seat, where Archie lies between us and instantly falls asleep. Mum gets in the front with Boris, and Dad puts Mac in the boot, from where he hangs his head between us, not wanting to miss any of the action.

For the next three days I am convinced I have shin splints. I wake up in the middle of the night and in the morning I'm in agony. 'I think I've fractured my leg,' I say.

'That's quite dramatic,' says Alice. 'Here, rub some of this on it and you'll be fine.'

She hands me some Deep Heat. It isn't quite the level of sympathy I'm expecting, but it is all I'm going to get. Two days later, I feel fine again.

'My fracture has healed itself,' I confirm.

'Gosh,' says Alice. 'You are a medical miracle. And so brave.'

Wayfarer's Walk

12

Unbelievable

It was barely a quarter of a mile, probably only eight hundred steps.
But it was one of the most important walks of my life.

I was wearing a white tracksuit bearing a sticker with the number
053. In my hand was a gold, conical torch about two feet in length. I
was unbelievably nervous, my hands sweating and my legs judder-
ing. I was just one of the eight thousand people chosen to carry the
Olympic flame and I was going to do it down a section of the high
street in my home town of Newbury.

Newbury – the place where Dad did his Christmas shopping in
one mad dash in Camp Hopson on Christmas Eve, weaving in and
out of the people on the pavements as if he was dodging tackles in
a high-paced game of rugby, with Andrew and I trying to keep up.
Newbury – where I passed my driving test, where I went to the doctor, where I won an amateur race on Song of Sixpence in 1990 and

appeared on television for the very first time, red-faced and out of breath.

On 11 July 2012 the high street was packed with children in school uniform, people with cameras and casual onlookers caught up in the moment. The crowds were five and six deep and among them were my parents, my sister-in-law, Anna Lisa, my nephews, Jonno and Toby, and Alice. Dad hadn't really wanted to come – he thought it would be difficult to park – but my mother had eventually talked him into it.

I had been nominated to carry the torch by my bank manager at Lloyds, which was one of the supporting sponsors for the torch relay. I have no idea whether it was a reward for not being overdrawn or not bouncing a cheque, but it was a wonderful act of kindness. If it was intended to ensure I bank with them for infinity, it's worked.

I left early in the morning to go to the meeting point, which I thought was in Newbury but in fact was the village hall in Thatcham, so, half an hour later than everyone else, I walked into a large room where everyone was having a briefing. There were about thirty of us and we had to introduce ourselves to the group. Everyone else was being rewarded for raising huge amounts of money for charity or being a pillar of the community or had been nominated by their co-workers. I tried to think of a good story or a solid reason why I should carry the Olympic torch, but I'm not a very good liar so I just told the truth.

'I was nominated by Brendan, my bank manager,' I said.

They all laughed. I think they thought I was joking.

Aaron, one of the enthusiastic, healthy-looking young things working full time on the torch relay, told us what would happen. He made sure we appreciated the honour we had been given.

'Remember that, when you're carrying the torch,' he said, 'you're the only person in the world in charge of the Olympic Flame.'

Aaron explained how the lighting process would work – essentially, they would do it all for us and there was no need to worry, as it would absolutely, definitely work and we would not be left holding an empty torch, knowing that the Olympic Flame had become extinguished in our hands. This was a relief.

I met Emma, a sixteen-year-old who has raised thousands for research into the rare kidney disease from which she suffers, and Reg, a former RAF navigator who has also worked tirelessly for charity. Emma would pass the flame to me, and I would hand it on to Reg. When the torches touched and the flame went from one to the other (with a lot of help from Aaron's team), it was known as 'the Kiss'.

I went into a room to get changed out of my jeans and into my tracksuit and found two men with a bunch of toy cars. I thought it a bit strange until they explained that they used the toy trucks and cars to show us how the convoy would work. I had missed that bit because I'd arrived late, so they gave me the benefit of a personal demonstration. Eventually I asked them to leave so that I could change into my special Olympic torch-bearing tracksuit.

The tracksuit fitted (always a relief) but I instantly regretted my choice of shoes. Everyone else was wearing smart white trainers. The woman I met when I came out of the changing room told me she'd bought hers especially for the occasion. She looked at my scruffy brown trainers with frayed laces from ten years of wear and I think I saw pity in her eyes. I had gone for comfort in the mistaken belief that I would have to walk or run a long way. I should've favoured style.

I went to the loo three or four more times before we were finally called into our white minibus with 'Moment to Shine' written on the side of it. I took photos of everyone else and of the array of twenty-four torches in their special holders. There were people on the streets of Thatcham and all along the A4, the crowds building up as we got towards Newbury. After weeks of rain we had a gap in the weather and the sun was shining. It seemed like a miracle, and it meant that everyone waiting had a smile on their face.

We cheered as fourteen-year-old Tom got off for the first leg, and wished him luck. The clapping and hollering got louder per person but quieter in total as each person disembarked. I was glad I wouldn't be the final one left on board. I'm not sure I could've taken the pressure.

Emma got off the minibus looking calm and controlled. She is a very together young woman. I was a wreck, and I knew it was my turn next. I stood up to take my torch from Aaron. I looked out of the window at the crowds, their faces full of expectation and excitement. My legs went wobbly. I took the torch in my hands and felt its latticed sides, grateful that the thousands of little holes meant it wasn't a slippery surface and that it shouldn't fall out of my sweaty hands. It was heavier than I expected but I couldn't tell if that was the torch or the weakness of my own muscles.

'Are you OK?' asked Aaron.

I nodded back, incapable of speech. I kept looking at all those people and thinking how special this was. It was a moment I wanted to last for ever and yet couldn't wait to get over and done with. I stumbled down the stairs of the minibus and, in the crowd, as I recovered myself, I saw Uncle Toby with my cousin Camilla, who had driven up from London to bring him. I had no idea he would be there and it was pure luck that the bus had stopped right opposite where he was standing.

Uncle Toby had a stroke a few years ago and he is nearly blind, but he has always made an effort to be there for important occasions and he doesn't let lack of sight stop him. He was at Towcester when AP McCoy (whose first job in the UK was riding for him) rode his record 4,000th winner, and he wanted to be in Newbury when I carried the Olympic torch. I let him hold it, and he leaned over to whisper in my ear.

'Well done, girl,' he said. 'I'm very proud of you.'

Well, that set me off. The schoolchildren around him wanted to hold the torch, so everyone got a go and as many photos as we could manage. I crossed the road to try to find Alice, and finally saw her. My nephews had made their way to the front with Anna Lisa, and my parents weren't far behind. Jonno held the torch and couldn't understand why it wasn't lit yet. I explained that the flame would pass to me like a relay baton. I looked at my father, and his bottom lip was wobbling. My mother smiled as she said, 'For God's sake, don't get over-emotional. Try to pull yourself together.'

The crowds started to clap as they saw the Olympic Flame coming down the high street, grey-tracksuited runners on either side of Emma, a yellow-and-white car behind and then a big bus. It looked very different to the toy trucks on the table.

Emma was nearing the end of her leg and, as she came jogging towards me, I tried to control the tears and grinned as wide as I could. We met in the middle of the high street and I put my torch out to hers. Someone fiddled with buttons and suddenly her flame had gone out and mine was lit. It was like magic, but with less sleight of hand. I held the torch up high and the crowd roared.

I walked at first – until one of the grey-shirted guardians of the flame whispered, 'It looks better if you run . . .'

The 350 metres went in a flash. Beaming faces, people shouting, children waving, three people wearing Royal Family masks hanging out of a window above Boots. It was overwhelming. I passed the flame on to Reg and stared at my torch, now empty of fire and its wires clipped so that it can never be lit again. People sent me photographs after the event that showed the crowds, and in every one all I can see are smiling faces.

I have no idea what I said afterwards to Radio Berkshire, or how I got home. It seems like a precious dream.

Later that day I took the torch to Kingsclere Primary School, where thirty years before I had been reprimanded for fighting in the playground. The children all wanted to touch it and we spent an hour having photos taken of them holding it. It had a magic quality, that torch, and the relay connected people to the idea of the Olympics long before the athletes arrived in this country. It made us all feel included, as if we were part of this great big team that would deliver a sporting spectacular. It embodied the essence of teamwork, the result of years of planning and the cooperation of people in towns and villages up and down the land. And I got to be a part of that relay thanks to Brendan the bank manager. Funny how life works.

That short walk with the Olympic torch started the most significant adventure of my working life, but the build-up to the Games didn't all go smoothly.

I hosted a ceremony to unveil a massive Countdown Clock in Trafalgar Square. There was dry ice, and Olympic rowers pulled a rope which moved a screen to reveal the clock counting down to the hour of the opening ceremony. I interviewed the London mayor, Boris Johnson, and Jess Ennis, heptathlete star and gold-medal favourite. The crowd whooped.

Twenty-four hours later, the clock stopped.

There was a comedy called *Twenty Twelve* on the BBC in the weeks before the Olympic Games started. It satirized the planning behind the Games, and the script included a similar scenario about a countdown clock. I messaged Hugh Bonneville, who played the lead role of the 'Head of Deliverance', saying, 'You are acting out my life.'

Then it started raining, and it didn't stop for weeks. Perhaps because of the rain, the Hammersmith Flyover, which provides the main route from Heathrow Airport into Central London, developed a fracture and was closed for repair work. The security firm G4S admitted that they didn't have the staff to cover the venues, so the army had to be drafted in. Then, at one of the first events, staged early to get the football tournament off and running, the North Korean women's team walked off the pitch and refused to play after their images were shown on the big screen next to the South Korean flag.

We all started to get nervous. Would the nay-sayers be proved right? Could London 2012 be a complete farce?

Finally, the day of the opening ceremony arrived. I had been to one of the rehearsals two days before, when we were urged to 'Save the Secret' by not revealing any of the details on social media. We saw the trees and grass disappear and, in their place, appearing from underground came the chimneys and wheels of the Industrial Revolution, we heard Emeli Sandé sing 'Abide With Me', we saw nurses and children bouncing on beds, but most of the key elements, such as Bradley Wiggins tolling the bell or Rowan Atkinson playing the repeated note of the *Chariots of Fire* theme or the Queen jumping out of a helicopter, were kept completely secret.

I was back in the stadium for the real thing, standing at the bottom interviewing Suffragettes and factory workers, talking to members of the public, who were being allowed to stand on the infield of the athletics track, trying to give an idea on TV of what it was like to be in the midst of it all. And how would I sum up that opening ceremony? It was brave, it was beautiful and it was bonkers. When the green and pleasant land transformed into the Industrial Revolution, it was as if a wand had been waved.

London 2012 had begun.

From that moment, we were in a bubble – a miraculous, uplifting bubble. There are times when I wish I could tap back into that stream of pride and confidence. London was the centre of the world and we were showing our very best face.

I was determined to enjoy every second. I hadn't realized until London 2012 that there is a difference between covering an event and immersing yourself in it. That you can be professional and capable, if a little distant, or you can dive right in and not just see the event but feel it. It's a bit like the way I think about Cornwall. If you can transmit that, make it travel down the line into people's sitting rooms, then they'd feel as if they were sitting right there in the stadium with you.

There is a thing actors call 'breaking the fourth wall'. It refers to a performer on stage breaking off script and talking to the audience. That's what I wanted to do. I wanted to reach through the screen and pull people right into the action. It might work, or it might make me look like an idiot – that was a risk I was prepared to take, because one of the tricks to live presenting is not being afraid.

You can't always know the answers, you certainly don't know what's going to happen next and you have to react as a human being, not as a polished performer.

In many ways, the pressure was off me at the Olympics. I wasn't one of the main studio presenters; after covering the swimming I would be on familiar territory doing the dressage and showjumping at Greenwich, and covering historic events like the first Olympic boxing medals awarded to women. I had presented a series on Radio 4 called *The History of British Sport*, so I had a bit of background knowledge.

My father always said that the best way of getting fit to ride in a race was by riding in a race. The same is true of Olympic broadcasting – the best way of preparing for one is to cover one. You clock up the hours, work out what you need to know, who to turn to for help, and how to negotiate the infernal transport systems.

My first Olympics was in Atlanta in 1996. Everyone told me that I had missed the best one, in Barcelona, and that Atlanta was awful, but for me it was the most exciting thing ever. I reported for radio on the eventing, showjumping, modern pentathlon and, weirdly, mountain biking, because it came through the Horse Park in Conyers where all the equestrian events were held. I interviewed Bo Derek because she was watching the showjumping. My ISDN kit melted in the sun.

BBC Radio 5 Live had started in 1994 and I had been taken on as a trainee sports reporter. My brief was to cover every shift and every sport. They tried to keep me away from racing, because my boss, Bob Shennan, wanted me to expand my knowledge and take me into areas where I wasn't dependent on people and facts that I already knew. I presented football, cricket and rugby union, wrote and read sports bulletins every half-hour for 5 Live and occasionally for Radio 4. For a while, I presented the sport on Chris Evans's breakfast show on Radio 1. This made me, in my brother's eyes, 'cool'.

I'd moved out of Kingsclere to a flat in West London, which I shared with Char, a friend from school. Finally, I was growing up – or at least growing away. In 1996 I did a screen test for the BBC and got a few days working as a reporter on the racing coverage with Julian Wilson.

That same year, a new racing channel started on satellite TV, and they offered me a job as the main presenter. The salary they proposed was three times what I was earning at 5 Live. I turned it down.

'You're making the biggest mistake of your life,' said their controller.

'But you can't send me to the Olympics,' I tried to explain. 'And I really want to go to the Olympics.'

'Fine,' he said. 'We'll make a star of someone else and, mark my words, you'll regret it.'

I can't say I ever have.

The BBC had been stealthily planning ahead for London 2012, without quite telling me those plans. In 2009 I'd quietly been sent to cover a swimming event, and after that I'd done world short-course championships, European championships and world championships; at the Commonwealth Games in Delhi I presented the swimming with Mark Foster and Ian Thorpe. I was very happy to be presenting all this swimming, but I can't pretend that I'd worked out why I was. The answer became clear in London.

In America and Australia, swimming had always been box office. Mark Spitz winning seven gold medals in Munich or Michael Phelps winning eight in Beijing were the headline stories. In the pool in London, Phelps would bow out of international competition by going for the all-time-record medal haul. And Britain had a host of swimmers who might actually win something, including Becky Adlington, who was defending her titles in the 400 and 800 metres.

I got to know the swimmers and mugged up as best I could, but I was still nervous about London. I could cover the equestrian sports with my eyes shut, and I knew all the people. This was different. I was being thrown in at the deep end with no life jacket.

So I came up with a plan. First I would make sure that no one could fault me for knowledge. I would do my homework, read around the subject, take notes in a hardback A4 book so I couldn't lose it, and I would ask questions. Lots of them.

The BBC swimming team is full of experts – Adrian Moorhouse is an Olympic gold medallist and four-times European champion, Andy Jamieson is an Olympic bronze medallist and European champion, Sharron Davies is an Olympic silver medallist and double Commonwealth champion and Mark, lovely Mark, is a six-times world champion and world record holder. They know their stuff. We were also helped by a brilliant researcher, Jonathan, who gave us start lists with added information in a code that I gradually deciphered.

I decided that it wasn't my job to know more than they did. Instead I should try to know *different* things about the swimmers and I should ask questions that would make swimming come alive for people at home.

Swimming is a strange sport because it gives the competitors no scope for personality. They walk out of the changing room in a dressing gown, they have a hat and goggles on, sometimes headphones as well, then they dive into a pool, swim up and down and get out again. There are no team tactics, no chat, no scope for doing anything different or playing to the crowd. It is a very basic sport in that way, and the characters can only live large outside the pool.

I knew I had to make people care about the competitors, otherwise it would be just a bunch of people swimming up and down lanes. In that sense, it was like horse racing, which is not an easy sell. If you haven't had a bet, why would you care about a bunch of horses running round and round in circles? And how do you tell one jockey from another when they're all wearing helmets and goggles?

For me, 2012 had already been a busy year, with the usual regulars of Cheltenham, Aintree, Epsom, Royal Ascot, Challenge Cup rugby league, Wimbledon, the Boat Race, the Open Golf, Crufts, Trooping the Colour – I've probably forgotten something, but you get the picture. By the time I arrived at the International Broadcast Centre, four days before the opening ceremony, I was terrified that I just didn't know what I needed to know about the Olympics. I would be caught out, exposed as a fraud. I would let the BBC down, let Britain down, let myself down.

With fear looming large in my mind, I decided something had to give: sleep. We had live coverage of morning sessions from 9 a.m. and evening sessions until 10 p.m. There was a gap between them when, in theory, I could have a nap, but that meant going back to a very average hotel four stops east of Stratford. More bother than it was worth.

So I stayed sat in the make-up room by the studio, which was the only place that had a sofa, a TV, a kettle and a pile of newspapers, watched the other events and read up for the evening races. That gave me time for another four hours' homework every day. Bingo.

The days passed, the notes grew, and I could find the stories to bring the swimming alive. I had my A4 book, my start sheets from Jonathan and my highlighter pens on a glass table in front of me. On screen, it looked like a bit of a mess, but I needed it all and I was damned if I was going to sacrifice substance for style. I had been given a GB Team stuffed toy called Pride the Lion, so Mark and I put a pair of his goggles on it and taped him to the wall behind us.

Mark got access to the Olympic family lounge so we could pilfer coffee and cake in the mornings, when no one was in there. I worked out that I could get an extra hour in bed if I reported in for duty at 8 a.m., then quickly did my own make-up before appearing on air at 8.45. The light wasn't great in the ladies' loo at the Aquatics Centre, and ticket holders were surprised to see me peering into the mirror, applying my mascara. But it did the job.

As it happens, British success in the pool was limited. There were more British finalists than ever before, but only two managed to win medals – Michael Jamieson with a silver in the 200 metres breaststroke, and Becky Adlington with two bronzes in the 400 metres and the 800 metres. So the swimming coverage wasn't about British victories. It had to be broader.

The day that everyone remembers is Tuesday 31 July. The men's 200 metres butterfly. Michael Phelps's signature event, the race he'd dominated for ten years. He was trying to become the first swimmer to win gold in the same race three Olympics in a row, and also to equal the record of eighteen medals. It was all about Phelps. Alongside him in lane five was a 20-year-old South African wearing a bright-green hat and goggles that made him seem like Kermit from *The Muppets*. He had been to a Youth Olympics but never a fully fledged Games, and Michael Phelps was his hero. He was called Chad Le Clos.

Though Le Clos got a fast start, by the halfway point Phelps was leading and gunning for his fifteenth gold medal. But the rest of the field would not go away. Butterfly is all about timing (so Mark tells me) and Phelps wasn't quite on it. His last stroke fell short of the end of the pool and, instead of taking another half-stroke and crashing into the timing pads with force, he glided. Le Clos pounced and touched the wall five hundredths of a second ahead.

It was a massive upset. The cameras focused on Phelps as he looked up at the scoreboard, and then his mother, who was ever present in the stands. I love a parental reaction. It brings home the ordinariness of the extraordinary athletes and, if the parents speak well, they will always say more about the champion than he or she can say about themselves. In Sydney, I was in the crowds with Steve Redgrave's wife, Anne, his kids and his parents as he won his fifth gold medal. We had snuck a camera into the family stand and the reaction we got became part of the archive.

So there was Michael Phelps's mum trying to look brave, but to her left and a little higher in the stands there was a right racket going on. There was a large man with a flushed face and a goatee beard waving a South African flag and screaming at the pool. He was going berserk.

As the medals ceremony took place right below us, the excited man moved closer to our presentation position. I said to Mark, 'That's got to be Le Clos's father. Go and get him!'

Having chatted every day to our security gateman, I was fairly confident he would let the man through to our presentation position without the right accreditation.

Sometimes in life you just get lucky – and sometimes you can shift the luck your way by making sure everyone understands the sense of urgency. I said excitedly on talkback to the production team, 'You have to stay with us. Mark's got Chad's dad, and this is going to be brilliant.'

At that point, Mark didn't actually have Chad's dad, but I knew how charming he could be and I trusted him to pull it off. As always, we were tight for time, but I wanted them to stay with us rather than shooting off to another sport. We showed a shot of the man, the South African flag now draped around his shoulders, then Mark was in shot, too, talking to him. So I said, on air, 'Mark's asking him to come and talk to us, so keep watching – anything could happen.'

I could hear the editor cursing in my ear. They couldn't leave the pool now.

And so Bert Le Clos, Chad's dad, arrived at the BBC's presentation point above the pool and gave one of the most memorable interviews on live television.

'This is *unbelievable*! Look at my boy – look at him. He's *bootiful*. He's the most down-to-earth, beautiful boy you will ever meet. Look at him! He's crying, like me.'

He blew him kisses and said: 'I love you!'

The words 'unbelievable' and 'bootiful' were repeated a few more times, but it's not the words so much as the emotion that you remember. Here was a father just brimming over with joy that his son had achieved something so unexpected. He knew how much training had gone into this moment, how much his son had given of his teenage years to swimming up and down a pool, and he shared that with us. His love was contagious, and there can't have been a person watching who didn't smile.

Down below us, Michael Phelps was guiding Chad through the protocol of showing your medal to the crowd. He put an arm around the man who had toppled him and made sure he enjoyed the moment. I admired Phelps as much for that as for the gold medal he won in the 4 x 200 freestyle relay later that evening, which took him to the outright record.

 What also made the interview with Bert so special was his humour and lack of self-awareness. He didn't perform for the cameras. When he saw himself on screen, he looked appalled, patted his tummy and said, 'Argh, don't show me, I am fat. Show my boy. There he is. Isn't he bootiful? Unbelievable. Unbelievable.'

After about two minutes, he said, 'Are we live?'

When it's going well on air you need say very little. Just keep smiling, ask the odd question and hold the microphone. Bert was a gift.

A couple of evenings later, I bumped into him at Westfield Shopping Centre, where we went after the evening session for supper. He was still draped in the South African flag and clearly loving his new-found fame.

'Clare, my *darling*!' Bert hollered. 'We are famous! We have gone viral, you and me.'

13

Home Turf

London stretched out below me, the river's U-bend containing the Isle of Dogs with its high-rise office blocks reaching upwards, the pyramid top of Canary Wharf blinking. To the left a little was the pale-grey dome of St Paul's, the skinny body and bulbous head of the BT Tower and, seemingly directly behind it, the white arch of Wembley Stadium. (I had lost my sense of direction, as I often did in London, but I must be looking west rather than north if Wembley was right behind the BT Tower.)

I love London. I love the variety of the buildings, the expanse of the river and the open green spaces, which all make it fresher and more vibrant than any other capital. I particularly loved London in the summer of 2012 and was delighted that the rest of the world seemed to agree.

I was walking from the hotel in Blackheath across the expanse of Shooters Hill and into Greenwich Park.

It was the second week of the Olympics and I was enjoying the moment, gazing across to the Olympic Park, which I knew would be humming with people. I could see the main stadium and the red twist of the Orbit to its right. In Greenwich, I walked to work every morning. It was probably no more than a couple of miles, but it gave me time just to *be*. The walk back up the hill was tougher, but with the sun fading, it was worth the effort.

When the London Organising Committee were planning venues for the Games, they came to the National Maritime Museum and decided that it would make a magnificent backdrop for an arena. They then went up the hill to the Royal Observatory and realized that the view from there across the Thames to Canary Wharf, the City and beyond was the equivalent of the Barcelona 10-metre diving board, which was outdoors and placed in such a way that the bright lights of the city at night formed the backdrop to the twirls and twists of the divers. Behind their somersaulting bodies were the iconic buildings of Barcelona, including the Gothic spires of Gaudí's Sagrada Família.

Greenwich Park would provide a similar effect. This was the chance to show off London to the world, and with Seb Coe a supporter of equestrian sport, it was the perfect site for the cross-country course.

That decision caused quite a stir both in Greenwich (they didn't want their park disrupted) and in horsey circles (they would rather go to Windsor, where the infrastructure already existed, than to south-east London), but Seb's motivation was to bring dressage, showjumping and eventing back into the heart of the Olympic Games. In Atlanta, Sydney, Athens and Beijing, the horse sports had been getting further and further away from the main events, and becoming more expensive (for Beijing, they weren't even in the same country: they were a four-hour flight away, in Hong Kong). London wanted to prove that a cross-country course could be built anywhere and that the fences could be reused afterwards at other venues.

I walked through the park towards the press centre, which was in the Maritime Museum, thinking that it had been a brave move, but it had worked. People who had never seen dressage bought tickets, people who had watched horses all their lives came to south-east London for the first time and, most importantly, the horses and their riders were enjoying world-class facilities.

It all seemed gentler than the frenzy at the Olympic Park. I was back with my horsey people, I had friends working on the host coverage to hang out with, I had my evenings free again, and I thought I'd got through the toughest part of the Games. Now I could relax the reins and gallop home, I hoped.

I had been covering showjumping for a long time and never seen the British team win a medal at the Olympics or the World Championships (the European Championships had been a tale of frustration and near-misses). The British team of Nick Skelton, Ben Maher, Scott Brash and Peter Charles had the right blend of youth and experience. Ben and Scott were the most exciting young talents in world showjumping, Peter was renowned for his confidence under pressure, while Nick was competing at his sixth Olympics.

I had been there in Athens when Nick had led going into the final round on Arko, only to make catastrophic, uncharacteristic errors. I knew how long he had been trying to win an Olympic gold.

The final session of the team competition had a sense of destiny about it. The last time Britain had won a team gold was in 1952 in Helsinki. This time, they stayed level with the Netherlands and went into a jump-off.

Peter Charles, who was last to go, said to his team mates, 'Don't worry. I'll jump clear. We've got this in the bag.'

He was right. Clear he went and they had won.

Nick Skelton ran over to my interview position and threw his arms around me in an enormous bear hug. Showjumpers have gained a reputation for being all about the big-money game and never showing emotion. At the Olympics, it's about pride, honour and history. I won't pretend my voice didn't crack a little as I tried to ask them questions that would make all those sentiments come through to an audience that was desperate to share the moment.

Showjumping wasn't the only equestrian success story. The

Three Day Event team had had plenty of attention, partly because it included Zara Phillips and partly because it was a strong team, with William Fox-Pitt, Mary King, Tina Cook and Nicola Wilson. They won silver in the first week.

Then it came to the lowest profile and most technical of all the equestrian disciplines: dressage.

Dressage had always been a mystery to my father. His life had revolved around making horses go as fast as they could. He had no time for getting them to dance around in circles, however much I tried to persuade him that obedience and balance learned in an arena were also useful when you're galloping towards a 5-foot hedge or turning on a sixpence into an upright gate.

Many shared his view. At *BBC Sports Personality of the Year* the previous winter, I had been working for 5 Live, and John Inverdale was hosting a panel that included Michael Vaughan and Matt Dawson. He asked us which sport would be the surprise hit of London 2012, and I said, 'Dressage.' They all laughed.

As it turned out, dressage *was* the 'dark horse' of the second week. The stands were packed as Carl Hester, Charlotte Dujardin and Laura Bechtolsheimer won Britain's first-ever gold in the team competition. It was Britain's twentieth gold of the Games, taking us past the tally set in Beijing and marking the best performance by a British team in more than a hundred years.

There was more to come, and Charlotte, on her bay gelding Valegro, followed up with gold in the individual competition. She and Valegro performed a stirring routine to a montage of uplifting music, including the themes to *The Great Escape* and *Live and Let Die* and finishing with 'Land of Hope and Glory'. It was inspired, and the judges rewarded her accordingly with an Olympic record score.

The dancing horses had caught on.

Dad had his epiphany, too. Until that day, he had thought dressage was for sissies and boxing was for tough guys. Just after Dujardin knocked the judges for six with that stunning routine to win the freestyle dressage, Nicola Adams won the first-ever gold medal in women's boxing.

My father was in tears. He gets emotional quite easily now, but still. It was a major moment for him. He realized that women can box and that dressage is a beautiful, complicated, technically difficult sport.

Dad wrote to Charlotte Dujardin, asking her to come to Kingsclere to ride a racehorse. I thought this a little forward of him and that she would dismiss him as a nutter. To her credit, she answered and said that, as she had never galloped fast, she would love to.

He now has a massive photo in the downstairs loo of himself and his new pin-up, Charlotte Dujardin, galloping upsides on the Downs. He asks me for updates on dressage championships around the world and keeps an eye on Charlotte's results.

Oh that he had shown such interest when I was trying to become an Olympic event rider. Dressage was my downfall. The judges never thought much of my tests and, to be honest, I was pretty hopeless at them, lacking the patience, the concentration and the technical ability to make it look effortless.

The one thing I thought I ought to be able to do was remember the moves. That at least did not involve anything more complicated than doing things in the right order at the right markers.

'What the hell are you doing?' my father would bark at me from the drawing-room doorway.

'I'm learning my dressage test,' I'd say, gesturing at the bits of paper on the floor. 'Obviously.'

'Well, put the furniture back where it belongs when you've finished.' He'd shut the door, leaving Lily the boxer inside with me.

Lily, our gorgeous brindle boxer, was my imaginary judge at 'C'. She sat there solemnly as I hopped around in my dressing gown doing transitions from trot to canter, changed legs, did a half-pass across the diagonal and a shoulder-in down the long side of the room (this is damned difficult when you only have two legs).

There were letters on pieces of paper in a rectangle around me. I was wearing my thinking hat. (This was a floppy green one my parents had brought back from safari, which I was convinced helped to keep information in my brain. I wore it throughout my O- and A-level revision. In hindsight, it did not have the desired effect.)

I was reaching the end of my practice test, so I trotted up the centre line, halted at X and saluted Lily with a flourish. One hand down by my side, the other on the imaginary reins of my imaginary pony, I bowed my head for three seconds and then calmly moved off, patting him down the neck and acknowledging the loud and long applause of the crowd.

My imaginary dressage tests were invariably better than the real thing.

In between the horsey events, I was covering as many other sports as I could. I reported from the open-water swimming in Hyde Park one morning, where Keri-Anne Payne had finished, agonizingly, just out of the medals, in fourth. I then rushed off to the ExCeL Centre to present the boxing. I got there just in time to hear the commentary of Dujardin's dressage test and knew she'd won gold. Less than half an hour later, Nicola Adams lifted her arms aloft. In a single afternoon, the full range of sporting options open to women were on show.

Female membership of gyms and sporting clubs has risen since the Games. I see a renewed ambition among young girls to succeed because they have followed the likes of Nicola Adams, Charlotte Dujardin, Jessica Ennis and Katherine Grainger. Sport is a powerful motivator, and it gives girls a much more honest reflection of the range of their strengths than they will find in a fashion magazine.

Sport is about what your body can do for you, not what it looks like. A sportswoman can be tall, she can be muscular, she can be competitive, she can be tough, and, thankfully, these are considered positive attributes – a welcome rejoinder to a media that has reduced women to an idealized form of femininity. There is a spirit of determination in women's sport at the moment to increase sponsorship so that funding of events such as the women's FA Cup or the Netball Super League or the women's Ashes can increase and perhaps the women competing can have the facilities, the time and the quality of training that would make a real difference to their performance. Increased funding leads to improved performance leads to increased interest and press attention, which then attracts more companies to want to put funding into sport, and so it goes on.

At the Olympics, coverage is equally split, because the medals are won by both men and women. Funding of Olympic sports is determined by performance, and so medals are precious not just to the individual who wins them but to those who hope to follow. British women were performing superbly in London and there was one final event in which a medal might be won. I was given the choice of going back to the Olympic Park to be part of the closing ceremony or reporting from the women's modern pentathlon in Greenwich. I chose the latter, because I wanted to stick with live sport and to know I had worked on the very last event of the Games.

Samantha Murray of Great Britain started the combined run/ shoot in fourth place. Modern pentathlon has a thrilling finale, because the competitors start at staggered intervals, with the leader going first and everyone else seconds behind according to their score. The first past the line is the winner, unlike in heptathlon or decathlon, where you have to work out the points.

Murray set off on her loops, pausing in the arena to shoot and then running off up the hill again. When she moved into third place and then into second, I realized how keyed up I had been for seventeen days. I started cheering for her and, when it was clear she was going to win silver, I burst into tears. I didn't want it to end. I knew nothing would ever match this.

I had no idea of the impact London 2012 would have on me until the following week. I had succeeded in avoiding most of the columns by TV critics; only on the final weekend, when I was reading up on the modern pentathlon, did I see a column in one of the Sunday papers that awarded me a gold medal for presenting. I rang my mother and asked her to save it for me.

'Oh,' she said. 'I wasn't going to tell you about that.'

As it happens, she had seen and saved every single mention of me in every single newspaper but, quite rightly, hadn't wanted to distract me while the Games were still going on. Halfway through, when I was on a weekend shift presenting from the studio, my old Radio 1 breakfast boss Chris Evans ran in and said, 'Hey, you're getting amazing press! You must've seen it.'

I told him I hadn't, and I could see he didn't believe me – but I really hadn't. There was so much to take in and so many other articles to read that I didn't want to be thrown off course. I am also wary of the draining impact of negative energy: I didn't want to see anything bad, so I just avoided all of it.

Public opinion can turn at any time. I have been on the wrong end of it, and I try to ignore the extremes. The only true indication of whether you are good at your job is whether you get booked again. I said after the Games that being 'flavour of the month' by definition only lasts about a month. I wasn't being falsely modest. I was bathing in the reflected glory of the Games and I didn't think I deserved plaudits for just doing my job.

What I hadn't banked on was the change in association. I wasn't 'the horsey lady' any more, I was 'the Olympic lady'.

The bestselling author and cultural commentator Malcolm Gladwell has popularized the 10,000-hour rule. You have to have practised something for ten thousand hours before you become a true expert and can break through. I wonder if it is particularly true in TV, a medium that allows you into people's homes and into their lives.

Most regular sports presenters will do about a thousand hours of television a year, so it takes at least ten years, probably longer, to reach a level where you know enough about your job *and* the audience is comfortable enough with you not to be distracted by how you look or what you sound like. Whether they like you or not, you are familiar. Des Lynam, Sue Barker, David Coleman – all of them earned their place as iconic presenters by putting in the hours, year after year. I am nowhere near their level of popularity or achievement, but I know you can't get there without doing the graft. The timing of London 2012 was right for me, so in that sense I was lucky – but the preparation for that moment had taken years. As the film producer Samuel Goldwyn and many others have said: 'The harder I work, the luckier I get.'

The day after the closing ceremony, Alice and I packed up the car, took Archie and headed down to Cornwall. It was when we stopped at a service station on the A303 that I realized things had changed. Alice went in to pay for the fuel and, as she was standing in the queue, she saw someone reading the paper in front of her. There was a picture of me and the man was pointing out of the window and saying to the rest of the people in the garage, 'Look! That's her.'

When Alice came out, she found me surrounded by a group of children who were all asking excitedly about the Olympics. I was telling them about my favourite events and asking them which sports they liked. We got back in the car.

'Have you got a baseball cap with you?' she asked.

'I think so,' I said.

'Good. You might need it.'

Generally speaking, being recognized doesn't bother me one way or the other. I don't mind if I am, because people are very nice (unless they are drunk) and just want to talk about sport, but it's a bit of a relief when I'm not. We were on holiday recently in Mauritius and a woman came rushing up to our table.

'Hello! When did you get here?' she asked as she leaned forward to kiss me. She was halfway towards my cheek when it dawned on her that she didn't actually know me at all. She went through with the kiss, blushed, asked a couple more questions and then left.

'Nope. No idea who she is,' I said to Alice.

'She has two options now – she'll either apologize tomorrow

and we'll laugh about it, or do the British thing and completely ignore us.'

We spent the next three days watching her avoid us.

Seventeen days after the Olympics finished, I was back at the same venues for the Paralympics. The Games themselves were also back where they started – after a Stoke Mandeville doctor called Ludwig Guttmann fought the accepted wisdom that paralysed servicemen were not to be moved, not to be reintegrated into society and not to be challenged. He refused to allow them to lie in a bed for the rest of their lives and used sport as therapy for body and mind.

In 1948, on the same day as the opening ceremony of the post-war London Olympic Games, sixteen injured service personnel took part in an archery competition at Stoke Mandeville. A year later, the competition expanded, and Guttmann said, 'I foresaw the time when this sports event would be truly international and the Stoke Mandeville Games would achieve world fame as the disabled person's equivalent of the Olympic Games.'

His prediction started to come true in 1960 when the 'International Games' moved from Stoke Mandeville to Rome. They took place one week after the Olympics and included four hundred athletes from twenty-one nations. They all had spinal-cord injuries. In 1976, the criteria were broadened to include athletes with a visual impairment, and amputees. In 1980, athletes with cerebral palsy were added and, in 1984, a new category came in called 'les autres'.

I first worked on the Paralympics in Sydney in 2000 and in the intervening years had watched it grow from a curiosity that was sometimes seen as an inconvenience to the host city (Moscow in 1980 and Los Angeles in 1984 had refused to stage it) into a huge international competition with headline names and awe-inspiring performances.

In China, the 2008 Paralympics was an eye-opener for a nation that had previously ignored, or hidden, disability. They shipped in crowds to Beijing to watch, perhaps unaware of the lasting impact that would have. For the first time, large numbers of Chinese people saw that amputation, paralysis or cerebral palsy was not the end of a life but the beginning of a new one.

London was the first time the venues and the village had been designed to be fully integrated and access-friendly. The number of competitors and nations represented had never been higher and, for the first ever time in Paralympic history, tickets sold out. Thriller Thursday – the night on the track when Hannah Cockcroft, Jonnie Peacock and David Weir all won gold medals – stands out, while Ellie Simmonds, Sarah Storey and Sophie Christiansen set new standards in swimming, cycling and para-dressage.

I presented from the studio with Ade Adepitan, who went to two Paralympic Games as part of the wheelchair basketball team and won a bronze medal in Athens. He's a live wire with a keen interest in all sports and a desire to do the job with enthusiasm and knowl-edge, but he's also wildly unpredictable. It was a bit like working with Willie Carson, in that I was never quite sure what he might say next, but it would probably be funny or left-field.

I suggested that every day we should go out into the park for the start of the programme to get a feel of the place. A studio can be antiseptic, removed from the atmosphere and the action; I much prefer to be in among the crowds, even if it makes broadcasting less predictable.

We started a daily 'Ask Ade' session, where people could pose any question they wanted about Paralympic sport. The kids (and there were a lot of them in the park) loved it.

'Who's the fastest runner?'

'Who's the best swimmer?'

'How much does a racing wheelchair cost?'

'How far can you throw a club?'

The questions came thick and fast and, after a few days, I realized that not one of them had asked about injuries, illness or inher-ited conditions. They didn't see the Paralympics as being about disability at all. It was a major sports event in which people tried to run, swim or cycle as fast as they could. If they were racing in wheelchairs, that involved tactical decisions and a different technique – but a wheelchair was just a vehicle, it didn't represent anything else.

There is a glorious clarity to children's thinking. Anna Lisa and Andrew brought my nephews along for a day and they wanted to ride in Ade's chair, which of course they were not allowed to do.

The night when I knew the Paralympic Games had struck home was the night Oscar Pistorius got beaten by Alan Oliveira of Brazil in the T43/44 200 metres. It was a stunning race, with Oliveira closing down Pistorius and storming past him in the final thirty metres. We were shell-shocked, but more surprising than the result was Oscar's reaction.

I had known him fairly well, having interviewed him twelve years earlier in Sydney and, at his request, I hosted his press conference at the start of the Paralympics. We spent half an hour in the green room chatting before that conference started, and he was relaxed and amiable. I remember being impressed with how he handled being asked the same questions over and over and how he dealt with the incessant flashbulbs. Oscar was a natural performer, saying, doing and wearing the right things, right down to the sponsored sunglasses on his head, despite the fact that he was indoors.

So I was surprised when he lost his cool and his dignity in the interview straight after that race. We had gone to an advert break, so I was watching the monitor – I could see Oscar hopping from foot to foot (runners on their competition blades don't have a flat surface to rest on). He had time to compose himself and deal with defeat; a minute is long enough to calm down if you want to calm down. But Oscar wanted to strike out. He accused Oliveira of using illegally long blades and argued that it wasn't a fair race.

'Not taking away from Alan's performance,' he said, about to take it all away, 'he's a great athlete, but these guys are a lot taller and you can't compete [with the] stride length. You saw how far he came back. We aren't racing a fair race. I gave it my best.'

I shouted at Stephen Booth, who was editing our programme.

'Boothy, are you listening to this? This isn't like Oscar. This is extraordinary.'

I knew we had a story. When I get that feeling it's like a shot of electricity. I wrote down Oscar's words so that I'd have a clear reference when we came back to the studio, and I reacted as honestly as I could. Within a couple of hours, the Pistorius PR machine had swung into action and he had apologized, but the damage to his image was done. Twitter went into overdrive, with some accusing him of bad sportsmanship and others pleased to see an angry response to defeat. The Paralympics had a genuine sporting controversy, and the reaction was as it would be in football, cricket or racing – heated.

We were at the centre of a true live event, and the next two hours flew by. Nights like that are why I adore live television. There is no script, the running order has been ripped up and you're relying on your wits. It's scary, but if you nail it it's the biggest thrill on earth.

The whole episode was surprising, but even weirder was Oscar's behaviour the next day.

At the medals ceremony, he was a different man. Superman had turned back into Clark Kent. Gone were the designer stubble, the sunglasses and the ruffled hair; here was a clean-shaven man in black-rimmed spectacles with slicked-down hair. He bowed his head throughout the ceremony, looking close to tears. If contrition had an image, this was it. Oscar has always known the power of a picture, and he did what he thought was the right thing to try to win back the public.

The heat haze of the loser's interview I could forgive as a perfectly natural response (albeit a sore one) to a result he did not expect. The medals ceremony was a different thing altogether. I remember saying to Ade that I thought he'd either been told to appear as respectful and remorseful as he could, or he'd decided to himself.

On the final night of competition in the Olympic Stadium, the stubble and the sunglasses were back as Pistorius cruised to victory in the T44 400 metres, beating Oliveira easily. He stretched both arms out sideways like an albatross, pointing his fingers and looking defiant. I was pleased he had won, and so was the majority of the crowd. He may have offended our British sense of sportsmanship, but he was the big draw and had completed a historic double in running the 400 metres at the Olympics (where he reached the semi-finals) and the Paralympics. Pistorius has always promoted his ability above his disability: he is not defined by being a double amputee but by being a sportsman.

After the events of Valentine's night 2013, Oscar Pistorius finds himself defined very differently.

Alice gets up earlier than me and listens to Radio 4. When she heard the news that he had shot and killed his girlfriend, Reeva Steenkamp, she came running upstairs.

'You won't believe it,' she said. 'Oscar has killed his girlfriend.'

'Not Oscar. He couldn't have,' I replied. 'Are you sure?'

Whatever he thought or intended, he shot and killed the woman he professed to love. Two lives were destroyed by those bullets: Reeva lost her life and Oscar shattered his own.

Those of us who admired his sporting achievements hope that there will be no more victims of that crime. The pin-up boy of the Paralympics has destroyed himself, but the organization and its members are bigger and stronger than just one man.

Since the first Paralympic Summer Games in Rome in 1960, Paralympic sport has grown in terms of the numbers competing in it and in profile. China has developed from a nation that hid disability into one that regularly tops the medals table, while Russia hosted the Winter Paralympics in Sochi to great commendation (they had refused to for Moscow 1980). Progress comes eventually.

My big hope is that the US will take more of an interest in the Games and start funding their own athletes. NBC invests millions of dollars in Olympic coverage but barely bothers with the Paralympics. It seems nonsensical to me; the Paralympics has the perfect blend of sporting achievement, personal stories, high drama and atmosphere. If only they would notice.

London 2012 was the coming of age of the Paralympic Games. At the closing ceremony, the president of the International Paralympic Committee called it 'the greatest Paralympic Games ever'. He wasn't exaggerating and, although there are still improvements to be made (including the woeful lack of commitment from US television), Rio promises much. Two new sports, para-canoe and para-triathlon, will make their debut.

Both the BBC's coverage of the Olympics and Channel 4's coverage of the Paralympics were nominated for BAFTAs at the glitzy awards ceremony the following May. I was in the weird position of having a foot in both camps; although I was disappointed for the BBC team, I was thrilled for Channel 4 when they won, because they had invested so much in new, disabled talent – people like Alex Brooker, Arthur Williams, Rachael Latham and Daráine Mulvihill, who had only had limited television experience before 2012.

I was sitting next to Ade in the front row of the Royal Festival Hall, and I cheered louder than anyone as the production team took to the stage to accept the award. There was no ramp, so Ade was taken backstage and lifted up (off screen) by two men. Ade never complained about the lack of a ramp, but it reminded me of how often in life he and every wheelchair user has to find a way to be where they want to be, even if it means arriving a little late.

Ade paid tribute to the London Organising Committee for giving Channel 4 the chance to cover the Paralympics and to the belief of the bosses who invested in the marketing of the Games, making heroes of athletes who had hardly enjoyed any profile beforehand. Finally, he said, 'When I was growing up we used to say, "One day people are going to respect us Paralympians. They are going to look at us as athletes." So thank you, Channel 4, for allowing us to be ourselves.'

The day after the closing ceremony of the Paralympics, there was a parade through the streets of London. I was working for Channel 4 as a roving reporter, which meant I got to hop from bus to bus. It was the perfect job for me, as it meant I could roam around, talking to athletes.

The satellite system was under pressure from the demands of all the various news outlets, so the radio microphones were working only intermittently. There was a whole hour when I couldn't do any broadcasting because the kit wasn't working; I just went with the flow and enjoyed being part of the parade.

I was shattered, having been on the go since the Boat Race on 7 April. I could see how an exhausted athlete can be lifted by the crowd: the noise and the numbers gave me the biggest boost imaginable.

I felt like a balloon, floating above all this mayhem, looking down on someone who looked like me doing the Mobot with Mo Farah (he thanked me for inventing it, by the way), taking photos of Tom Daley and Zara Phillips, hugging Chris Hoy, waving with David Weir and marathon runner Richard Whitehead at the thousands and thousands of people.

When we got to Trafalgar Square, I thought of the countdown clock that had stopped, the one I'd helped to unveil in March 2011. I tried to take a mental picture, to hold this moment for ever. I looked at that mass of people, all of them cheering the athletes who had brought them hope and joy through the summer of 2012. I looked at the athletes, waving back at them and thanking them. I looked at big, strong Chris Hoy, and his bottom lip was wobbling. That's when I went. I started to cry proper tears.

A voice said, 'Oi, Balding, are you getting a bit wobbly?'

It was Zara Phillips, who has a wonderful ability to make people laugh, even when they're on the verge of meltdown. I pulled myself together and got off the bus as we went under Admiralty Arch. The satellite signal was still intermittent, so I ran down the Mall, body-surfed into a bunch of schoolchildren and high-fived them all the way along. The cameras covered what they covered but I didn't really notice. I just did what I would do whether they were filming or not.

When it was all over, I took off my microphone, said thanks to the outside-broadcast team and left. I had been offered transport, but I didn't want to get into a car. I needed to walk.

I wanted time to gather my thoughts. I needed to find a last bit of energy, because that evening was the launch party for *My Animals and Other Family*. I had to be bright and sparkly for that. So I walked past Clarence House and St James's Palace, down Pall Mall and round the back of Trafalgar Square, up St Martin's Place and Charing Cross Road.

As I walked, I tried to remember moments, to recall what people had said. But all I felt was a surge of love: the love that had come from everyone on those streets and the love that had been shown back to them from the men and women in the parade. I was neither a participant nor an observer: I was right in the middle. That seemed the one place I wanted to be.

Athletes often say that, when they win, they just want to win again. But I don't want ever to try to repeat what happened in London 2012. I may do versions of the same thing, but the alchemy of time, place and people will never be re-created. And that's just fine by me.

Ladle Hill–Watership Down–Kingsclere

When she died, Grandma left the contents of her house to my mother, my brother and me. I suspect she laughed writing her will, imagining the rows as we tried to sort out what we each wanted. She'd have laughed even harder if she'd seen Uncle Willie trying to organize what he needed to keep, then piling up the remainder into the rooms he was meant to be preparing for his new bed and breakfast.

As it happens, we all wanted slightly different things. My brother needed furniture and likes art, my mother wanted the desk and some of the pictures, and I wanted a bowl of glass eggs that was always in the hall, and the books. Grandma had rather a fine collection of hardbacks, including a specially bound limited edition of *Watership Down*. It is encased in a marbled box, the inside sleeves have the same marbled paper, the pages

Wayfarer's Walk

are gilt edged and it is signed in red ink by Richard Adams. It is a beautiful book: the outside is lovely to look at, but the inside is even more precious to me.

To most people, *Watership Down* is a book about rabbits. To me, it's a book about home. In the Foreword to the Special Edition, Richard Adams wrote:

> *I was born in Watership Down country – copse and ploughland, streams and hills, chicory, cowslips and harebells. If the book has a theme apart from the story, that is it . . . the story became an excuse for writing with affection about the country I have always loved. It's still there at the moment, thank God. May it always remain.*

That was written in 1976, when I was five and living a few miles away, in Kingsclere. When I was a child I rode along Watership Down in search of rabbits, but I had never walked it. We had missed that section of the Wayfarer's Walk when Alice, Mum and I had been diverted to Litchfield and then got lost. It meant that there was one more walk home from the west.

Aunt Gail is over from America for Easter. She is my father's youngest sister and (entirely independently) my mother's best friend. They went to prep school together, until Aunt Gail got expelled for bringing her pony into the dormitory. They, probably sensibly, went to different boarding schools but remained close friends. Aunt Gail used to come and stay for the summer holidays and, when my mother went to America after she left school, she of course went to see Aunt Gail.

That she ended up marrying her best friend's brother was sort of a coincidence. Dad had come to work at the stables, and although they'd met as children, the age gap of ten years meant that at first my mother was just one of his sister's squitty little friends. Things changed, obviously, as my mother grew up, and Aunt Gail was probably the happiest person at my parents' wedding. She was certainly happier than my grandmother.

Aunt Gail adores my father. I don't really know why, as he was beastly to her when she was little and all he does now is tease her about her strangely shaped thumbs and tell her she's bow-legged. Her thumbs *do* look as if they've been squashed in a press and her legs *are* a little bandy, but there are many other qualities that are more worthy of note. She takes her brother's jibes with remarkable grace and seems pleased just to spend time with him. I can't fathom why.

I suggest that Aunt Gail come with Mum, Alice and me for the last section of the Wayfarer's Walk. She has been visiting Kings-clere for nearly fifty years but has never walked from Ladle Hill to home. I think she'd enjoy it. I also ask our nephews along. Both of them, to my surprise, say yes.

So off we drive to Sydmonton and park up outside the Lloyd Webbers' ornate black gates, behind which stretches a perfect avenue leading to their house.

'Hide your bag,' my mother warns Aunt Gail.

Wayfarer's Walk

'Mum, we're in the middle of the country. I don't think thieves are going to smash your car windows in and nick her bag, I really don't. And I'm pretty sure Andrew Lloyd Webber won't take it either.'

My mother raises her eyebrow at me. God, I wish I could do that.

'Just hide the bag.'

I once walked with a man in Cornwall who, immediately afterwards, ordered Doom at the pub. I thought he couldn't abide my company, but it turned out that it's a type of ale: Doom Bar. My mother would order a pint of that. She's like an insurance broker, who always sees the worst possible outcome. Sometimes it's quite useful: for example, if you're planning a sophisticated crime she can work out exactly where you're going to slip up. If you're not planning a sophisticated crime, it can be quite depressing.

Aunt Gail hides her bag. She finds it easier to go with the flow. I have yet to learn this art.

We have Boris (on the lead) and Archie (off the lead), Jonno and Toby (both off the lead) and four vaguely sentient women to keep the boys in order. The ground is wet and sticky from more rain, so I'm wearing wellington boots. For once, my mother has not foreseen the worst-case scenario and is wearing trainers.

'Bollocks,' she says loudly as we get to the first puddle. The boys laugh.

'It's OK, Nini,' says Jonno. 'There's a way round here.'

(My nephews and my niece, Flora, all call my mother Nini,

pronounced 'Nee-nee' rather than 'Ninny'; although if she's been listening to rap music or watching American cartoons, Flora calls her Neens. Mum didn't want to be 'Grandma' or 'Granny', so Nini just sort of happened. My father is 'Grumpy', which is easier to explain.)

Jonno leads us through the trees on a curving path and then decides that we should get right out the other side and walk along the edge of the field, where it is drier. We march up the side of Ladle Hill, where the tumuli reveal the remains of an unfinished Iron Age hill fort that has never been excavated. Jonno tells me that the army based on Ladle Hill used to fight the army based on Beacon Hill, which we can see on the other side of the A34.

'He remembers so much,' says my mother. 'It'll get him into terrible trouble, you know.'

Andrew said he might join us for some of the walk, but I know he won't. He has a meeting with the accountant at 12.30 p.m. and Mum is due to meet the same accountant at 2.30 p.m. She looks at her watch as we get to the top of Ladle Hill and says, 'Do you think I'll make it back in time?'

'Absolutely. I think the walk is just short of six miles, and we'll do it in well under two hours, even with the boys,' I say, without factoring in the worst-case scenario of one of us breaking a leg and having to hop the whole way home.

It's a fresh day, not warm enough to encourage Easter-holiday families out into the open, so we have the place to ourselves. Toby explains earnestly that there are coins under the ground

Wayfarer's Walk

and so we should bring up metal detectors and find them all – then we could buy a new car. He finds a flint that he is convinced was a tooth from an enormous animal. I say it was probably a mammoth and it might still be around. His eyes turn wide as saucers and he starts to scan the fields.

I love being an aunt. You get all the fun with none of the responsibility. It's even better than being a grandparent, because you haven't had to give birth to anyone and you don't have a view on parenting. Alice and I were born to be aunts. We can read to the children, play with them, tease them, advise them, teach them stuff that may or not be strictly true or useful, and love them unconditionally. I never knew it could be so satisfying.

Jonno is very tall for his age, with great long legs that stride over the ground. Toby is much smaller, but he's tough and he's fit, so he keeps up as best he can. He has decided he wants to wear a visor for the walk; he fancies himself as a tennis player for the day. They mainly wear football kit, and I am riding sky high in their estimation because I've brought them each a Liverpool football shirt with 'Balding' written on the back of it. I was working there the day before and I took two penalties in front of the Kop.

Yes, I did. I really did. Alice has told me to point out that the mascot was in goal, but I would like to counter that by saying that the mascot, Mighty Red, is over six foot tall and very wide. He fills up a lot of the goal. He might not be able to bend down or move easily, but he is mighty. And red.

I was at Anfield to do my sports chatshow, and I'd agreed to take penalties with comedian John Bishop and a few others at half-time in the charity match to commemorate the lives of the ninety-six fans killed at Hillsborough in 1989.

Anfield was packed with fans of all ages. They had bought special scarves with 'Celebration of the 96' written on them, and tied them to the Shankly Gates. It was a moving tribute to fans whose families are still fighting for honest explanations of what happened that day.

I explained to the boys all about the day and who was playing for the Liverpool Legends – Kenny Dalglish, Michael Owen, Steve McManaman, Robbie Fowler, Jan Mølby and John Barnes were on the pitch.

'Yes, but what happened when you took your penalty?' Toby asked.

'Yes, talk us through it, Auntie Clare. Did you go top left or top right?' added Jonno.

A week before, when the boys heard I was to take penalties at Anfield, they had looked at my brother with solemn faces.

'We think Auntie Clare needs some coaching,' they said.

So they had coached me, with the help of Dwayne, who works in the yard and is a mean footballer. He told me to put my left foot level with the ball, sweep through with my right, connect with my laces and keep my head down. Other people told me to pick my corner and stick with it. This assumed I could control the direction of the ball, which was ambitious. Alice told me to remember to look happy.

'Just keep smiling, whatever happens. You know how you can

Wayfarer's Walk

look when you're concentrating, and that wouldn't be good. Just smile.'

I bought myself my first-ever pair of football boots in Canterbury on Easter Saturday. I was there for Radio 2 live from Canterbury Cathedral, so I thought I'd better invest in the local economy. They were fluorescent green but they were reduced to £25, so who was I to quibble with the colour?

'Are you planning to blind the goalkeeper?' asked Alice, when I proudly showed them to the family.

I did not sleep well on Sunday night. I kept having visions of coming off a long run towards the penalty spot and slipping on my backside in front of the Kop, the most revered and famous stadium end in England. My lovely BT producer was worried on my behalf.

'Are you sure you want to do this, Clare?' he asked. 'We can get you out of it, you know.'

'They've made me a special kit with my name on and everything,' I said. 'Of course I can't get out of it. Anyway, I don't want to get out of it. It'll be fine. Look at my boots!'

I changed into my football kit. The first time I have ever worn a football kit. I pulled up my socks and tightened my laces.

'All the gear and no idea,' I said to myself.

Never mind, confidence is the key. Lots of people do things every day that they've never done before, and I'm sure they feel just like this. Terrified. I joined the other penalty takers in the tunnel. John Bishop was going first. He used to be a really good footballer, nearly a professional, and he's a lifelong Liverpool fan. This was his idea of heaven. I went out second and touched the Anfield sign, because I knew that's what players did. I needed a bit of luck.

They called out my name on the tannoy and I hoped people wouldn't boo, but they were a friendly crowd, here for a special event. John Bishop took his first penalty and hit it low and hard to the right. The keeper – sorry, the mascot – waved a wing at the ball but got nowhere near. John celebrated in style and whooped the fans up into a frenzy.

'Look at that, Clare, isn't it great?' he said to me, pointing at the sea of red behind the goal.

I swallowed hard. I wasn't sure I wanted all of them watching me taking my very first penalty in public. I decided to focus on one thing and one thing only. My left foot. Just plant that next to the ball and the rest will look after itself. Don't get all fancy with a run-up or muck about trying to pick a corner, just two steps and *boom*!

The ball flew forward, which was a good start. It went in the air a bit, then dipped down low and past the goalkeeper into the back of the net. I had scored! I had actually scored a goal at Anfield. I waved at the crowd and trotted into the goal to collect my ball. I thanked Mighty Red as I did so. I'm not sure if you're meant to thank the goalkeeper when you score a penalty, but it seemed the polite thing to do.

I re-enact the goal and the celebration for the boys.

'What happened with the second one, Auntie Clare?' asks Toby.

Wayfarer's Walk

'Well, do you know what?' I reply. 'The second one went straight through the keeper's legs and into the net. Two out of two!'

I do a little jig of celebration for the boys, who slap me on the back and grin.

'Phew,' says Jonno. 'We thought you were going to be really embarrassing, and then we'd have to pretend we didn't know you.'

We walk past a barrow on the right, an ancient burial mound that now sits quietly in the middle of a field, and turn left when we reach a row of trees. There is a glorious view down to Sydmonton Court and of Madeleine Lloyd Webber's stud paddocks. We wave hello to them.

'This is lovely,' says Aunt Gail. She says 'lovely' a lot, because the Americans tend to favour 'awesome' or 'great', and she prefers to protect her English heritage and her accent. She sounds more English than my mother, despite having lived in South Carolina for the best part of fifty years. She's also unfailingly positive, so most things in her world are 'lovely'.

The boys run ahead and then back to us, teasing Boris because he isn't allowed off the lead. Aunt Gail tells me that when she came down for breakfast that morning she found Boris lying on the kitchen table. Not just sitting in the chair by the side of the table, but actually lying across the middle of the table. Mum pats his head and says, 'Bad boy, Boris.'

He looks very pleased with himself.

We amble along, chatting to the boys to keep them interested and to stop them trying to kill each other. There is a sign on the fence that reads 'Do not leave valuables in your car. Thieves operate in this area.' My mother reads it out slowly and deliberately, puts her head on one side and looks at me as a QC would in court. I scrunch up my face and say, reluctantly, 'OK. You were right. I was wrong.'

'I'm sorry?' she says. 'I couldn't hear you. Can you say that again?'

'*You were right and I was wrong!*' I shout into the air around us, my voice reaching up to the branches bursting into life, across the lumpy, short-grassed slopes, up into the sky, where a buzzard is wheeling, his finger-like wings stretched out beside him.

'This is fun,' says Toby.

I start to tell him about *Watership Down*, about Fiver and Hazel and Bigwig and Silver and how they had to find a new home, so they came here, right where we are walking.

I tell them about Nuthanger Farm, which is down on the Ecchinswell Road about a mile away. There's a footpath very close to it and I promise them we'll walk there another time. Mum tells them that the book has been turned into a film and a TV series and that Art Garfunkel sang a song about the rabbits called 'Bright Eyes'.

'So what happened to the rabbits?' they ask.

We walk alongside a row of huge beech trees to a gate and cross the narrow country lane on to Watership Down.

'They're here,' I say, pointing to the slopes on our left and the

Wayfarer's Walk

thickets of trees and bushes ahead of us. 'They're all under here in a massive warren. It's a palace of a warren, the biggest one in the world, and they come out early in the morning and just as the sun is setting in the evening to have a party in the open air. They'll be safe, because there will never be any houses built here. It will all stay just like this for ever.'

Boris suddenly pulls Mum sideways. He has seen a rabbit disappearing down one of the myriad holes that pockmark the north-facing slope of the Downs.

'Hold on tight, Nini!' shouts Jonno.

She manages to stay upright and prevents Boris from re-enacting one of the gorier scenes from *Watership Down*.

We come up to the top of the Downs and cross on to Cannon Heath Down. Mum suggests we walk next to the new all-weather gallop my brother has just put in for the racehorses. It's made of oiled sand and rubber, and it is clearly the best thing Archie has ever smelt, because he dives into the middle of it and rolls and rolls until he can't roll any more. He has sticky, oily sand all over him and a piece of chopped-up red electrical cable on the end of his nose.

As we are on home soil and have a fence between us and the public footpath, Mum finally relaxes and lets Boris off the lead. He goes berserk, running as fast as he can backwards and forwards on the grass and bouncing on the all-weather gallop and back. Archie chases him and then rolls again, gets up and chases him some more. Within ten minutes, Boris is panting as if he's run a marathon.

'I see why you kept him on the lead,' Alice says to my mother.

'Indeed,' she replies, looking at me and once more raising an eyebrow. I don't bother saying anything. One 'You were right and I was wrong' a day is enough for me.

'Isn't it lovely?' says Aunt Gail, again.

Toby is starting to flag a bit. He's only five, after all: 'How much further is it, Auntie Clare?'

'Well, you can see your house down there, so I would say it's about another mile, and I think we'll be there in twenty minutes or so. How does that sound?'

'I'm hungry.'

We pass the point on the grass gallop where my father's Derby winner Mill Reef broke his leg in 1972. The boys want to know what happened and how he was saved by a vet from America who pinned the leg, how he recovered because he stayed so calm and how he learned to walk with the plaster cast on his leg (and then how it was cut off – the plaster, not the leg). That keeps them entertained until we cross on to the side of the Downs and cut down along the edge of the steep bowl-shaped slope we call the Cuckoo Pen. Boris is on the lead now, because he's done enough running for a week.

Jonno and I are at the back.

'I think we should walk backwards, Auntie Clare. Did you know a hundred steps backwards is equal to a thousand steps forwards?'

'I did know that, JJ, because it was me who told you.'

'Oh,' he says, turning round. 'Well, anyway, let's do it.'

Wayfarer's Walk

He and I walk down the steep slope backwards, counting our steps, which doesn't hurt any of the muscles that have been starting to ache but gives me some pain in very strange places the next morning.

Toby has an energy surge because we are going downhill and he knows where we are. We head towards Uncle Willie's farm, turn left down the grass track and right into Prince of Wales Avenue, planted in 1894 when Prince Edward (later Edward VIII, who abdicated) was born.

Mum looks at her watch. Perfect timing for her meeting. The boys race each other to the gate, because I've promised a prize to the winner. Toby has a head start and wins easily but looks a little disappointed to win only a pound.

'How many miles have we done?' he asks me.

I plug my Jawbone bracelet into my phone and wait for it to upload. It says 5.87 miles.

'Well, that was a lovely five point eight seven miles,' says Aunt Gail.

Mum goes to see the accountant; the boys run into Park House to tell Anna Lisa how far they have walked. Alice and I look at each other and smile.

'Cup of tea?' I suggest.

'Yes,' she says. 'And, by the way, if you want to live here one day, that's fine with me.'

After-Walk

We have just been recording the latest series of *Ramblings* for Radio 4. Lucy is producing half of the series, and Karen the other half. Lucy wrote on her notes for the Essex walk: 'You can take the train and I will leave my car at the station. I promise you won't have to be driven anywhere by me.'

During that walk, one of the group told me about her first husband, who had died at twenty-seven of lung cancer. Her second husband had died of prostate cancer (they were married for thirty-three years) and her third had also died of cancer. She did not tell me to elicit sympathy, nor was she sorry for herself, it was just a conversation you have when you're walking along, the sort of conversation you couldn't have anywhere else. Another told me about her search for a partner and how hard it is after the age of sixty, because you're so used to doing your own thing you don't want to compromise for another person. I told her about the walking club I had met that was designed for those looking for love.

'Oh, I might just try that,' she said. 'I did walk with the last one, and that was fine. It was just the other stuff that didn't work out!'

When we went to Devon for two days, I let Lucy drive from the station, because I had to finish writing an article. I regretted it almost immediately. She stalled the car three times before we reached Fingle Bridge, so I took over for the return journey. To be fair to her, it was one of those eco-friendly cars where the engine cuts out when you stop. The trick, I found, is to put your foot on the clutch, rather than keep turning the keys while bashing the wheel and swearing at the car.

We walked with a group called the Diamond Ramblers, who are all past or approaching their sixtieth birthday and have, between eleven of them, lost thirty-six stone in weight. They were incredibly revealing when talking about the shame of being overweight and how different they feel now that they are fitter and lighter. But, more than that, the bond they have as friends who walk together is unbreakable.

One of them, Jenny, had moved from Yorkshire to Devon to be near her ill daughter, and suddenly found herself with no friends; she had a dodgy hip and was miserable until she joined the Diamond Ramblers. After a bracing walk from Otterton to the Jurassic Coast, up to Ladram Bay and back to Otterton Mill for lunch, she tried to assess the impact the group had had on her.

'I can't even put it into words, but honestly' – her voice broke as she looked at the rest of them – 'you have changed my life.'

I have started reading *Walk! A Celebration of Striding Out* by Colin Speakman. I am happy to follow his example of becoming an evangelist for walking, of trying to turn around the misconception that it's somehow boring or low grade.

And it's an important mission: our over-reliance on the car means that, as a nation, we are becoming ever more sedentary. Our average walking distance per year has fallen in the past two decades from 244 miles to 189 miles, which is only 3.6 miles per week.

I try to do nearly double that per day, and it's made a huge difference to my life. My mind is clearer, my fitness has improved, my stress levels have reduced, my connection with Alice is better because we walk and talk together, our dog is fitter and we know our local area intimately. I have had adventures with my mother, my brother and my nephews. Flora is keen to come walking with us because the boys have told her it's fun. Even my father might, one day, be persuaded to join us.

I am excited just thinking of all the footpaths that I have yet to discover. I have been lucky to walk in some beautiful and remote places, from the Shetland Isles to the Isles of Scilly, from the Channel Islands to Northern Ireland, but the joy of it isn't in going too far or being extravagant. The joy is in allowing myself to slow down, to be close to the land, to smell the freshly cut grass or hear the willow warbler calling.

One of the new jobs in my life since London 2012 is presenting *Good Morning Sunday* on BBC Radio 2. It means a 5.30 a.m. alarm call every Sunday but, as I said to my book editor, Joel, it's not a time of the week that I'd be using to do anything else. It's a joy to present, as we have fascinating conversations about faith, spirituality, motivation and how to lead a meaningful life.

In the course of doing interviews for that show I met a remarkable woman called Roz Savage. She has rowed single-handed across the Atlantic, the Pacific and the Indian Ocean. She has spent over five hundred days at sea, on her own, undertaking a seemingly impossible challenge in order to raise awareness of environmental issues.

Roz had had a successful career in management consultancy, a husband and a sports car. It all looked good, but she wasn't happy, so, as an exercise, she wrote two versions of her own obituary – one for the person she wanted to be and one for the person she was becoming. It made her see that she needed a purpose, to make a difference in this world, so she took a fairly extreme course of action: she left her husband and her job, went on a retreat to Ireland, and then came up with her plan to row the Atlantic. She followed it up by becoming the first woman ever to row solo across the eight thousand miles of the Pacific, and then added the Indian Ocean, just for good measure.

Roz is not enormously tall or strong, nor is she bonkers (which you might assume). She is just like you or me: she is ordinary – apart from the fact she decided *not* to be. In her book, *Stop Drifting, Start Rowing*, she explains:

> If you don't keep pushing the boundaries, keep expanding your comfort zone, your comfort zone actually gets smaller and smaller, until you're shrink-wrapped in such a tiny comfort zone that you can't move, you can't achieve anything, you can't grow. And so I keep pushing, keep developing, keep evolving. I keep showing what an ordinary person can do when they put their hearts and minds and souls into it.

I have thought a lot about Roz, and about her belief that it is the search for meaning in our lives that gives us relevance. It doesn't matter how we do it, she says, it's more important that we engage in the process. 'It is the search itself that gives meaning to our lives, lends our existence a narrative arc, makes us feel that we are on a quest, a journey, a trajectory. Without that sense of life's great adventure, it would be hard indeed to feel that life has meaning.'

I am not about to row any of the great oceans, but I like to try to prove, on behalf of all women in the media, that nothing is impossible. We can take on a heavy workload, we can deal with pressure, master a complicated subject, engage with experts and we can present those subjects with joy and enthusiasm. I get called a 'workaholic', as if it's an insult. I just smile, knowing that a few dinosaurs in the press are still adjusting to the fact that women can do what men have been doing for decades – and they can do it without making it seem like hard work.

I will shift my focus to other challenges at some point, because I want to have new adventures and I want to keep improving as a broadcaster and communicator. Roz Savage's words keep ringing in my ears – if I don't push out of my comfort zone, I will suffocate.

Writing *My Animals and Other Family* and this book have been exercises in that cause. I always told myself that I didn't have the concentration or the ability to write a book, so it's nice to prove myself wrong.

Now for the next challenge – and for a bit of time every day to walk rather than gallop through life.

Acknowledgements

This book would not have been possible without the gentle persuasion, dedication and fine judgement of Joel Rickett and the team at Viking Penguin. I'd also like to thank Joel's wife, Sian, who has read every word and helped with the structure of the book. Gill Heeley has again produced some wonderful drawings that I think bring the book alive, and Sarah Day has given her time and expertise to copy-editing – I am extremely grateful to both of them.

Lucy Lunt and Karen Gregor have been wonderfully supportive of the idea of me writing about walking, and thanks also to Gwyneth Williams, the controller of BBC Radio 4, for continuing to commission *Ramblings*, without which I would never have explored so much of the country. Thanks also to Lucy for reading the first draft, not insisting that I be nice about her and for offering factual corrections in her usual no-nonsense style.

My parents are getting used to being the butt of my jokes, and they don't seem to mind, which is amazing. Most of all I want to thank them for giving me and my brother a home that we love and cherish. My sister-in-law, Anna Lisa, has been so supportive and has thrown herself and her children into the spirit of the book. Jonno and Toby have walked with me, and I know Flora will one day; I look forward to the adventures we will have together.

My poor brother has suffered constant teasing in the racing world for the stick he got in *My Animals and Other Family* – he will again, I fear, when this book does the rounds. I apologize to him for that, but also thank him for giving me at least a day to walk home with me and for allowing me (again) to abuse him in print. One day, I promise, we will do the whole of the Wayfarer's Walk.

My heartfelt thanks to Alice, who has cajoled and chided me, supported me and not minded that I've painted her as a fire-breathing dragon. I should point out that she's not – not all of the time, at any rate. We will continue to walk together, with Archie, enjoying life and being thankful that we get to spend it together.

Text Permissions

1	2	3	4	5	6	7	8	9	10
11	12	13	14	15	16	17	18	19	20
21	22	23	24	25	26	27	28	29	30
31	32	33	34	35	36	37	38	39	40
41	42	43	44	45	46	47	48	49	50
51	52	53	54	55	56	57	58	59	60
61	62	63	64	65	66	67	68	69	70
71	72	73	74	75	76	77	78	79	80
81	82	83	84	85	86	87	88	89	90
91	92	93	94	95	96	97	98	99	100
101	102	103	104	105	106	107	108	109	110
111	112	113	114	115	116	117	118	119	120
121	122	123	124	125	126	127	128	129	130
131	132	133	134	135	136	137	138	139	140
141	142	143	144	145	146	147	148	149	150
151	152	153	154	155	156	157	158	159	160
161	162	163	164	165	166	167	168	169	170
171	172	173	174	175	176	177	178	179	180
181	182	183	184	185	186	187	188	189	190
191	192	193	194	195	196	197	198	199	200
201	202	203	204	205	206	207	208	209	210
211	212	213	214	215	216	217	218	219	220
221	222	223	224	225	226	227	228	229	230
231	232	233	234	235	236	237	238	239	240
241	242	243	244	245	246	247	248	249	250
251	252	253	254	255	256	257	258	259	260
261	262	263	264	265	266	267	268	269	270
271	272	273	274	275	276	277	278	279	280
281	282	283	284	285	286	287	288	289	290
291	292	293	294	295	296	297	298	299	300
301	302	303	304	305	306	307	308	309	310
311	312	313	314	315	316	317	318	319	320
321	322	323	324	325	326	327	328	329	330
331	332	333	334	335	336	337	338	339	340
341	342	343	344	345	346	347	348	349	350
351	352	353	354	355	356	357	358	359	360
361	362	363	364	365	366	367	368	369	370
371	372	373	374	375	376	377	378	379	380
381	382	383	384	385	386	387	388	389	390
391	392	393	394	395	396	397	398	399	400